Copyright
for archivists
and records
managers

Copyright for archivists and records managers

Third edition

Tim Padfield

facet publishing

© Crown Copyright and T. R. Padfield 2001, 2004, 2007

Published by
Facet Publishing
7 Ridgmount Street
London WC1E 7AE

Facet Publishing is wholly owned by CILIP: the Chartered Institute of Library and Information Professionals.

First published 2001 by the Public Record Office as *Copyright for Archivists and Users of Archives*.
Second edition published 2004 by Facet Publishing.
This third edition 2007

British Library Cataloguing in Publication Data
A catalogue record for this book is available from the British Library.

ISBN-10: 1-85604-604-4
ISBN-13: 978-1-85604-604-6

Typeset in 10/13pt Elegant Garamond and Humanist 521 by Facet Publishing.
Printed and made in Great Britain by MPG Books Ltd, Bodmin, Cornwall.

Contents

Acknowledgements

Since receiving the degree of Master of Laws from the University of London, I have continued to benefit from the facilities provided by the University's Institute of Advanced Legal Studies; without them my use of case law would have been severely limited. I am grateful to the staff there for their unfailing helpfulness and courtesy. I have also continued to have the pleasure and benefit of many conversations and meetings with other specialists in this field, notably Peter Wienand, Graham Cornish, Charles Oppenheim and Naomi Korn; I am most grateful to them. Meetings, especially of the Libraries and Archives Copyright Alliance, which I have the honour to chair, of the Museums Copyright Group and of the Office of Public Sector Information's Licensing Forum, are always instructive and informative, and I am grateful to their members for many useful discussions. I have also continued to learn much about the problems faced by archivists, librarians, and museum and other information professionals from their comments at seminars and training sessions. I hope that with all this help I have managed to avoid serious error, both legal and archival, but if readers have comments to make on the text I should be glad to receive them at The National Archives for use in any future edition.

As before, I cannot do better than to dedicate this book to the four women in my life: Lucy, Clare, Emma and Poppy.

Preface

This book was written by a practising archivist (albeit with experience of only one institution) with limited legal training, and does not constitute formal legal advice. Archivists and records managers should seek advice from a specialist intellectual property lawyer if they are in any doubt about their legal position or the legality of any action they might wish to take. Also, archivists and records managers themselves should always make abundantly clear to those who consult them that any advice they offer on copyright issues, including the subsistence and ownership of copyright in particular works, does not constitute legal advice or authority to use material protected by copyrights that they do not administer.

Given that this is a book by an archivist for archivists and records managers and not for lawyers, it contains a lot of legal references. Although the primary authority for the law as set out here is statutes and statutory regulations, the UK legal system relies heavily for the interpretation of statutes on the decisions of judges in cases they have heard. As a result, the advice in this book on how the law is applied in particular circumstances derives largely from reports of those cases (as well as from publications of lawyers). The statutes and regulations alone are not enough.

The references to authorities (treaties, directives, statutes, statutory instruments, law reports) given in the footnotes to each paragraph are abbreviated; full citations appear in the table of authorities (see Chapter 11). Statutes are referred to simply by year (and, where necessary, a word or abbreviation), statutory instruments and regulations by their number and cases by title. There are also a few citations of legal opinions preserved in original documents; the full references are given at 10.1.

As well as advice on detailed points of law, the book contains worked examples (see 9.5 and 9.6): these are imaginary but are based on real-life enquiries answered by the author.

This is the third edition of this book, published only six years after the appearance of the first. That says something about the desire of archivists and records managers to do the right thing, but it is more an indicator of how the law keeps changing. This is unfortunate for professional people who need to be up to date, not only by training but also by spending money to maintain the currency of their bookshelves. It is with some regret that I have to say, again, that archivists and records managers should not rely on earlier editions of this book. More or less substantial changes to the text have been made to around half the numbered sections, and the entire text has grown by some 10%. Some of the more notable areas of change are:

- the meaning of the term 'copyright';
- originality, in particular in new editions of old works;

- international copyright, copyright outside the UK and qualification by country of origin;
- ideas and facts;
- university staff, academics and students;
- Crown and Parliamentary copyright, and public sector information;
- licences, assignments and contracts;
- 'orphan' works;
- exhibition;
- electronic signatures and declaration forms;
- records management;
- digital rights management systems;
- magistrates' courts;
- Ordnance Survey maps;
- electoral registers;
- databases;
- performers' and artists' rights, registered designs and privacy; and
- worked examples.

Every effort has been made to ensure that the advice given in this book, and the views expressed, are an accurate reflection of the law, but neither the author, nor The National Archives, nor the publisher accepts any liability for any damage, however caused, arising as a result of reliance on them. *If in doubt, consult a lawyer.*

Tim Padfield

1 What is copyright?

1.1 Nature of copyright

1.1.1 Introduction

Copyright is, to quote the *Oxford English Dictionary*, 'the exclusive right given by law for a certain term of years to an author . . . to print, publish or sell copies of his work'. Clearly, it is not merely the right to copy. Rather, the word 'copyright' derives from another meaning of copy, as in an advertiser's 'copy'. In this context, a copy is, as Dr Johnson put it in his *Dictionary* (1810), 'the autograph; the original; the archtype; that from which any thing is copied'. Copyright, then, is the right in the 'copy', the author's original work.

The right to enjoy copyright protection is regarded internationally as arising from natural justice, in accordance with the Universal Declaration of Human Rights of 1948, which says that 'everyone has the right to the protection of the moral and material interests resulting from any scientific, literary or artistic production of which he is the author'. Copyright also exists in order to benefit society generally, by encouraging learning and the arts. It originated, though, with the much more immediately practical purpose of outlawing the piracy of publications in the UK, where it has always been regarded as primarily an economic property right: the right of the owner to benefit from the fruits of his or her skill, judgment and labour. This is the 'common law' approach exported from the UK to Ireland, the Commonwealth and the USA, as distinct from the 'civil law', 'author's right' approach of most other European countries which emphasizes the protection of the author's personality as expressed in his or her work.

For most practitioners copyright continues to mean copyright in published works. There are relatively few people, even among lawyers specializing in intellectual property law, who are much interested in the intricacies of copyright in unpublished material, but that is what is of most concern to archivists, records managers and the users of archival materials. Copyright law in itself can seem bad enough, but when combined with limited expert commentary and the tangled web of different copyrights that might subsist even in a single file of correspondence, it is not surprising that many fight shy. The archivist or records manager cannot afford to, however, and this book is an attempt to show him or her a way through the maze.

Universal Declaration of Human Rights art 27(2); *Dr Johnson's Dictionary*, 10th edn, 1810

1.1.2   Definition of copyright

Copyright is (in very broad terms, and with exceptions as to details):

- a property right, one of a group of intellectual property rights (see 1.1.3)
- in certain types of work (see 1.1.4)
- which have been made in a certain way (see 1.1.5)
- which are the original products of skill, labour and judgment by their author (see 1.1.6)
- and whose duration is for a fixed period (see 1.1.7)
- which gives the owner (see 1.1.8)
- the power to control use (see 1.1.9)
- of a substantial part (see 1.1.10)
- but which does not give the owner a monopoly in facts or ideas (see 1.1.11) and
- which is subject to certain defined exceptions (see 1.1.12).

1.1.3   Intellectual property rights

Copyright is one of a group of rights known as intellectual (sometimes industrial and intellectual) property rights (IPRs) (see Figure 1.1.3). There is no distinct right called an 'intellectual property right' as such.

These rights fall, on the whole, into one of two categories. Rights in designs, trade marks and patents are monopoly rights, so that the owner of the rights may prevent anyone else using the design, mark or invention even if they thought of it independently.

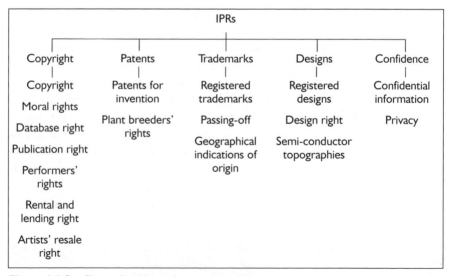

Figure 1.1.3   Chart of intellectual property rights

The other rights do not confer a monopoly; anyone else may create a work just the same so long as it is by their own effort, not by copying (see 2.1). This book is primarily about copyright, but gives some information about other intellectual property rights which are likely to affect archivists and records managers (see Chapter 8).

Copyright, like these other rights, is an exclusive property right. Much as with property in things, such as land or a book, it may be owned, sold and bequeathed, and permission may be given to others to use it. It is effectively a negative right to restrain someone else from exploiting the property: the positive right to exploit the work may actually be restricted in various ways. For instance, the author of a book may own the copyright in the text, which means he or she may prevent someone else copying it, but he or she will not own every published copy of the book, the publisher will own the copyright in the typographical arrangement and an artist might own the copyright in the illustrations. The permission of the publisher and artist would be needed before the author could republish the book, and the owner of each published copy is at liberty to sell it or give it away.

1.1.4 Scope of copyright

Copyright is extensive in scope, covering works of many kinds. It includes not only literary (that is, written, see 2.2) and artistic (that is, graphic, photographic or three-dimensional, see 2.3) works, but also dramatic works (such as plays, ballets, operas, see 2.2), musical works (see 2.2), films (see 2.4), sound recordings (see 2.5), radio and television broadcasts (see 2.6.1–14), computer software (see 2.2), and typographical arrangements of published editions (see 2.6.15–17). In effect it protects the expression of virtually any product of the mind as well as many products of investment which have had little or no intellectual input, if the work is capable of being copied or imitated, regardless (for the most part) of the aesthetic or technical quality of the work. Copyright may subsist in a list, a single entry in a diary, a sketch, a short poem or a business letter just as much as in a novel or a symphony.

British Oxygen v Liquid Air, 1925; *A v B*, 2000

1.1.5 Subsistence of copyright

Copyright is said to subsist in a work; it subsists, rather than exists, because it cannot exist independently of the work it protects. It does so automatically in all countries that have signed or that observe the Berne Convention (see 1.2.5, 3.1.4). While some countries (such as France) will protect even an unrecorded work, in the UK copyright arises (in most cases) as soon as the work is recorded in some way (see 2.1.3). There is no need for any formality or registration before copyright subsists or before action may be taken against someone infringing copyright (but see 1.2.9). There is thus no need to 'claim' copyright, although some sort of assertion may be helpful (see 3.4). On the other hand, an assertion of moral rights is necessary for some purposes (see 8.1).

1.1.6   Originality and authorship

Literary, dramatic, musical and artistic works must be original, not in the sense of being unique but in the sense of not having been copied from another work. The author of a work must have 'originated' it by investing some minimal quantity of his or her own skill, labour or judgment in creating it (see 2.1.5). So long as a work is original, it may attract copyright even if someone else has produced the same thing previously (see also 2.1.7). So, for example, consider two individuals setting out to survey Hyde Park. All being well, the resulting maps will show the same features in the same relative positions. If the surveyors choose the same scale and use the same set of mapping symbols their maps may well look virtually identical, but each will be a copyright work without infringing the other because each was created independently. In copyright terms, each is 'original' (see 2.1.7). It is also possible to create an original work which infringes copyright in a pre-existing work (see 2.1.11). Unfortunately for the author of the new work, the existence of a new copyright is irrelevant to a decision on whether there has been infringement of the copyright in the earlier one.

The term 'author' applies to the creator of any literary, dramatic, musical or artistic work, including for instance, composers of music, photographers and painters, and to the producer of a sound recording, the producer and principal director of a film, the person making a broadcast and the publisher of a published edition. For the role of the author in relation to duration see 2.1.16.

1988 (CDPA) s9; *Wilkins v Aikin*, 1810; *University of London Press v University Tutorial Press*, 1916; *Geographia v Penguin Books*, 1985; *Scottish and Universal Newspapers v Paul Mack*, 2003

1.1.7   Duration

The duration of copyright depends on a number of factors, though which ones apply depends on the circumstances:

- the type of work;
- the date of creation and (where applicable) when it was first made available to the public or first published;
- the date of the author's death; and
- ownership of the copyright (Crown and Parliamentary copyright, and copyright belonging to some international organizations, only, see 3.2.28).

Until the passing of the 1988 Act (see 1.2.3), most unpublished literary works and engravings enjoyed a term of copyright that was unlimited until first publication, irrespective of whether the author died in 1066 or 1966. This perpetual copyright, a relic of pre-20th-century common law protection (see 1.2.2), has now been abolished (see 2.2.19, 2.3.15), although the transitional provisions mean that the full effect of abolition will not be felt until the year 2040 (see 2.1.20). Perpetual copyright in unpublished works can be a problem in other common law (see 1.2.2) countries too (see 1.2.10).

In all cases, the duration of copyright includes the remainder of the year in which the triggering event takes place (death of the author, publication, creation, making available to the public or coming into force of the legislation) followed by a fixed term running from the end of that year. Details of duration in different circumstances are given in Chapter 2. Flow charts to simplify the calculation of the duration of copyright in literary, dramatic, musical and artistic works are in the Appendix (see 9.1).

Where duration is based on the life of the author, it is authorship, not ownership, that matters even if the author was an employee of the first owner (see 2.1.16). First or subsequent ownership of copyright by a person other than the author, or by a corporate body, does not affect duration. Where duration depends on the death of the author and there are joint authors, it is the death of the last surviving author that matters.

1.1.8 Owner

The first owner of copyright is normally the author, but where an author is an employee the first owner is the employer. The owner may also assign the copyright to someone else (see Chapter 3) even, in some circumstances, before the work is created.

1.1.9 Use

There is an exhaustive list of restricted acts, including copying, issue to the public, communication to the public (for instance on the internet), adaptation and performance, that may be done with a copyright work only by the copyright owner or with his or her permission (see Chapter 5).

1.1.10 Substantial

Copyright does not protect insubstantial parts of a copyright work, but 'insubstantial' does not necessarily mean 'small' (see 5.2.3).

1.1.11 Not a monopoly

Copyright is not a monopoly right. Identical works may each be protected (see 1.1.6), and copyright does not subsist in a fact or a general idea. Not until a collection of facts has been gathered together so that the sum means more than the parts, or a general idea has been formulated in a way that particularizes it, can copyright arise, and even then the original facts and ideas taken individually remain unprotected. The setting of this boundary between unprotected ideas and protected expression is one of the trickiest problems facing commentators and courts (see 2.1.4).

1.1.12 Exceptions

Parliament seeks to find a balance between the rights of copyright owners on the one hand and the interests of society in the ready exchange of information and ideas and the encouragement of creativity on the other. It therefore sets limits on the exclusive rights given to owners by allowing limited exceptions, which may apply to particular types of work or types of people, to particular circumstances and to particular kinds of use (see 5.2).

1.1.13 Other points

The following general points may be noted:

- After copyright has expired, the work may be copied, published, placed on a website, adapted or performed without infringement (see 5.2.2).
- The use of insubstantial quotations, suitably acknowledged, does not normally require permission from the copyright owner (see 5.2.3).
- More than one copyright may subsist in a single work, and frequently will in a documentary file (see for instance 2.1.2, 7.9.1).
- Neither the author of the work, nor the owner of the original document in which it is recorded, necessarily owns the copyright (see 3.2). Rarely will it be possible for an archivist to receive a collection of papers secure in the knowledge that the depositor was the owner of all the copyrights involved. Similarly, records managers should remember that, for the most part, only works created by employees in the course of employment are copyright of the employer (see 3.2.12); letters received from outside or the products of consultants will normally be the copyright of their authors (see 3.2.17).
- The availability of a document for public inspection and the supply of a copy of it (for instance under Freedom of Information Act provisions) does not imply that the works it contains or any copy of them are free from copyright restrictions.
- The owner or custodian of the original document may have the right to forbid inspection or reproduction of it, irrespective of the permission of the copyright owner (see 3.2.3).
- Ownership or custody of the original document does not confer the power to authorize its reproduction if that has been forbidden by the copyright owner (see 5.1.2).

- The authorization of someone to infringe copyright in a work, even if innocent, is in itself an infringement of the copyright (see 5.2.28).

1.1.14 National protection

The protection given by copyright varies around the world, particularly in terms of the scope of works protected and ownership. It is important to understand this, particularly now that international communications have become so simple and accessible, and it is becoming normal, even necessary, to make material available on the internet.

The Berne Convention (see 1.2.5) requires that the law that applies to a copyright infringement be, on the whole, the national law of the country in which the infringement occurs and in which protection is claimed. Occasionally, the courts have to consider whether UK law applies to an issue and whether the local (England and Wales, Scotland or Northern Ireland) courts have jurisdiction (see 6.2.6), but archivists and records managers will normally be safe to assume that local law and jurisdiction will apply to them.

As noted above (see 1.1.7) much archival material in the UK, no matter how old, is still protected by copyright. The placing of copyright works on the internet is an infringement if permission is not obtained (see 4.1.7). If the copyright owner has given permission, he or she should understand that the work will be accessible in places where UK law does not apply; it could even be that the law in the country of use does not recognize that the work qualifies for protection (see also 3.1.4) or makes a quite different person the author or the owner of the copyright.

This book deals primarily with copyright in the UK, with some limited comments on the differences and similarities between the UK law and provisions elsewhere in the British Isles including in the Republic of Ireland (see 7.7), but takes account of international and European law, and the laws of other countries, where appropriate (see especially 1.2.5–11). It does not attempt to deal with the problems that will arise if there is a conflict of laws (see also 6.2.6).

Berne Convention art 5(2); *Huston v Turner Entertainment*, 1992; *Blau v BBC*, 2002; *Sawyer v Atari Interactive*, 2006

1.2 Development of copyright

1.2.1 Statutes before 1911

Copyright was first given statutory force in the UK by the Copyright Act 1710, long before any other country introduced copyright legislation. The next country was Denmark in 1741; the USA acquired copyright legislation in 1790 followed by France in 1793. The Act of 1710 and subsequent Acts in the 18th and 19th centuries gave protection for a limited period to published works and also to certain categories of other material, including drawings and photographs, whether published or not. Some of these statutory copyrights (books and other written works, paintings, drawings, photographs, music) were enforceable only if they were registered with the Stationers' Company at Stationers' Hall. Registration covered both the initial ownership of copyright and any subsequent assignments, so the records of the Company are a valuable source for the pre- and early 20th-century history of intellectual and artistic material. Other types of work (engravings, sculptures) were protected only if the work carried the name of the copyright owner on each copy. Each statute was limited in scope to a specific category of material, so that, for instance, the author of a novel gained no copyright protection against the performance of a play that was based on it, and each statute defined the terms and duration of the protection it gave.

The statutory registers to 1842 are preserved at Stationers' Hall. Statutory registers from 1842 to 1912 (and in some cases to 1923) are in The National Archives (see 2.1.17).

Goubaud v Wallace, 1877; *Warne v Lawrence*, 1886

1.2.2   The common law

Unpublished works of every kind, including books, lectures, letters and photographs, were potentially protected under the common law until the passing of the 1911 Copyright Act, though the precise nature of the protection in any particular case was uncertain since it depended on the judge's interpretation of earlier decisions, if any, in similar cases. This protection was perpetual until the work was published, but any action to enforce it could result only in the payment of the cost of the actual damage that was shown to have been suffered. Until the late 19th century a separate action, in a different court, was required for an injunction to prevent new infringements.

In most cases the author seems to have been the first owner of the common law copyright (see 3.2.16). Publication was taken to mean the distribution of copies to the public or the communication of the work to the public generally (for instance, by delivering a sermon in church), but the giving of a university lecture or the performing of a play to a ticketed audience, for instance, did not count as publication.

Common law protection also extended to questions of privacy, protecting a person who commissioned photographs for private purposes from seeing them published by the photographer without permission. Similar protection for this purpose is now provided by the statute (see 8.1.10).

The common law is a creature of the English legal tradition, and its practices have been exported to many parts of the Commonwealth, to the USA and to Ireland, though not in the same way to Scotland. Scotland's legal system owes more to the civil, or Roman, law traditions to be found elsewhere in Europe. The term 'common law' may be applied specifically to non-statutory law or more generally to a shared legal tradition distinct from the civil law.

Prince Albert v Strange, 1848–9; *Mayall v Higbey*, 1862; *Pollard v Photographic Co*, 1889; *Stedall v Houghton*, 1901; *Mansell v Valley Printing*, 1908

1.2.3 Copyright law since 1911

The Copyright Act 1911 came into force on 1 July 1912, replacing all common law copyright with statutory copyright and replacing almost all the existing statutory rights with a single, uniform code. It also gave protection, for the first time, to sound recordings. It was needed not only so as to simplify and improve the law of copyright in the UK, but also to allow the UK to ratify the amendments made in 1908 in Berlin to the Berne Convention of 1886 (see 1.2.5). Most of the 1911 Act was repealed by the Copyright Act 1956, with the exception of the provisions covering the legal deposit of publications (now replaced by those in the Legal Deposit Libraries Act 2003). The 1956 Act was also required so that the UK could ratify international conventions; it came into force on 1 June 1957. It gave protection for the first time to films and broadcasts as distinct types of work. Subsequent amendments gave protection to cable programmes and computer software. The 1956 Act as amended was repealed by the Copyright, Designs and Patents Act 1988, which was intended to be flexible enough to cope with changes in technology and again to allow adherence to new international conventions. This is the statute currently governing copyright in the UK. It came into force on 1 August 1989, but has been very significantly amended since then following initiatives in the European Union and to take account of the WIPO treaties (see 1.2.7), themselves prompted by changes in communications technology.

1911 s37(2); SI 1957/863; SI 1989/816

1.2.4 Continuity of the law

Continuity of copyright protection has been a recurrent theme of UK legislation. The intention, at each major revision, has been to prevent works from suddenly losing copyright protection to which they had previously been entitled. From 1 July 1912, when it came into force, the 1911 Act substituted the new statutory rights for existing common law and statutory rights over materials created earlier and still protected on that date. The 1956 Act contained complex transitional provisions which allowed for continuity of protection for works entitled to it at commencement on 1 June 1957. The 1988 Act also contains transitional provisions for works still entitled to protection on 1 August 1989 when it came into force. These transitional provisions limit or modify the extent to which the new legislation applies to existing works and specify that certain matters are to be determined in accordance with the law in force at the time when a particular work was made. This means that earlier statutes continue to be of significance and archivists must have some awareness of them. Where appropriate, such provisions are taken into account in this book.

1.2.5   International law and the Berne Convention

Until the later 19th century, UK copyright works were not protected in many foreign countries and the UK did not protect the work of a foreigner who was not, at the time of publication, resident in a British dominion. Reciprocal protection between individual countries began to become available as a result of bilateral treaties but this was not of great assistance to publishers who suffered from pirated copies printed elsewhere. Eventually the Berne Convention for the protection of literary and artistic works was signed in 1886, laying down a minimum standard of protection to be provided by countries that were members of the Berne Union.

Today, any country that is a member of the World Trade Organization must be a party to the Trade-Related Intellectual Property Rights elements (the TRIPS Agreement) of the World Trade Agreement, which requires member states to comply with almost all of the current text (the Paris Act of 1971) of the Berne Convention even if they are not formally part of the Berne Union. Most countries of the world are now signatories of the Berne Convention or the TRIPS Agreement or both, giving reciprocal rights to protection (see 3.1.4).

Jefferys v Boosey, 1854

1.2.6   Other conventions

The Universal Copyright Convention (UCC) was signed in 1952 under the auspices of the United Nations and amended in 1971, and is now administered by UNESCO. It guarantees a lower level of protection to copyright owners than does the Berne Convention, and is much vaguer about the exceptions allowed for users, but was significant for bringing many countries, notably the USA, into the international copyright system. This was important in itself, but has since proved even more valuable as a preliminary to the near-universal acceptance of the Berne Convention through the TRIPS Agreement.

The Rome Convention (1961) provides for performers, producers of phonograms (records) and broadcasters in a similar way to Berne, and most EU member states are signatories (see 3.1.5); countries that were reluctant to give rights to performers subsequently agreed a more restricted Geneva Convention (1971) for record producers only.

1.2.7   The World Intellectual Property Organization

The Berne and Rome Conventions are administered by the World Intellectual Property

Organization (WIPO). This is a United Nations body, which sponsored the WIPO Copyright Treaty agreed in 1996. The purpose of that treaty was to update and clarify the Berne Convention in the light of technological and social changes, avoiding the almost impossible task of amending the Berne Convention itself. Accession to the WIPO Copyright Treaty means compliance with the whole of the Paris Act of the Berne Convention, including articles excepted by the TRIPS Agreement. In 1996, WIPO also sponsored a new Performances and Phonograms Treaty to supplement the Rome Convention.

1.2.8 The European Union

Copyright law in the UK has been significantly influenced in the years since the passing of the 1988 Act by developments in the European Union. Eight directives (see 11.1) have been passed as part of a programme to 'harmonize' aspects of copyright law that are thought to obstruct the free flow of goods and services throughout the EU's Internal Market or that discriminate between citizens of different member states, and others have had an impact while not requiring amendment of the 1988 Act. It should be noted that some or all of these directives apply not only in the EU but throughout the European Economic Area (EEA: the EU plus Norway, Iceland and Liechtenstein). They also apply, following bilateral agreements, elsewhere in Europe.

Judgments of the European Court of Justice are binding on UK courts, and have been taken into account where appropriate in this book.

A national of, or a person normally resident in, an EU member state enjoys the full protection of the local law in all other member states. It is not permissible to discriminate against an EU national or resident on grounds of his or her country of origin (see 2.1.23).

Directives 1986, 1991, 1992, 1993 (two), 1996, 2001, 2004; *Tod's v Heyraud*, 2005

1.2.9 Variations between countries

Despite the international conventions and the European directives there are wide variations in protection between countries even within Europe, and still wider ones beyond Europe. For instance, long as the standard term of protection now is in Europe (see 2.1.18–25, 9.1) in some countries (e.g. Spain) it may be even longer in some circumstances (see 1.2.10). The definition of the owner can also vary markedly, so that quite different people qualify as owners of copyright in the same work in different countries. Even the definition of a protected work can vary so that a work protected in the UK is not protected at all in some countries. The possibility of such differences should be borne in mind if works are exploited overseas (for instance on the internet).

1.2.10 Variations between countries: duration

Although UK law protects works that qualify for protection (see 3.1) but which were created overseas, it does not give that protection for any longer than would be given by the country of origin. The member states of the EEA (see 1.2.8), the USA, Australia, Switzerland and Turkey give protection for the life of the author plus 70 years, but this is more than elsewhere in the world. In most cases, therefore, protection for works created outside these countries will last only for the life of the author plus 50 years (the minimum requirement of the Berne Convention).

It is especially important to note that most countries do not offer the long duration enjoyed in the UK by unpublished literary, dramatic and musical works (see 2.2.17). However, in Australia unpublished literary, dramatic and musical works, and in South Africa unpublished literary, dramatic, musical and artistic works except photographs, all continue to have perpetual protection. In Canada, literary, dramatic and musical works and engravings which were unpublished on 25 July 1957 and whose author died on or after 25 July 1947 are protected until the end of 2017 at the earliest; unpublished works by earlier authors are now out of copyright.

In the USA, the standard term of life of the author plus 70 years applies to works created on or after 1 January 1978 and to works created but not published or 'copyrighted' (registered, see 1.2.11) before that date. Copyright in works which were created before 1 January 1978 and published or copyrighted between then and 31 December 2002 expires on 31 December 2047. There are special provisions for works published or copyrighted before 1 January 1978. For anonymous and pseudonymous works and works 'made for hire' (including by employees) which were created on or after 1 January 1978, the term is publication plus 95 years or creation plus 120 years, whichever is shorter.

1968 s33; 1976 (USA) ss301–5; 1978 (South Africa) s3; 1985 (Canada) ss6–7; 1988 (CDPA) ss12(6), 13A(4), 13B(7), 14(3)

1.2.11 Variations between countries: registration in the USA

Works created and/or published in the UK and other Berne Union countries (see 3.1.4) have protection in the USA under US law and for the period of protection provided by US law. This covers all unpublished works whatever the origin of the author, and all published works published in countries qualifying under US law (see also 3.1). It is necessary for a work of US origin (including a work published in the USA) to be registered ('copyrighted') with the Library of Congress before action may be taken in the USA against an infringement. This is not strictly necessary for a work that originated in the UK or another Berne Convention country but the redress available for infringement of an unregistered work is much less extensive and there could be other problems. It is most important therefore to register a work before an infringement action is started in the USA.

1976 (USA) ss104, 401, 411

1.3 Copyright and records

1.3.1 Context

Files and archival documents consist almost exclusively of materials that are or have been protected by copyright. The administration of that copyright will rarely be entirely in the hands of the archivist or records manager, and its ownership will often be obscure, not least because copyright persists for so long in unpublished works, which are what make up the bulk of files and archival collections. A knowledge of how copyright affects material for which they are responsible and what he or she may do with them is thus of vital importance to the archivist and records manager.

1.3.2 Why is copyright important to archivists, records managers and users?

Copyright protection is provided by the law, and infringement of copyright can lead to civil damages and even to criminal prosecution. An archivist or records manager will often be asked about copyright in a work, sometimes with the assumption that because the work is in a file or in the archive the institution holding it owns the copyright too. In such circumstances, the archivist or records manager needs to know something about copyright, and needs to know not to authorize, or appear to authorize, acts that could infringe.

1.3.3 The dangers of infringement

Many copyright owners, or their representatives, are increasingly assertive of their rights, particularly in the face of the growth of electronic media which can enable the mass distribution of perfect copies of copyright works. Universities, schools, companies and copy-shops have all discovered to their cost that unauthorized use of copyright works can prove to be an expensive option, even where the actual damage to the copyright owner has been very small. Almost all infringement cases are settled out of court, but the settlements can result in costs of tens of thousands of pounds, including substantial payments for damages. Scholarly purposes, even within a single institution, are not always sufficient to justify the unauthorized copying of works: the limits of fair dealing in copyright materials are quite narrow, and licences must be obtained for more extensive use.

Moorhouse v University of New South Wales, 1976; *Sony Music Entertainment v Easyinternetcafé*, 2003

1.3.4 Archives and libraries

All archivists, but especially those who are closely associated with library materials, including librarians who are working with special collections among a library's holdings, will need to ensure that they are fully aware of how copyright affects library materials and services. Much guidance is available for this purpose (see 10.2), and it should be studied carefully.

The worked examples (see 9.5 and 9.6) are imaginary, but are based on real-life enquiries, and may help archivists, records managers and users to understand how some of the rules apply in practice.

1.3.5   Digitization

Archivists and records managers should be extremely wary of demands from users and superiors that their material be copied without authority, but especially of demands that they be digitized for access electronically or that electronic records be made widely available electronically (see Chapter 6). The ready availability of journals and other works on the web should not be accepted as evidence that archival works and electronic files can be similarly made available without a lot of effort (and often cost) to secure the many permissions that will usually be needed (see 5.4.20–22, and for detailed guidance see 10.2). Copyright must thus be an issue that is considered at the very beginning of any project to digitize archival material or to make electronic records available remotely (see 6.5.3); if digitization can be directed towards works in which copyright has expired (such as early photographs) the difficulties will be much reduced.

1.3.6   Duration of copyright: a summary

Copyright material created since 1988 is all still protected. In broad terms, it is fair to say that most written records and artistic material (such as maps) created before 1988 will be in copyright as follows:

- Most unpublished literary materials where the author is known will be in copyright until at least the year 2039 (see 2.2.16–18).
- Most artistic works (except engravings), whether published or not and where the author is known, will be in copyright for 70 years after the death of the author (see 2.3.12).
- Most unpublished works of any sort where the author is unknown will be in copyright at least until the year 2039 (see 2.2.19–20, 2.3.16–19).

There are many variations and details, particularly for photographs, films and sound recordings, for published material and for material whose country of origin is outside the EEA and certain other countries, so if the duration of copyright in a work is particularly important, do not rely on this summary.

1.3.7 Checklist of copyright queries

Archivists and records managers are likely to receive enquiries from colleagues and members of the public about copyright restrictions on particular documents. The following checklist suggests an approach to the problem, but it must be emphasized that they should give advice on the answers to these questions only in general terms unless they are quite sure about what they are saying (see 5.2.28).

- Is it a work that qualifies to be protected by copyright? Relatively few items in an archive or in files will not, but remember that a file or document may contain many separate copyright works, and that a copyright work can be as small as a single letter, a short poem or (perhaps) a signature (see the definitions in Chapter 2). Might other rights apply (see Chapter 8)?
- Who was the author (see the sections on authorship in Chapter 2)? This can affect duration, ownership and moral rights.
- Is it still in copyright (see the sections on duration in Chapter 2)?
- Is copying of the work allowed? Public records may be copied without formality (see 5.3.1) but non-public records may in many cases only be copied if they are out of copyright or if the purchaser has completed a declaration form (see 5.3.10). Copyright artistic works in archives, that are not public records (including maps or photographs), should not normally be copied on their own without permission (see 5.3.18). Records that are not yet in an archive may be copied under fair dealing if appropriate (see 5.2.7ff.) or perhaps for educational purposes (see 5.2.15), but in many cases will require a licence (see 5.4.1).
- Is what is being requested allowed without permission, because the use is insubstantial (see 5.2.3), because a particular exception applies (see 5.2), or because copyright may be presumed to have lapsed (see 3.3.20)?
- Who was the first owner of the copyright (see 3.2) and who is the owner now (see 3.3)?

1.3.8 Checklist for publishing

Following on from the basic checklist above, if publication is intended there may be, depending on the answers to the initial questions, some further things to think about when using a copyright work. The same considerations apply whether the prospective publisher is a member of the public or the institution itself.

- How do I trace the copyright owner (see 5.4.20)?
- Do I need to bother (see 5.4.21)?
- Do any other intellectual property rights apply and how do I trace the owners (see Chapter 8)?
- Have I secured permission to cover everything that I want to do with the work?

- Have I acknowledged the permission given, the author and title of the work (see 5.2.7, 5.2.10–11) and the author's moral rights (see 8.1)?
- Have I acknowledged the custody of the institution holding the work and given its document reference?
- Where what I am publishing is sufficiently original and substantial to qualify for protection itself (see 2.1.5ff.), have I asserted my moral rights in it and announced in it that I have done so (see 8.1.5), and have I properly claimed my own copyright and all other relevant intellectual property rights in it (see 3.4)?

2 Copyright protection

2.1 Protection for works

2.1.1 Types of work

Copyright law classifies works into defined types, for which the provisions differ. For archivists and records managers, the most important are literary, dramatic, musical and artistic works, films and sound recordings. Other types of work (broadcasts and typographical arrangements) will less often present problems. The definitions themselves have varied with successive legislative changes, but those in the 1988 Act (as subsequently amended) are normally applicable to all works created and still in copyright at commencement and are thus the only ones that need be of concern for most purposes. Cases where earlier definitions still apply (notably pre-1957 films, see 2.4.1) are set out in the description of the appropriate categories.

1988 (CDPA) Sch 1 para 3

2.1.2 Nature of works

A single item may consist of more than one work, of different types. An academic journal, for instance, might contain several articles, each of which could be a separate literary work, together with illustrations, each of which could be a separate artistic work, and some music, which could be a musical work. The journal as a whole might qualify for protection as a compilation (see 2.1.9, 2.2.3), and will certainly have protection for its typographical arrangement (see 2.6.15). Similarly a song consists of music and words; each has its own copyright and there is no distinct copyright in the song as a whole although the same person may be the author of both. Also, each separate entry in a diary is a separate copyright work while the diary as a whole is another. In an archive, deeds, for instance, will be primarily literary works, but any plans in or on them are separately protected as artistic works. Likewise, a single file might contain minutes and papers produced by the creating body, letters, drawings and photographs received from private individuals or other bodies and companies, and published papers and maps including some in Crown copyright. Each separate item would qualify as a copyright work with its own authorship, duration and ownership, so the use of the whole file could require permission from many different people and bodies.

A single work may also qualify for copyright under more than one description (see 2.2.2, 2.3.2). Thus a computer circuit diagram is an artistic work, but because it consists of notation identifying the various component parts it can also be a literary work. Similarly, Chinese calligraphy or a poem arranged on the page to form the shape of a cat could qualify under both heads. This can be significant because copying of the work (for example taking a list of components from the circuit diagram, or the making of a copy by an archivist, see 5.3.10, 5.3.18) could infringe copyright in one description of work but not the other. Note, though, that if a work is a dramatic or musical work it cannot also be a literary work (see 2.2.2).

1988 (CDPA) ss1, 3(1); *Chappell v Redwood Music*, 1981; *Anacon v Environmental Research Technologies*, 1994; *Electronic Techniques (Anglia) v Critchley Components*, 1997; *Aubrey Max Sandman v Panasonic UK*, 1998; *Mackie Designs v Behringer*, 1999; *A v B*, 2000

2.1.3   Material form

Before a literary, dramatic or musical work can attract copyright, it must be recorded in a material form. This means that there is no copyright in (say) improvized music or an impromptu speech unless someone writes it down or makes a recording (in which case it could also be a sound recording, see 2.5), nor in ephemeral images on a computer screen (though there would be in the computer program which generated the images as a literary work, and in a screen layout or design recorded in a program as an artistic work, see 6.6.1).

There is no equivalent requirement for other kinds of work. Some (artistic works, typographical arrangements, films and sound recordings) must in practice be in a material form because of the terms in which they are defined, so that (for instance) something which was fluid rather than static did not qualify (in Australia) as a work of artistic craftsmanship (see 2.3.5). Broadcasts do not have to be in a material form but must be transmitted or re-transmitted before they attract copyright.

1988 (CDPA) ss3(2), 4(1), 5A(1), 5B(1), 6(1), 6(5A), 8(1); *Komesaroff v Mickle*, 1988

2.1.4   Ideas and facts

In 1854, a judge said: 'The subject of property is the order of words in the author's composition; not the words themselves, they being analogous to the elements of matter, which are not appropriated unless combined, nor the ideas expressed by those words, they existing in the mind alone, which is not capable of appropriation.' This has been an element of copyright law ever since: there can be no copyright in a general idea, but there can be copyright in the way the idea is developed and expressed.

Exactly where the border lies between the idea and the expression depends on the circumstances of any individual case, but it is clear that once a general idea is expressed or developed in a material form, so as to add something significant to the idea, that form of expression or development can be protected, whether the expression or development was by the originator of the idea or someone else. The courts are inclined nowadays to consider the 'level of abstraction' or of 'generality' in an idea to see whether it is sufficiently well developed to be protected. The more abstract the idea the less likely the protection. Thus, the making of a translation of a work does not merely take abstract ideas, so there can be infringement even though not a single word of the source work is used. On the other hand, a general theme (for instance a historical theory, an outline for a play, the approach to be adopted in making a design, the message conveyed by a brochure, a technique) cannot be protected. Examples of unprotected ideas have included:

- the former legal principle that a person may not be tried again for a crime for which he or she has already been convicted or acquitted, used in a play and a novel;
- a simple drawing of a hand holding a pencil, to show an illiterate voter where to put his or her cross; anyone was welcome to copy the idea so long as the new drawing was not identical to the earlier one;
- the thoughts and memories of the nominal author of ghost-written articles; the ghost-writer was author of the articles, though in appropriate circumstances there could be joint authorship (see 2.2.14);
- the mood of a film and the techniques used in making it;
- the theme of a computer game.

Even harder to distinguish are the idea behind the 'look and feel' of something and the expression of that idea in the work. People have found it difficult to persuade the courts that the look and feel of computer systems (as distinct from the actual software or the on-screen displays, see 6.6.1) can be protected, and the look and feel of works which use commonplace materials is likely in any case to be found to be unoriginal (see 2.1.5).

In a similar way, there can be no copyright in an individual fact. For instance, facts taken from a diary or a letter, maybe about where a person was and what he or she was doing or thinking, are unprotected, as are facts about a historical event, individual facts about a person in a register of births (see 7.2.4) or a directory, or the facts of an item of news. On the other hand, the precise words the person used in the diary or letter, an account of the historical event and a news article would all be protected and the contents of the diary might also be protected as confidential information (see 8.7.3). Further, a deliberately assembled collection of unprotected facts could be protected as a compilation (see 2.2.3); the legitimate use of such a compilation is not unlimited. So, the taking of facts, amounting to a substantial part, from a map or a directory, in order to make a rival map or directory, would be an infringement, while the use of those facts to find a route to a place or to locate organizations would be legitimate.

Erle J in *Jefferys v Boosey*, 1854, at 702; *Kenrick v Lawrence*, 1890; *Walter v Steinkopff*, 1892; *Springfield v Thame*, 1903; *Philip v Pennell*, 1907; *Tate v Fulbrook*, 1908; *Byrne v Statist*, 1914; *Wilmer v Hutchinson (Publishers)*, 1936–45; *Donoghue v Allied Newspapers*,

1938; *Ravenscroft v Herbert*, 1980; *Geographia v Penguin Books*, 1985; *Express Newspapers v News UK*, 1991; *Waterlow Publishers v Rose*, 1995; *Designers Guild v Russell Williams (Textiles)*, 2000; *Norowzian v Arks (No 2)*, 2000; *Ashdown v Telegraph Group*, 2001; *IPC Media v Highbury-SPL Publishing*, 2005; *Navitaire v Easyjet Airline Co*, 2005; *Baigent v Random House*, 2006; *Nova Productions v Mazooma Games*, 2006; *USP v London General Holdings*, 2006

2.1.5 Originality

To attract copyright a literary, dramatic, musical or artistic work must be original, which means, as a judge said in 1916, it must 'originate' with the author, rather than be copied from the work of someone else. In the common law tradition (see 1.2.2) this originality does not normally require creativity: 'original' does not mean 'new'. Instead, for a work to be original the author must have used his or her own skill, knowledge, taste, judgment or labour to produce it. A Canadian judge has defined skill as 'use of one's knowledge, developed aptitude or practised ability', and judgment as 'use of one's capacity for discernment or ability to form an opinion or evaluation by comparing different possible options'.

The position is different in civil law countries (see 1.1.1), including most member states of the EU, and also in the USA, and this is reflected in the stricter definition of originality for copyright in a database where some intellectual creativity is required, as a result of a European directive (see 8.2.4). The UK has not so far implemented a similar EU provision for artistic (as distinct from documentary) photographs. It is quite likely that over time, and under the pressure of the programme to harmonize intellectual property law in Europe, the UK will move further in this direction, giving more emphasis to the skill, knowledge, taste and judgment involved and less or even none to the labour, but for the moment the EU appears content to leave originality unharmonized.

Directive 1993 (Term) art 6; Directive 1996 recital 15; Peterson J in *University of London Press v University Tutorial Press*, 1916, at 608–9; McLachlin CJ in *CCH Canadian v Law Society of Upper Canada*, 2004, at para 16

2.1.6 Originality and material changes

Because original does not mean new, the author may produce an original work which is not unique, using existing general ideas or by developing an earlier work, so long as he or she uses his or her own skill to express those ideas and is not simply copying. On the other hand, a slavish copy of another work cannot be original, so there can be no copyright in it. The copy must be sufficiently different from its source to make it a new work. Examples might be a change of medium, a translation, a transcript of an old manuscript in an obscure or difficult language, or a performing edition of various difficult versions of old musical works (see also 4.1.9, 5.1.7). One judge said in 1923: 'It is necessary that the labour, skill and capital expended should be sufficient to impart to the product some quality or character which the raw material did not possess, differentiating the product from the raw material.' In 1988 another said that it did not follow 'that that which is an exact and literal reproduction in two-dimensional form of an existing two-dimensional work becomes an original work simply because the process of copying it involves the application of skill and labour. . . . Whether it does so or not is a question of degree having regard to the quality rather than the quantity of the addition.'

Where a derivative work does qualify for copyright protection it is an entirely new work with its own author and owner. The author and owner of the source work have no rights in the new one. Nevertheless, the creation of the derivative work could be an infringement of the copyright in the source work unless the use was authorized. Subsequent use of the derivative work could also infringe that copyright. The owner of the copyright in the source work is thus likely to be entitled to a share in the royalties from the derivative work, in proportion to what has been taken.

1988 (CDPA) s1(1)(a); *Tree v Bowkett*, 1896; *Walter v Lane*, 1900; *Evans v Tout*, 1905–10; *Byrne v Statist*, 1914; *Lord Atkinson in Macmillan v Cooper*, 1923, at 188; *Redwood Music v Chappell*, 1982; Lord Oliver in *Interlego v Tyco*, 1988, at 371–2; *Gabrin v Universal Musical Operations*, 2004; *Sawkins v Hyperion Records*, 2005

2.1.7 Originality and independent creation

Again, since original does not mean new and copyright gives no monopoly, it is possible for two independently produced works to be virtually identical (see 1.1.6). A photographer may take a photograph of a scene which almost exactly reproduces another photograph by someone else, and will still be entitled to copyright without any infringement because the photograph is a copy of the scene, not of the earlier photograph.

1988 (CDPA) s1(1)(a); *Walter v Lane*, 1900; *Corelli v Gray*, 1911–16; *King Features Syndicate v O and M Kleeman*, 1941; *Bauman v Fussell*, 1978; *Creation Records v News Group Newspapers*, 1997

2.1.8 Originality in copies

Where a copyright work consists of material copied from elsewhere, those parts that are copies are unoriginal and can have no new copyright protection. Anyone wishing to copy the earlier material (for instance a poem in an anthology or a letter in a volume of collected works) will need permission only if it is still in copyright, and then only from the earlier copyright owner, unless the typographical arrangement is copied (see 2.6.15).

Warwick Film Productions v Eisinger, 1969

2.1.9 Originality in compilations

Although gaining no new protection for the individual works it contains, a work which contains copies of earlier material can attract copyright as a compilation if the compiler has used enough skill, judgment or labour to select the material (see 2.1.5). A compilation which has required no skill in selection or arrangement (such as the information tables often found in diaries, and the contents of parish registers, see 7.2.4) is unlikely to be sufficiently original. A compilation is a form of literary work, regardless of the nature of the material it contains (see 2.2.2–3), but many are likely now to be defined as databases (see 8.2).

An abridgement or paraphrase, in the words of the editor using the ideas from the original, will also attract copyright, but a simple condensation or precis of an existing work is less likely to do so (see also 5.1.10).

1988 (CDPA) s1(1)(a); *Macmillan v Cooper*, 1923; *Cramp v Smythson*, 1944

2.1.10 Originality in photographic and digital copies, and photocopies

Because of the requirement of originality there can be no copyright in a photocopy of an existing work, even if it has been enlarged or reduced. The level of skill and labour required to produce any other form of copy, and possibly how far the medium has been changed, will determine whether it can qualify for copyright. In the case of photographs or drawings of three-dimensional objects, such as wax seals or antique vases, the positioning of the object, the angle at which the picture is taken, the lighting and the focus are 'all matters of judgment, albeit in many cases at a very basic level'. It is therefore probable that all such photographs would qualify.

A photograph of a significantly faded and damaged two-dimensional original, using 'great talent and technical skill' with appropriate lighting and filtration techniques, will qualify, but a simple photographic facsimile copy, a single frame from a microfilm, or an unmodified digitized image of a flat document would probably not. Quite where the borderline is between these two extremes is uncertain: 'one has to consider the extent to which the "copyist" is a mere copyist – merely performing an easy mechanical function. The more that is so the less is his contribution likely to be taken as "original".' A US judgment found that there was no copyright in facsimile photographs of paintings, but it has had no influence in the UK, which remains bound by the very first judgment under the Fine Arts Copyright Act in the 1860s.

Even if there is no infringement of copyright in a particular copy, reproduction might infringe any copyright in the original document itself and might be contrary to any contract entered into when the copy was purchased (for instance, the conditions imposed by an archive on purchasers of copies of materials in the collection, see 5.4.34).

1988 (CDPA) s178 'facsimile'; *Graves' case*, 1868–9; *Walter v Lane*, 1900; *LB (Plastics) v Swish Products*, 1979; *Reject Shop v Manners*, 1995; *Bridgeman v Corel*, 1997; Neuberger J in *Antiquesportfolio.com v Rodney Fitch & Co*, 2001, at 59; Jacob LJ in *Sawkins v Hyperion Records*, 2005, at 827–8

2.1.11 Originality: piratical copying

The question of originality inevitably becomes entangled with the question of infringement if one work copies a substantial part of another (see 5.2.3), unless the source work is no longer in copyright. The nature of the copying will determine the result. A simple pirated copy of a work (that is, one that duplicates an earlier copyright work, without permission) will not itself enjoy copyright protection because it is not original. On the other hand, something like a translation, or an arrangement of a piece of music, would normally qualify for its own protection even if unauthorized, because it will certainly be original. As a result, the use of the translation or arrangement would require permission from the copyright owners of both versions.

The principles are similar with artistic works. If a photographer re-creates from an earlier photograph, painting or other copyright image a scene that did not exist in nature, for example by setting up afresh a still-life or portrait in a studio, the resulting image (depending on the circumstances) might not be original and will probably infringe.

If one person produces a work that appears to the judge to be a copy of an earlier one, it is up to the author of the later work to prove that it was not produced by copying in order both to gain copyright protection for it as an original work (see 2.1.7) and to defeat an action for infringement (see 5.1.2). In rare cases a court might deny the owner of copyright in a pirated work the power to enforce the copyright if there are public interest issues involved (see 5.2.25).

1988 (CDPA) ss1(1)(a), 21(2), 171(3); *Turner v Robinson*, 1860; *Wood v Boosey*, 1868; *Byrne v Statist*, 1914; *Gross v Seligman*, 1914; *Redwood Music v Chappell*, 1982; *Creation Records v News Group Newspapers*, 1997; *ZYX Music v King*, 1997

2.1.12 Originality in sound recordings and films

A sound recording or film does not have to be original as such, but any part of a recording or film that is a copy of a previous recording or film does not attract copyright. In this context, copy means a direct copy from the earlier work; so a new film can be a re-make of an earlier one and be protected by copyright.

1988 (CDPA) s5(2)

2.1.13 Originality in broadcasts

A broadcast or a repeat of a broadcast does not have to be 'original' to attract copyright, but the copyright in a repeat expires on the same date as the copyright in the first transmission. However, if the repeat also includes new material, that part of it is entitled to its own copyright for the full term. There can be no copyright in a repeat of a broadcast in which the copyright has already expired, and there can be no copyright in a broadcast which infringes the copyright in another broadcast.

1988 (CDPA) ss6, 14(5); SI 1995/3297 reg 7

2.1.14 Originality in typographical arrangements

There is no requirement of originality in the typographical arrangement of a published edition (see 2.6.15). However, there is no copyright to the extent that the edition reproduces the typographical arrangement of a previous edition.

1988 (CDPA) s8

2.1.15 Triviality

The courts have decided that some works are too trivial to qualify for copyright; examples include the names of companies, the titles of books, magazines and songs, advertising slogans and simple forms. There is no copyright either in a personal name: anyone may adopt another's name without infringement of copyright. The courts have found that a signature is too trivial to qualify as a literary work, but that it might qualify as an artistic one (see 2.3.2).

Du Boulay v Du Boulay, 1869; *Francis Day and Hunter v Twentieth Century Fox*, 1940; *Exxon Corporation v Exxon Insurance*, 1982; *Elvis Presley Trade Marks*, 1997, at 558

2.1.16 Author

In most circumstances, the author is the person who creates the work, and is the first owner of the copyright in it. The circumstances where the author is not the first owner are considered in Chapter 3. The definition of the 'author' depends on the nature of the work in question, as discussed for each category below, and can be more than one person (see 2.2.14, 3.2.7–9). The identity of the author is important, even if he or she is not the first owner and regardless of any assignments of ownership, since the term of copyright normally depends on the length of his or her life.

There are some general difficulties with authorship and first ownership which should be recognized:

- It is not always easy to determine who is the author or the first owner, because it depends on the particular circumstances as well as on the law in force at the time the work was made or completed.

- When the author is an employee, there can be significant difficulties in discovering when he or she died, and thus the duration of the copyright. Since employees leave and in most cases will be untraceable thereafter this can be a major problem not only for potential users but also for their former employers, who are the first owners of the copyright (see 3.2.12ff.). The Master of the Rolls suggested in 1883 that employers should ensure that their employees were young and healthy, so as to prolong the period of copyright protection, but he offered no advice on how to discover when a former employee died. In most cases it will probably be necessary to make assumptions about the age of the author at the time the work was created and his or her life expectancy (probably 100 years nowadays) and to take a risk. The risks would be either that the court would disagree with the assumptions made or that the date of death is subsequently discovered and the assumption is shown to be wrong.

1988 (CDPA) ss9(1), 11(1), Sch 1 paras 10, 11; *Nottage v Jackson*, 1883

2.1.17 Author of anonymous or pseudonymous works or works of unknown authorship

Any sort of work may be of unknown authorship because the author is unidentified or used an impenetrable pseudonym. A work is of unknown authorship if it is not possible to ascertain the identity of the author, or of at least one of the authors if the work is of joint authorship (see 3.2.7), by reasonable enquiry. If, before copyright expires, the identity of the author or one of the authors becomes known, the work can no longer be treated as one of unknown authorship. In some older works, the copyright could immediately lapse. There are special provisions for the duration of copyright in some works of unknown authorship (see 2.2.19–20, 2.3.15–19, 2.4.16–17). There is also a special provision allowing use of works of unknown authorship in some circumstances (see 5.3.17, 5.4.25–26).

Reasonable enquiry is not defined in the Act but must include contacting the owner of the copyright or the publisher, or their successors (if identifiable) (see 3.3.20, 5.4.21). It would also be necessary to follow up any evidence given in the work itself as to who the author might have been, for instance initials or references to an office he or she held. For some pre-1912 works there are the statutory registers maintained by the Stationers' Company under the 1842 and 1862 Acts. These covered books (in a very wide sense, including maps, see 7.12.3), some dramatic and musical works, paintings, drawings and photographs, and some sculptures. They record the name and address of the copyright owner, the author and any assignor together with a description (and sometimes a copy) of the work. They are now preserved in The National Archives (registers in document reference COPY 3 and application forms with attached copies in document reference COPY 1). Some photographs were wrongly registered before 1883, incorrectly identifying the author, so these will be anonymous despite registration.

1842 s11; 1862 s4; 1988 (CDPA) s9(4–5); *Nottage v Jackson*, 1883

2.1.18 Duration

Establishing the duration of copyright is notoriously difficult, though some standardization has now simplified matters for recent works. The calculation of the duration of copyright in older literary, dramatic, musical and artistic works is especially difficult, particularly where expired copyrights have been revived (see 2.1.22) and where the duration provided by earlier statutes gives a later terminal date. For most literary, dramatic, musical and artistic works and films the basis is normally the life of the author. Duration of copyright in sound recordings, broadcasts and typographical arrangements owes nothing to the life of the author. Details are given under 'duration' for each type of work. The charts in the Appendix (see 9.1) show how the rules are applied to literary, dramatic, musical and artistic works and the following notes seek to explain the principles applying to them.

2.1.19 Duration: standard rules for literary, dramatic, musical and artistic works

The duration of copyright in the UK is governed by the Copyright, Designs and Patents Act 1988 as amended (but see 1.2.10). The basic rule is that copyright is for the life of the author plus 70 years, whether the work is published or not. If the author is unknown, the duration is either 70 years after the year of creation or, if it is made available to the public (including by being published, see 4.1.10) within that period, 70 years after being made available. However, the Regulations also say that these standard rules do not apply if copyright would last longer under earlier provisions, either those of the unamended 1988 Act or those of earlier Acts as set out in Schedule 1 to the 1988 Act. The durations given in this book thus reflect the standard rules and their possible variations.

1988 (CDPA) s12; SI 1995/3297 regs 5, 15

2.1.20 Duration: the variations for literary, dramatic, musical and artistic works

The three principal variations that apply are calculated as follows (remembering that in every case copyright expires at midnight on 31 December of the year in question):

- In some works of known authorship (see 2.2.17, 2.3.13), copyright expires in 2039 (50 years after the 1988 Act came into force), provided the author died before 1969. If the author died after 1969, the standard rule (life plus 70 years) would give a final date after 2039. Death in 1969 would give a terminal date of 2039 whichever rule applies.
- In some works of known authorship (see 2.2.18, 2.3.14), copyright expires 50 years after the year of publication, provided the author died more than 20 years before publication. If the author died at any time after the year 20 years before publication, the standard rule (life plus 70 years) would give a later date. Death precisely 20 years

earlier would give the same terminal date whichever rule applies.

- In some works of unknown authorship (see 2.2.20, 2.3.16, 2.3.18) copyright expires in 2039 (50 years after the 1988 Act came into force). If the work was created, first published or first made available to the public (see 4.1.10) after 1969, the standard rule (creation plus 70 years or publication/made available to the public plus 70 years) would give a later date. Creation, first publication or first being made available to the public in 1969 would give the same terminal date whichever rule applies.

2.1.21 Duration: films

Similar variations apply to some films, except that for the purposes of duration a film is anonymous when none of the 'persons connected with the film' (see 2.4.9) is known. The principal director is one of these persons, and also a joint author, but while the producer is the other joint author for the purposes of ownership his or her life is irrelevant to duration.

2.1.22 Extended and revived copyright

Until 1 January 1996, the standard term of copyright in literary, dramatic, musical and artistic works and films in the UK was 50 years from the death of the author, or 50 years from the year in which the work was first made available to the public if the author was unknown. When this standard term was changed in 1995 to 70 years under the EU directive of 1993, not only were copyrights and moral rights still subsisting on 31 December 1995 extended, but also some copyrights and moral rights that had expired before then were revived even if they had expired many years earlier. Archivists and records managers would be well advised to assume that, for most purposes, all works in their care are covered by the provisions as set out in this book, since those provisions will cover works whose copyright has been extended or revived in the UK (though see 1.2.10). They should however be careful if they wish to publish a work in another country which has even longer terms (such as Spain, which gives life plus 80 years in certain instances, and France and Belgium, which give extended coverage to some works published during or between the two world wars).

Until 31 October 2003, the term of copyright in a sound recording was 50 years from the end of the year of its creation or 50 years from the end of the year in which the recording was released, if it was released during the first 50 years after creation. Under the 2003 regulations, the concept of release has been removed, and the 50-year term now starts at creation, publication or the first playing or communication to the public. This has resulted in the extension of copyright in some unpublished sound recordings (see 2.5.12).

Directive 1993 (Term); 1988 (CDPA) ss12, 13(A), 13(B); SI 1995/3297 regs 16, 17; SI 2003/2498 reg 29

2.1.23 Application of extended and revived copyright

Copyright in a literary, dramatic, musical or artistic work or a film was extended or revived only if, on 1 July 1995 (the date the directive came into force), the work qualified for and was still protected by copyright somewhere in the EEA (see 1.2.8). The directive made elaborate provisions for revival, but two subsequent cases before the European Court of Justice have simplified matters. Thus:

- Copyright was extended or revived, even if only for a few months, in any work whose author was a national of an EEA member state who died after 31 December 1924, no matter how many years earlier copyright had expired under the old provisions. This is because Germany and Spain both already had 70-year terms, and they are obliged to apply those terms to nationals of all member states, not merely their own nationals.
- Where by 1 July 1995 copyright had expired in the UK in a work whose author was not an EEA national, the copyright was probably not revived.
- Copyright was extended in an anonymous work which was created or first made available to the public (see 4.1.10) in the UK after 31 December 1944.
- Copyright was revived in the UK in an anonymous work which once qualified for copyright in the UK (see 3.1), which was created or made available to the public in another member state of the EEA prior to 1 January 1945, and which still qualified for copyright there on 1 July 1995. In Germany prior to the directive, literary, dramatic and musical works were protected for 70 years after publication or (apparently) perpetually if unpublished. Anonymous photographs were protected in Germany for only 25 years from creation or publication, but other anonymous artistic works were given no special term at all.

The owner of the revived copyright is the person (or body) who was the owner immediately before the copyright expired, unless that person has died in the meantime (or the body has ceased to exist). If the last owner has died (or ceased to exist) the owner of the revived copyright is:

- for literary, dramatic, musical and artistic works, the author, or his or her heirs; and
- for films, the principal director, or his or her heirs.

Thus the rules about ownership by employers no longer apply in such cases. There are further special provisions to protect people from infringement of revived copyright, if they legitimately started to exploit a work when it was out of copyright; to extend the term of licences granted for the full life of the original copyright (irrespective of whether the copyright owner has changed as a result of the death of the person who made the grant); and to ensure that assertions or waivers of moral rights continue unchanged.

Copyright in sound recordings still in copyright on 31 October 2003 was extended in a few cases, but the ownership was unaffected. Existing licences were extended where appropriate.

1965 (Germany) art 66; SI 1995/3297 regs 16, 17, 19, 21, 23; SI 2003/2498 regs 29, 38–39; *Phil Collins v Imtrat*, 1994; *Land Hessen v G Ricordi*, 2003

2.1.24 Works affected by revived copyright

Revived copyright does not apply to the bulk of records, including:

- literary, dramatic and musical works and engravings of any date that were unpublished on 1 August 1989, photographs taken and films made after 1 June 1957, and other artistic works of unknown authorship of any date that were unpublished on 1 August 1989, all of whose copyrights were set to expire later than 1994;
- works in Crown copyright, whose duration and ownership is not dependent on authorship;
- copyright in broadcasts and typographical arrangements, whose duration was not extended by the 1993 directive.

Works most clearly affected were (bearing in mind that some revived copyrights will since have expired again) those whose copyright had expired under the old law but whose authors died sufficiently recently to be caught by the new. They include:

- literary, dramatic and musical works that were published and whose author had died between 1924 and 1944 (see 2.2.16);
- photographs, including those taken before 1 July 1912, and most other types of artistic work of known authorship taken by an author who died between 1924 and 1944 (see 2.3.12, 2.3.15);
- films (as sequences of photographs) of known authorship made by an author who died between 1924 and 1944 (see 2.3.12, 2.4.10).

Pre-1912 photographs have caused much confusion, since commentators used to be able to assert that all the copyrights had expired: the 1911 Act provided for their expiry at the latest 50 years after creation, with no reference to authorship, and so did the 1956 Act. For photographs of known authorship at least, that simple assumption no longer holds good.

1911 ss3, 21; 1956 Sch 2, Sch 7 paras 2, 16

2.1.25 An example

For example, suppose a photographer took a graphic picture of the General Strike in 1926 for a UK newspaper. The photographer died in 1942 and the newspaper ceased to exist in 1993. Copyright in that photograph would have expired on 31 December 1976 (50 years after creation) under the terms of the Copyright Act 1911, and the owner of the copyright at that date would have been the newspaper. Copyright in the photograph would have revived on 1 January 1996, because although out of copyright in the UK it was still in copyright in Germany, where rights already lasted for 70 years from the author's death. The owner of the revived copyright would be the author's heirs and it would finally expire on 31 December 2012 (70 years after the author's death).

1911 s21; 1956 Sch 7 para 2; 1988 (CDPA) s12(2), Sch 1 para 12(2)(c); SI 1995/3297 regs 5, 16(1), 19(2)(b)

2.2 Literary, dramatic and musical works

2.2.1 Definition

Although literary, dramatic and musical works are defined differently, they are treated in the same way for most purposes. In practical terms the main reason to take note of the distinctions is that a single composition can have separate authors and owners for each of the different copyright works of which it is composed. Thus an opera is both a dramatic work (the libretto) and a musical work (the music), and the words of an individual aria (a poem) might be a separate literary work. Moreover, when the opera is performed on stage the sets will be artistic works.

2.2.2 Literary works

A literary work is an original work of any date which is not a dramatic or musical work, which may be written, spoken or sung and which has been recorded in writing or otherwise (see 2.1.3). Clearly then, 'literary' does not mean any high or erudite quality. Instead it means something 'which was intended to afford either information or instruction, or pleasure in the form of literary enjoyment'. 'Writing' includes any form of notation or code, so a literary work does not have to be expressed in words, and can include mathematical formulae, numbers and ideograms (such as Chinese calligraphy, which will also be an artistic work, see 2.1.2, 2.3.2), messages in cipher, circuit diagrams (as notation of components) and stories told as strip cartoons without any words (though each picture will have a distinct artistic copyright). Literary works include:

- a table, such as a list of document references or a railway timetable, unless it is a database (see 8.2);
- a compilation, but a work that is a database, such as a catalogue, is not a compilation (see 2.2.3, 8.2);
- a database (see 8.2);
- a computer program, which is a series of instructions controlling a computer (see 6.6)
- design material for a computer program;
- the words, but not the music, of a song.

1988 (CDPA) ss1(1)(a), 3(1), 178 'writing'; Davey LJ in *Hollinrake v Truswell*, 1894, at 428; *University of London Press v University Tutorial Press*, 1916; *Exxon Corporation v Exxon Insurance*, 1982; *Anacon v Environmental Research Technologies*, 1994; *Aubrey Max Sandman v Panasonic UK*, 1998

2.2.3 Compilations

A compilation is a form of literary work, regardless of the nature of the material of which it is composed, so it may consist entirely of non-literary works, such as pictures, numbers or samples of music (which themselves might enjoy separate copyrights), and it may be, for instance, a form. For a compilation to qualify, the process of compilation must have involved skilful arrangement, judicious selection and/or comprehensive coverage, but the skill and labour used simply to collect information is irrelevant (see also 8.2.7). Thus a production which brings more than one work together will not be a compilation if the skill lies in creating those separate works rather than in bringing them together. In all cases, a song consisting of words and music comprises two separate copyrights in those works but none in the song as a compilation (see 2.1.2).

The definition of a compilation made on or after 27 March 1996 has been curtailed by the wide definition of a database (see 8.2). The definition of a compilation made after that date would probably include a form, map (as a compilation of various pieces of information), advertisement or poster including any pictures, but in some cases might no longer include:

- a collection of other works (such as a poetry anthology or a book of photographs);
- a microfilm;
- a trade catalogue or directory;
- a printed catalogue of the documents in an archive.

1988 (CDPA) ss1(1)(a), 3(1)(a); *Southern v Bailes*, 1894; *Whitaker v Publishers Circular*, 1946–9; *Chappell v Redwood Music*, 1981; *Geographia v Penguin Books*, 1985; *Autospin v Beehive Spinning*, 1995; *Waterlow Publishers v Rose*, 1995

2.2.4 Dramatic works

A dramatic work is an original work of movement or action of any date, which is capable of being performed before an audience and which is recorded in writing or some other form (see 2.1.3). 'Writing' includes any form of notation or code. A dramatic work includes not only works of acting (plays, operas), dancing (choreography) or mime, but also many films. In practice, most administrators of copyright in films regard only fiction films as dramatic works, but the law does not actually seem so restrictive so long as they are works of action and are capable of being performed before an audience. It follows that the whole libretto of an opera (containing directions for action as well as words to be performed) is a dramatic work, but that the words of an individual aria are probably a literary work since they do not comprise a work of action (the aria contains no directions for actions, merely the words to be sung). Similarly, a comedy film may be a dramatic work, but individual verbal jokes are probably literary works.

1988 (CDPA) ss1(1)(a), 3(1), 178 'writing'; *Creation Records v News Group Newspapers*, 1997; *Norowzian v Arks (No 2)*, 2000

2.2.5 Musical works

A musical work is an original work combining melodies and harmonies, of any date, which is capable of being performed to produce sounds appreciated by the ear, and which is recorded in writing or some other form (see 2.1.3). Writing includes any form of notation or code, including musical notation. A musical work does not include any words that are to be performed with the music, such as those of a song, nor any actions intended to be performed with the music, which have separate literary and dramatic copyrights, nor any elements of performing style, which have no copyright at all though they might be protected by performers' rights (see 8.5), but it does of course include the musical symbols indicating volume and so on.

1988 (CDPA) ss1(1)(a), 3(1), 178 'writing'; *Coffey v Warner and Chappell Music*, 2005; *Sawkins v Hyperion Records*, 2005

2.2.6 Author

The person who creates a literary, dramatic or musical work is the author, in whatever manner the work is recorded in material form. In this context, the person who 'creates' means the person who originates the actual language, notes or collection of ideas used. See also 2.1.16.

1988 (CDPA) ss3(2), 9(1)

2.2.7 Nature of author

In the case of literary, dramatic and musical works, as in artistic works (see 2.3.10), the author can normally only be a 'natural person' (that is, a human) or persons. There is one exception. The author of a computer-generated work is the person who made the arrangements for its creation, and could be a company (see 2.2.13).

1988 (CDPA) s9(1)

2.2.8 Author of an exact transcript of impromptu words or music

The speaker or player is the author of a work first recorded word-for-word or note-for-note by someone else (for instance, shorthand notes of a letter or speech, a text dictated to a secretary or amanuensis, a tape recording of a song, or a tape recording of the interviewee in an oral history interview), whether or not the person making the recording is an employee and even if the speaker or player has not given permission or does not know that the recording is being made.

1988 (CDPA) ss3(2) and (3), 9(1); *Donoghue v Allied Newspapers*, 1938

2.2.9 Author of words spoken impromptu

If a listener makes the first record of a work (such as an impromptu speech) in a material form by writing it down in his or her own words from general ideas expressed by a person speaking without notes, the person making that record will be the author of the work. It does not seem that this could apply to a musical work, and could probably only apply to the outline theme of a dramatic work.

1988 (CDPA) ss3(2), 9(1); *Walter v Lane*, 1900

2.2.10 Author of the recorded version

Separately from the copyright in the work recorded, the person who makes the recording may have a distinct right as the author of the recorded version itself. Thus, a person giving a speech would be the author of the speech if recorded as text by another, but the person who writes the speech down might be the author of the text as a distinct literary work if there has been some use of skill in the making of them (even, perhaps, if they are verbatim). Similarly, the player of a new musical work, a person giving a speech or the people taking part in an interview for an oral history project which is first recorded as a sound recording would be the author of that musical work, speech or interview, while the producer of the sound recording of it would be the author of the sound recording (see 2.5.4ff.). It follows that the interviewer and interviewee in an oral history recording would be authors of their respective parts of the interview, while the interviewer would be the author of the sound recording. Because of the existence of copyrights in any works recorded, there may be restrictions on the use that the author of the recording may make of it (see 2.5.2).

1988 (CDPA) ss3(3), 9(1); *Walter v Lane*, 1900

2.2.11 Author of a composite work

Where a work is a composite work in which the contribution of each person is separately identifiable (such as a collection of essays, an encyclopedia, a CD-ROM), there will be several authors, of the individual component parts and perhaps of the whole composite work (see 2.15, but see also 8.2).

1988 (CDPA) s9(1)

2.2.12 Author of computer-generated works before 1989

For computer-generated material created before 1 August 1989 for which there was no human author, there can be no copyright since this was not recognized as a distinct type of work.

2.2.13 Author of computer-generated works after 1989

For computer-generated works created on or after 1 August 1989 for which there was no human author, the author is taken to be the person by whom the arrangements necessary for the creation of the work are undertaken. In many cases this will be the author of the computer program which generated it.

1988 (CDPA) ss9(3), 178, 'computer-generated'; *Nova Productions v Mazooma Games*, 2006

2.2.14 Joint authors of works

Where two people have collaborated to create a work and their contributions are indistinguishable, they will be joint authors (see 3.2.7–9). Thus when someone writes an article based on an interview with someone else, using the interviewee's ideas and opinions but expressing them in his or her own words, they will probably be joint authors of the resulting work. Similarly, a solicitor and his or her client could be joint authors of a will drafted on the basis of the client's precise instructions (but see 7.3.9). The contributions do not need to be equal, but an insubstantial contribution will not qualify, nor will the wrong kind of contribution. For instance, the director and actors who have contributed to a play merely by their manner of performing it have not done enough to qualify as joint authors.

1988 (CDPA) s10(1); *Hadley v Kemp*, 1999; *Brighton v Jones*, 2004

2.2.15 Author: Crown and Parliamentary copyright

The significance of the author of a Crown or Parliamentary copyright literary, dramatic or musical work is merely to determine the copyright status of the work (see 3.2.28–35), though such authors can have moral rights (see 8.1.5, 8.1.7).

1988 (CDPA) ss163, 165

2.2.16 Duration: known authorship: standard term

Copyright expires 70 years after the end of the calendar year of the author's death, whether the work is published or unpublished, unless earlier provisions would give a later date (see 2.1.18–25).

1988 (CDPA) s12(2); SI 1995/3297 regs 5(1), 15

2.2.17 Duration: known authorship: unpublished before 1989

Copyright expires on 31 December 2039, if the work was created, but had not been published, performed in public, offered for sale to the public in the form of records or broadcast, before 1 August 1989, and the author died before 1 January 1969 (see 2.1.20, 2.1.22).

1956 s2(3); 1988 (CDPA) Sch 1 para 12(4)(a); SI 1995/3297 reg 15

2.2.18 Duration: known authorship: published before 1989

Copyright expires 50 years after the end of the calendar year in which the work was first published, performed in public, offered for sale to the public in the form of records or broadcast, provided that act took place before 1 August 1989 and the author died more than 20 years earlier (see 2.1.20, 2.1.22).

1956 s2(3); 1988 (CDPA) Sch 1 para 12(2)(a); SI 1995/3297 reg 15

2.2.19 Duration: unknown authorship: standard term

Copyright expires 70 years after the end of the calendar year in which the work was made, or, if it is made available to the public (see 4.1.10) during that period, 70 years after the end of the calendar year in which the work was first made available. If the identity of the author becomes known before the expiry of copyright, the work will no longer be regarded as of unknown authorship and the provisions for known authors will apply (see 2.2.16–18). Earlier provisions will apply if they would give a later expiry date (see 2.1.18–25). However, see 5.4.25–26.

1988 (CDPA) s12(3); SI 1995/3297 reg 5

2.2.20 Duration: unknown authorship: unpublished before 1969

Copyright expires on 31 December 2039 (see 2.1.20) for all works created before 1 January 1969 and unpublished before 1 August 1989, of which the identity of the author does not become known before copyright expires, if:

- they are not made available to the public (see 4.1.10) before 1 January 2040; or
- they were first made available to the public but not published (see 4.1.2) before 1 January 1969.

However, for some relief from these long terms see 5.4.25–26.

1988 (CDPA) Sch 1 para 12(3)(b); SI 1995/3297 reg 15

2.2.21 Duration: Crown copyright: unpublished before 1915

For unpublished works created before 1 January 1915, copyright expires on 31 December 2039.

1988 (CDPA) s163(3)(a), Sch 1 para 41(3)

2.2.22 Duration: Crown copyright: created after 1914 but unpublished

For unpublished works created on or after 1 January 1915, copyright expires 125 years from the end of the calendar year in which the work was created.

1988 (CDPA) s163(3)(a)

2.2.23 Duration: Crown copyright: created and published before 1989

For works created and published before 1 August 1989, copyright expires 50 years from the end of the calendar year of first publication.

1956 s39(3)(b); 1988 (CDPA) Sch 1 para 41(2)(a)

2.2.24 Duration: Crown copyright: created before but commercially published after 1989

In the case of works created before 1 August 1989 but first published after that date, where they are published commercially (see 4.1.4) and such publication is less than 75 years from the end of the calendar year in which the work was created, copyright expires 50 years from the end of the calendar year of first publication.

1988 (CDPA) s163(3)(b)

2.2.25 Duration: Crown copyright: created before but non-commercially published after 1989

For works created before 1 August 1989 but first published after that date, where they are published non-commercially (see 4.1.4) and such publication is less than 75 years from the end of the calendar year in which the work was created, copyright expires 125 years from the end of the calendar year of creation or on 31 December 2039, whichever is later.

1988 (CDPA) s163(3)(a), Sch 1 para 41(3)

2.2.26 Duration: Crown copyright: created before but published after 1989

In the case of works created before, but first published on or after 1 August 1989, at a date more than 75 years from the end of the calendar year in which the work was created, copyright expires 125 years from the end of the calendar year of creation or on 31 December 2039, whichever is later.

1988 (CDPA) s163(3)(a), Sch 1 para 41(3)

2.2.27 Duration: Crown copyright: created and commercially published after 1989

In the case of works created on or after 1 August 1989 and published commercially (see 4.1.4) less than 75 years from the end of the calendar year in which the work was created, copyright expires 50 years from the end of the calendar year of first commercial publication.

1988 (CDPA) s163(3)(b)

2.2.28 Duration: Crown copyright: created and non-commercially published after 1989

For works created on or after 1 August 1989 and published non-commercially (see 4.1.4) less than 75 years from the end of the calendar year in which the work was created, copyright expires 125 years from the end of the calendar year of creation.

1988 (CDPA) s163(3)(a)

2.2.29 Duration: Crown copyright: created and published after 1989

For works created on or after 1 August 1989 and published more than 75 years from the end of the calendar year in which the work was created, copyright expires 125 years from the end of the calendar year in which the work was created.

1988 (CDPA) s163(3)(a)

2.2.30 Duration: Parliamentary copyright

Parliamentary copyright (including copyrights of the Scottish Parliament and the Assemblies of Wales and Northern Ireland, see 3.2.33–36) in a literary, dramatic or musical work expires 50 years after the end of the calendar year in which the work was made.

1988 (CDPA) s165(3, 7)

2.2.31 Duration: computer-generated works

Copyright expires 50 years after the end of the calendar year in which the work was made.

1988 (CDPA) s12(7); SI 1995/3297 reg 5

2.2.32 Duration: universities and colleges

The Copyright Act 1775 gave perpetual copyright in books bequeathed or given to the two universities in England (Oxford and Cambridge), the four universities in Scotland (Aberdeen, Edinburgh, Glasgow and St Andrews) and the colleges of Eton, Westminster and Winchester. This copyright was curtailed by the 1988 Act, to end on 31 December 2039. However, according to the Whitford Committee, only Clarendon's *Rebellion* and *Life*, published by Oxford, are now believed to be covered by it.

1911 s33; 1956 s46(1); 1988 (CDPA) Sch 1 para 13(1); Whitford Report (Board of Trade) para 648

2.3 Artistic works

2.3.1 Definition

There are several different forms which an artistic work can take.

2.3.2 Graphic work

A graphic work includes:

- a painting, drawing, diagram (including a circuit diagram, but see 2.2.2), graph, map, chart or plan
- an engraving, etching, lithograph, woodcut or similar work
- a typeface, being a graphical image representing a single letter, numeral, character or ornamental motif.

All such works are covered, irrespective of artistic merit, though what seems to characterize them is that they are things to be appreciated by the eye. Thus a logo is likely to be an artistic work even though the purpose is to identify the organization, rather than to create a work of art.

An artistic work can, in some circumstances, be composed entirely of text, such as a poem arranged on the page to form the shape of a cat (which will also be a literary work, see 2.1.2, 2.2.2). The courts seem to think that a person's signature qualifies as a graphic artistic work, but probably only if it is more distinctive and personal than mere cursive writing, so the more illegible it is the better it seems. A map is an artistic work of which the written elements form an intrinsic and 'visually significant' part, and an advertisement or poster would similarly qualify as an artistic work if it is primarily graphic and any text is decorative and/or too insubstantial to qualify for copyright as literary material. Technical information on engineering or architectural drawings is not part of the artistic work because, no matter how important it may be technically, it is not 'visually significant'. However, an advertisement or poster might be a literary work (a compilation) if it consisted of an assembly of graphic and other elements (see 2.2.3). In these sorts of case the nature of the work will depend on the balance of the elements and the extent to which they are artistic in the relevant sense.

An engraving or similar work is not merely the print taken from the plate but also the plate itself (see also 7.12). A typeface is the design of a single character in a font; there is no copyright protection for the font as a whole, and clearly a typeface is not the same as a typographical arrangement (see 2.6.15). For typefaces as designs see 8.6.2.

1988 (CDPA) ss4(1)(a), 4(2), 54(1), 178 'typeface'; *Wham-O Manufacturing v Lincoln Industries*, 1985; Lord Oliver in *Interlego v Tyco Industries*, 1988, at 367; Whitford J in *Rose Plastics v William Beckett (Plastics)*, 1989, at 123; *Anacon v Environmental Research*

Technologies, 1994; *Elvis Presley Trade Marks*, 1997, at 558; *Anne Frank Trade Mark*, 1998, at 389; *Aubrey Max Sandman v Panasonic UK*, 1998; *Vermaat and Powell v Boncrest*, 2001

2.3.3 Photograph

A photograph is a recording of light or other radiation (including, for example, X-rays and heat) on any medium on which an image is produced or from which an image may by any means be produced, and which is not part of a film (see 2.4.2). This definition applies only to the negative image (or the slide, or the original digital file, as appropriate); a print from that original is merely a copy and will attract its own distinct copyright only if there is some degree of skill and judgment required to make it. A single frame of a motion-picture film qualifies as a photograph only if it was made before 1 June 1957 (see 2.4.1).

Thanks to their quasi-mechanical nature, photographs have not always been treated as fully fledged artistic works, hence the variations in the definition of an author under successive Acts (see 2.3.7), though they are now all protected in the UK irrespective of artistic merit. In some countries, such as Switzerland, the courts have to apply a test of artistic quality to a photograph: it might not be regarded as original, and thus as qualifying for copyright protection, if it was obvious and could have been taken by anyone or if the purpose was not artistic.

1988 (CDPA) ss4(1)(a), 4(2); *Mayer & Pierson v Betbeder & Schwabbé*, 1862; *Courier Lithographing v Donaldson Lithographing*, 1900; *Apple Corps v Cooper*, 1993; *Blau v BBC*, 2002

2.3.4 Sculpture, collage and architecture

A sculpture includes a cast or model, including a medal. A collage must be formed of items stuck to a surface; a mere co-location of loose objects will not qualify. Both sculptures and collages are protected irrespective of artistic merit.

A work of architecture is a building, including any fixed structure, and a model for a building. The copyright in it is distinct from any copyright in design drawings from which the building was made. It is unclear whether a work of architecture must have artistic merit.

1988 (CDPA) ss4(1)(a) and (b), 4(2); *Reliance (Nameplates) v Art Jewels*, 1953; *Creation Records v News Group Newspapers*, 1997

2.3.5 Works of artistic craftsmanship

A work of artistic craftsmanship is undefined by the Act, and the courts have failed to provide any consistent definition either. The term probably means a work which required skilled craftsmanship to make (so a machine-made item, a flimsy prototype or crude work by a hobbyist amateur probably would not qualify), which was intended to have (and has) aesthetic appeal, and which gives emotional or intellectual satisfaction to a section of the community. Examples might be stained glass, bookbinding and needlework. A designer dress was found to qualify, but a poorly made baby cape, intended to protect the baby rather than to be appreciated by the eye, was not. This requirement of artistic merit is a notable and subjective hurdle which is not put in the way of most other kinds of artistic work. The courts seem to have decided that the artistry and the craftsmanship do not have to be combined in a single person, so there may be joint workmanship by an artist (designer) and craftsman. For works of artistic craftsmanship as designs see 8.6.2ff.

1988 (CDPA) s4(1)(c); *Radley Gowns v Costas Spyrou*, 1975; *Hensher v Restawile Upholstery*, 1975; *Merlet v Mothercare*, 1986; *Bonz Group v Cooke*, 1994; *Creation Records v News Group Newspapers*, 1997; *Vermaat and Powell v Boncrest*, 2001

2.3.6 Author

The author of an artistic work (see also 2.1.16) other than a photograph (see 2.3.7) is the person who is responsible for the actual design. This means that both a painter who uses his or her own skill to paint a work under the general instructions of someone else, and an architect whose designs are realized as a building by a builder, are the authors. If a builder erects a building without reference to plans, he or she is the author of the resulting building, whereas if a scene-painter paints scenery according to specific designs of the designer, the designer is the author.

1988 (CDPA) s9(1); *Kenrick v Lawrence*, 1890

2.3.7 Author of a photograph

- Photographs, of any date: for the purpose of determining the duration of copyright and for the purposes of moral rights (see 8.1.3), the author is the person who created the photograph (normally the photographer).
- Photographs created before 1 July 1912: for the purpose of determining the first owner of the copyright, the author is the person who created the photograph (normally the photographer).
- Photographs taken between 1 July 1912 and 31 July 1989: for the purpose of determining the first owner of the copyright, the author is the person who, at the time when the photograph was taken, was the owner of the material (for instance, the negative) on which it was taken.

- Photographs created since 1 August 1989: for the purpose of determining the first owner of the copyright, the author is the person who created the photograph (normally the photographer).

Thus in photographs taken before 1912 and since 1989 the photographer is normally the author and first owner (see 2.1.16), but the courts have at times had difficulty in deciding who the 'photographer' actually is. In the context of professional studios, for instance, the person who presses the shutter release may be only an assistant, acting on the instructions of the photographer. It is not the mechanical act of taking the photograph that decides authorship but the work of 'the inventive or master mind' in charge. If the photograph is merely a reproduction of another work, there will probably be no copyright at all (see 2.1.10).

1862 s1; 1911 s21; 1956 s48 'photograph'; 1988 (CDPA) s9(1); SI 1996/2967 reg 19; Cotton LJ in *Nottage v Jackson*, 1883, at 635; *Melville v Mirror of Life*, 1895; *Stackemann v Paton*, 1906; *Creation Records v News Group Newspapers*, 1997

2.3.8   Author of computer-generated works before 1989

For computer-generated works created before 1 August 1989 for which there was no human author, there can be no copyright since these were not recognized as a distinct type of work.

2.3.9   Author of computer-generated works after 1989

For computer-generated works created on or after 1 August 1989 for which there was no human author, the author is taken to be the person by whom the arrangements necessary for the creation of the work are undertaken. Composite images made up of bitmap files, as in a computer game, are computer-generated, and the author is the author of the program who devised their appearance.

1988 (CDPA) ss9(3), 178; *Nova Productions v Mazooma Games*, 2006

2.3.10 Nature of author

In artistic works, as in literary, dramatic and musical works (see 2.2.7), the author can normally only be a 'natural person' (that is, a human) or persons. There are exceptions:

- a computer-generated work, since the author is the person who arranged for its creation, and this could be a company (see 2.3.9)
- a photograph made on or after 1 July 1912 and before 1 August 1989, since under the 1911 and 1956 Acts the author was the owner of the material on which the

photograph was taken, which could be a corporate body (see 2.3.7)

- a film made before 1 June 1957, since although it enjoyed no protection as such, individual frames were treated as photographs (see 2.4.3).

Artistic works may also be works of joint authorship, and the same considerations apply as to literary, dramatic and musical works (see 2.2.14).

1911 s21; 1956 s48 'photograph', Sch 7 para 16; 1988 (CDPA) s9(1)

2.3.11 Author: Crown and Parliamentary copyright

The significance of the author of a Crown or Parliamentary copyright artistic work is merely to determine the copyright status of the work (see 3.2.28–35), though such authors can have moral rights (see 8.1.5, 8.1.7).

1988 (CDPA) ss163, 165

2.3.12 Duration: known authorship: standard term

Copyright expires 70 years after the end of the calendar year of the author's death, whether the work is published or unpublished (see 2.1.18–24), except in the case of some photographs taken between 1 June 1957 and 31 July 1989 and some engravings created before 1 August 1989 (see 2.3.13–14).

1988 (CDPA) s12(2); SI 1995/3297 reg 5; SI 1996/2967 reg 19

2.3.13 Duration: known authorship: unpublished photographs and engravings created before 1989

Copyright expires on 31 December 2039 (see 2.1.20), if the work:

- had not been published before 1 August 1989; and
- the author died before 1 January 1969; and it was either
- a photograph taken on or after 1 June 1957 and before 1 August 1989; or
- an engraving made before 1 August 1989.

For the duration of copyright, and revived copyright, in photographs of known authorship taken before 1957 and especially before 1912, see 2.1.19, 2.1.22–24.

1988 (CDPA) Sch 1 para 12(4)(b) and (c); SI 1995/3297 reg 15; SI 1996/2967 reg 19

2.3.14 Duration: known authorship: photographs and engravings published before 1989

Copyright expires 50 years after the end of the calendar year in which the work was first published (see 2.1.20), if the work:

- was published before 1 August 1989; and
- the author died more than 20 years before publication; and it was either
- a photograph taken on or after 1 June 1957; or
- an engraving made before 1 August 1989.

1956 s3(4)(a) and (b); 1988 (CDPA) Sch 1 para 12(2)(b) and (c); SI 1995/3297 reg 15; SI 1996/2967 reg 19

2.3.15 Duration: unknown authorship: standard term

Copyright expires 70 years after the end of the calendar year in which the work was made, or, if it is made available to the public (see 4.1.10) during that period, 70 years after the end of the calendar year in which the work was first made available (see 2.1.18–24). If the identity of the author becomes known before the expiry of copyright, the work will no longer be regarded as of unknown authorship and the normal provisions will apply. Earlier provisions will apply if they would give a later expiry date (see 2.1.20). However, see 5.4.25–26.

1988 (CDPA) s12(3); SI 1995/3297 reg 5

2.3.16 Duration: unknown authorship: unpublished before 1969

Copyright expires on 31 December 2039 (see 2.1.20) for all works (except photographs) created before 1 January 1969 and unpublished before 1 August 1969, of which the identity of the author does not become known before copyright expires, if:

- they are not made available to the public (see 4.1.10) before 1 January 2040; or
- they were first made available to the public before 1 January 1969.

However, for some relief from these long terms see 5.4.25–26.

1988 (CDPA) Sch 1 para 12(3)(b); SI 1995/3297 reg 15

2.3.17 Duration: unknown authorship: photographs before 1957

For photographs of unknown authorship created before 1 June 1957, copyright expires 70 years after the end of the calendar year in which the photograph was taken, or, if it was made available to the public (see 4.1.10) during that period, 70 years after the end of the calendar year in which it was first made available, unless the identity of the author becomes known before copyright expires (see 2.1.18–24). However, for some relief from these long terms see 5.4.25–26.

1911 s21; 1956 Sch 7 para 2; 1988 (CDPA) s12(3), Sch 1 para 12(2)(c); SI 1995/3297 regs 5, 16

2.3.18 Duration: unknown authorship: unpublished photographs, 1957–1969

Copyright expires on 31 December 2039 for photographs created on or after 1 June 1957 and before 1 January 1969, which were not published before 1 August 1989 and which are not made available to the public (see 4.1.10) before 1 January 2040, provided the identity of the author does not become known before copyright expires (see 2.1.20).

1988 (CDPA) Sch 1 para 12(4)(c); SI 1995/3297 reg 15

2.3.19 Duration: unknown authorship: published photographs 1957–1989

Copyright expires 70 years after the end of the calendar year in which the work was published, for photographs created on or after 1 June 1957 and published before 1 January 1989, unless the identity of the author becomes known before copyright expires.

1956 s3(4)(b); 1988 (CDPA) s12(3)(b), Sch 1 para 12(2)(c); SI 1995/3297 regs 5, 16

2.3.20 Duration: Crown copyright: before 1989

Works, other than engravings and photographs, created before 1 August 1989, whether published or unpublished: copyright expires 50 years from the end of the calendar year of creation.

1956 s39(4); 1988 (CDPA) Sch 1 para 41(2)(b)

2.3.21 Duration: Crown copyright: unpublished engravings before 1989

Engravings created but not published before 1 August 1989: copyright expires on 31 December 2039.

1988 (CDPA) Sch 1 para 41(4)(a)

2.3.22 Duration: Crown copyright: published engravings before 1989

Engravings created and published before 1 August 1989: copyright expires 50 years from the end of the calendar year of first publication.

1956 s39(4); 1988 (CDPA) Sch 1 para 41(2)(b)

2.3.23 Duration: Crown copyright: photographs before 1957

Photographs taken before 1 June 1957, whether published or unpublished: copyright expires 50 years from the end of the calendar year in which the photograph was taken.

1956 s39(4), Sch 7 para 30; 1988 (CDPA) Sch 1 para 41(2)(d)

2.3.24 Duration: Crown copyright: published photographs 1957–1989

Photographs taken on or after 1 June 1957, and published before 1 August 1989: copyright expires 50 years from the end of the calendar year of first publication.

1956 s39(4); 1988 (CDPA) Sch 1 para 41(2)(d)

2.3.25 Duration: Crown copyright: unpublished photographs 1957–1989

Photographs taken on or after 1 June 1957 and before 1 August 1989, but not published before 1 August 1989, whether or not published thereafter: copyright expires on 31 December 2039.

1988 (CDPA) Sch 1 para 41(4)(b)

2.3.26 Duration: Crown copyright: created and unpublished after 1989

Unpublished works created on or after 1 August 1989: copyright expires 125 years from the end of the calendar year in which the work was created.

1988 (CDPA) s163(3)(a)

2.3.27 Duration: Crown copyright: created and published after 1989

Works created on or after 1 August 1989 and published more than 75 years after the end of the year in which the work was created: copyright expires 125 years from the end of the calendar year in which the work was created.

1988 (CDPA) s163(3)(a)

2.3.28 Duration: Crown copyright: created and commercially published after 1989

Works created on or after 1 August 1989 and published commercially (see 4.1.4) less than 75 years after the end of the calendar year in which the work was created: copyright expires 50 years from the end of the calendar year of first publication.

1988 (CDPA) s163(3)(b)

2.3.29 Duration: Crown copyright: created and non-commercially published after 1989

Works created on or after 1 August 1989 and published non-commercially (see 4.1.4) less than 75 years after the end of the calendar year in which the work was created: copyright expires 125 years after the end of the calendar year of creation.

1988 (CDPA) s163(3)(a)

2.3.30 Duration: Parliamentary copyright

Parliamentary copyright (including copyrights of the Scottish Parliament and the Assemblies of Wales and Northern Ireland, see 3.2.33–36) in an artistic work expires 50 years after the end of the calendar year in which the work was made.

1988 (CDPA) s165(3, 7)

2.3.31 Duration: computer-generated works

Copyright expires 50 years after the end of the calendar year in which the work was made.

1988 (CDPA) s12(7); SI 1995/3297 reg 5

2.3.32 Duration: typefaces

The general term of copyright in typeface designs is the same as for any other graphic works, but the effect is limited after a time. Once a typeface design has been used for the production of materials to reproduce that typeface (such as printer's type, a computer font), and those materials have been marketed, it has full protection for only 25 years from the end of the calendar year in which it was first marketed. However, all typefaces marketed before 1 August 1989 have full protection until the end of 2014. Legitimate purchasers have an implied licence to reproduce the typeface in printing. Thereafter, the use of the design to make type or fonts, or as the basis of the design of new typefaces, is not an infringement. It would, however, be an infringement to copy the typeface for purposes not connected with composing text (for example, as an illustration in a book).

1988 (CDPA) s55, Sch 1 para 14(5)

2.3.33 Artistic works and design right

Some artistic works qualify for design right protection as well as for copyright. This can have implications for the use that may be made of the work and even for the duration of copyright in it (see 8.6.3–6).

2.4   Films

2.4.1   Definition: before 1957

Films as such did not appear in the Copyright Act 1911, so those made before 1 June 1957 do not qualify for copyright protection in their own right. However, the 1911 Act did provide that a 'cinematograph production' that consisted of arrangements, acting or a combination of incidents of an original character (an original fiction film) qualified for protection as a dramatic work. Also, since there was no other protection for non-fiction films from that period, the 1956 Act provided retrospectively that the individual frames of a film made before 1 June 1957 qualified for protection as photographs. The sound track has separate protection as a sound recording (see 2.5), and possibly also as an original musical work (see 2.2.5). There may be distinct copyrights ('underlying rights') in the written screenplay of a fiction or non-fiction film and in the written script of a non-fiction film as original literary or dramatic works, as well as in such things as set designs (see 2.4.6).

1911 s35(1) 'dramatic work'; 1956 Sch 7 para 16; 1988 (CDPA) Sch 1 para 7

2.4.2   Definition: since 1957

A film made on or after 1 June 1957 is a recording on any medium (including film, video, computer disk, or a series of images assembled as a flick-book) from which a moving image may by any means be produced. Note also that:

- a film includes its sound track, although the sound track may also have a separate and independent existence as a sound recording, with a different author (see 2.5.3);
- a film must exist as a recording: a sequence of moving images generated by a computer for example, but never fixed in a recording, cannot be protected by copyright;
- the individual images of a film cannot be separately protected as photographs, so unauthorized reproduction of a single frame could be an infringement of the

copyright in the film as a whole if that frame were found to be a substantial part of the film (see 5.2.4). However, the equivalent restriction does not apply to non-photographic forms of 'film', so that, for instance, each cartoon making up a flick-book would be an artistic work.

As with earlier films, there may be distinct copyrights ('underlying rights') in the component parts of the film (see 2.4.6). The film itself may also still be a dramatic work (see 2.2.4). There are also the rights of performers, both actors and musicians (see 8.5).

1988 (CDPA) ss4(2) 'photograph', 5B, Sch 1 para 8(1); SI 1995/3297 regs 9, 26(1); *Norowzian v Arks (No 2)*, 2000

2.4.3 Author: before 1957

Films made before 1 June 1957 have no author, as they were not recognized as works in themselves. However, where a film was an original dramatic work (i.e. a work of fiction, see 2.2.4), it qualifies for protection as such, and the author, that is (probably) the director, would be defined as the author of a dramatic work. The writer of the script or screenplay might share this authorship, and would in any case be the author of the written script as a dramatic work in its own right. At the same time, in any film before this date the author of the individual frames comprising the film would be defined as the author of each of them as photographs. For films made before 1 July 1912 the author of the photographic frames would normally have been the director and perhaps the cinematographer, while after 1 July 1912 the author is the owner of the material on which the film was shot (see 2.3.7), which in most cases was the production company. There could thus be one or two copyrights in film materials of this period, depending on whether the film was a work of fiction or not, not to mention further 'underlying rights' in works used in the film (see 2.4.6). In many cases, the director, screenplay writer, designer and others would have been employees of the production company, so that company would be the first owner of all the copyrights in a film (see 3.2.12), but this would not always be true; the director in particular could have been working on commission (see 3.2.17–18). In the case of amateur films, the person making the film would normally be the author of a film made before 1 July 1912, and the same person would normally have owned the film stock and would thus also be the author of a film made after that date.

1862 s1; 1911 ss21, 35(1) 'dramatic work'; 1956 Sch 7 paras 15–16; 1988 (CDPA) Sch 1 para 7(1), (2)

2.4.4 Author: 1957–1994

The author of films made between 1 June 1957 and 30 June 1994 (in the 1956 Act, the 'maker') is the person or body who made the (normally financial) arrangements necessary for the making of the film (that is, the producer). In identifying this person or body, it might help to identify who initiated the project and was responsible for ensuring that the necessary arrangements were made. In the case of amateur films and videos, this person is likely to have been the person who paid for the equipment and the film or tape.

1956 s13(10); 1988 (CDPA) s9(2)(a); *Century Communications v Mayfair Entertainment*, 1993

2.4.5   Author: after 1994

The author of films made on or after 1 July 1994 is the producer and the principal director jointly unless the producer and principal director are the same person in which case that person is sole author (see 3.2.7–9). It seems that it is possible for the producer, though presumably not the director, to be a company. In the case of amateur films and videos, it would be quite possible for the producer to be one person (the person who paid for the equipment and the film or tape) and the director another (the person wielding the camera or recorder), but in many cases they are likely to be the same person.

1988 (CDPA) ss9(2)(ab), 10(1A), 178 'producer'; SI 1996/2967 regs 18, 36; *Century Communications v Mayfair Entertainment*, 1993

2.4.6   Author: underlying rights

Any film is likely to involve copyrights and other rights in material besides the film itself. If the sound track is removed from the film, it is protected as a sound recording (see 2.5). The composer of music used for the film, and the writer of the script or screenplay may be the authors of those parts as musical and dramatic works respectively (see 2.2.6–15). The designers of sets, costumes and other visual aspects of the film may be authors of them as artistic works (see 2.3.6–11). The performers may have performing rights in the recording of their performances (see 8.5). The necessity for clearing all these and other rights may depend on the extent of the permissions and rights obtained by the producer.

2.4.7   Author: component elements

Where no recording, in any form, of a literary, dramatic or musical work previously existed, and a recording is made as a film, the author of the literary, dramatic or musical work so recorded is normally the speaker, player or director (see 2.2.6). However, the producer and principal director of the film may have a separate right as the authors of the film (see 2.4.5), and the director might have another copyright in the film as a dramatic work (see 2.2.4, 2.4.2).

1988 (CDPA) ss3(2), 9(1); *Norowzian v Arks (No 2)*, 2000

2.4.8 Author: Crown and Parliamentary copyright

The identity of the author of a Crown or Parliamentary copyright film determines both the copyright status and (unlike with literary, dramatic, musical and artistic works) the duration of copyright, and is decided as for other films. However, Parliamentary copyright may subsist only in a film made on or after 1 August 1989, so the authorship of an earlier film made by an employee of Parliament will determine its first ownership in accordance with the normal provisions (see Chapter 3).

1988 (CDPA) ss163, 165, Sch 1 para 43(1)

2.4.9 Duration: standard term

Copyright in the film as such expires 70 years after the end of the calendar year in which the last of the following individuals, described in the literature but not the Regulations as 'persons connected with the film', where they are known, dies:

• the principal director
• the author of the screenplay
• the author of the dialogue
• the composer of music specially created for and used in the film.

The standard term applies to all films made since 1 June 1957, with some variations (see 2.4.11–18). However, this term applies only to the film as such; each of the other copyrights that might subsist in aspects of the film (see 2.4.6) will have its own duration.

1988 (CDPA) s13B; SI 1995/3297 regs 6, 15

2.4.10 Duration: before 1957

The duration of copyright in films made before 1 June 1957 depends on the nature of the rights that subsist in it (see 2.4.1, 2.4.3). These are the copyright in the photographs comprising the film (see 2.1.24, 2.3.12ff.) and in the dramatic work (see 2.2.16ff.).

2.4.11 Duration: 1957–1989

The 1956 Act gave copyright protection to films as such for the first time. Films could fall into three categories: registered, unregistered but published, and unpublished.

2.4.12 Duration: registered films 1957–1985

Starting on 1 January 1928, under the Cinematograph Films Acts 1927–57 and the Films Acts 1960–80, the showing of British films in cinemas was encouraged by a requirement that cinemas show a minimum quota of British films. This called for a scheme of registration for all films shown to the public in cinemas, run by the Board of Trade. Registration under this scheme ceased on 23 May 1985.

Copyright in registered films made on or after 1 June 1957 is for the standard term. Films shown after 23 May 1985 but before 1 August 1989 have duration as unpublished films (see 2.4.14).

1956 s13(3)(a); 1960 s8(1); 1985 (Films) s1(1); 1988 (CDPA) Sch 1 para 12(2)(e); SI 1995/3297 reg 15

2.4.13 Duration: unregistered published films 1957–1989

Films not shown in public, but published (that is, copies were issued to the public, as small-format films or as videos for home viewing, for instance, see 4.1.2): copyright is for the standard term unless the last to die of the 'persons connected with the film' (see 2.4.9) died more than 20 years before publication, in which case it expires 50 years after the end of the calendar year of publication.

1956 s13(3)(b); SI 1995/3297 reg 15

2.4.14 Duration: unpublished films 1957–1989

Films made but not shown or published (see 4.1.2, 4.1.5) between 1 June 1957 and 31 July 1989: copyright is for the standard term unless either:

- the last of the 'persons connected with the film' (see 2.4.9) died before 1969 and the film remains unpublished until 31 December 2039, in which case copyright expires on that date; or
- the film is published between 1 August 1989 and 31 December 2039 and the last of the 'persons connected with the film' died more than 20 years before publication, in which case copyright expires 50 years from the end of the calendar year of publication.

1988 (CDPA) Sch 1 para 12(5)(b); SI 1995/3297 reg 15

2.4.15 Duration: 1989–1995

Films made between 1 August 1989 and 31 December 1995: copyright is for the standard term unless the last of the 'persons connected with the film' (see 2.4.9) died more than 20 years before the film was made or released, in which case copyright expires 50 years after the end of the calendar year in which the film was made or released (see 4.1.12).

1988 (CDPA) s13(1) before amendment; SI 1995/3297 reg 15

2.4.16 Duration: anonymous films: standard term

If the identity of none of the 'persons connected with the film' (see 2.4.9) is known, copyright expires 70 years after the end of the calendar year in which the film was made, or, if it is made available to the public before that period has expired, 70 years after the end of the calendar year in which the film was made available to the public (see 4.1.10). If no such people worked on the film, copyright expires 70 years after the end of the calendar year in which the work was made, whether it is made available to the public or not.

1988 (CDPA) s13B; SI 1995/3297 reg 6

2.4.17 Duration: anonymous films: variations

If an anonymous film had been made and was still unpublished by 31 July 1989, copyright will be for the standard term for anonymous films unless either:

- it was made or released before 1969 and it remains unpublished until 31 December 2039, in which case copyright expires on 31 December 2039; or
- it is published between 1 August 1989 and 31 December 2039 and it was made or released (see 4.1.12) more than 20 years before publication, in which case copyright expires 50 years after the end of the calendar year of publication.

1988 (CDPA) s13(1) before amendment; SI 1995/3297 reg 15

2.4.18 Duration: Crown and Parliamentary copyright

Duration is as for other films except in the case of Crown copyright films made between 1 June 1957 and 1 August 1989 that were both unpublished and unregistered at the latter date (see 2.4.12, 2.4.14). In these, copyright expires on 31 December 2039 unless they are published before that date, in which case copyright expires 50 years after the end of the calendar year of publication.

1988 (CDPA) Sch 1 para 41(5)

2.5   Sound recordings

2.5.1   Definition

A sound recording is either:

- a recording of sounds, from which the sounds may be reproduced; or
- a recording of the whole or any part of a literary, dramatic or musical work, from which sounds reproducing the work or part may be produced, regardless of the

medium on which the recording is made or the method by which the sounds are reproduced or produced.

The copyright in a sound recording is thus explicitly in the recording itself, and not in the work (if any) recorded. In order to infringe the copyright in a sound recording (by copying, for instance), the actual sounds must be copied. A transcription of words spoken in the recording might infringe copyright in a literary work, but would not infringe the copyright in the sound recording.

1956 Sch 7 paras 11, 12; 1988 (CDPA) s5A; SI 1995/3297 reg 9(1)

2.5.2   Definition: variations

It should be noted that:

- there might (if it is still in copyright) be a separate copyright (as a literary, dramatic or musical work) in a work recorded in a sound recording;
- a recording of signals that were not originally sounds (for example, on a computer tape) cannot be a sound recording under the first part of the definition;
- under the second part of the definition an object would qualify as a sound recording if it was created to reproduce a literary, dramatic or musical work even if it did not consist of a recording of actual sounds, such as a musical box roll carrying the pins to play a musical work; and
- a recording of an oral history interview is likely to involve at least three distinct copyrights (see 2.2.8, 2.2.10).

1988 (CDPA) s5A(1); SI 1995/3297 reg 9(1)

2.5.3   Film sound tracks

The sound track of a film made before 1 June 1957 has distinct protection as a sound recording, but a sound track made on or after that date was treated under the 1956 Act as part of the film. The 1988 Act reclassifies all film sound tracks as sound recordings, but gives those made before 1 August 1989 the same duration, authorship and ownership as the films to which they were attached (see 2.4). Sound tracks of films made since that date are both part of the film and separate works in their own right, so that they can have two separate copyrights with different authors and durations.

1911 s19(1); 1956 ss12(9), 13(9), Sch 7 para 14; 1988 (CDPA) ss5A(1), 5B(2), Sch 1 paras 5(1), 8; SI 1995/3297 reg 9(1)

2.5.4 Author: before 1912

Sound recordings made before 1 July 1912: the author is the person or body who on 1 July 1912 was the owner of the original plate on which the recording was made.

1911 s19(8)

2.5.5 Author: 1912–1957

Sound recordings made between 1 July 1912 and 31 May 1957: the author is the person or body who at the time the recording was made was the owner of the original plate on which it was made.

1911 s19(1)

2.5.6 Author: 1957–1989

Sound recordings made between 1 June 1957 and 31 July 1989, and sound recordings commissioned before but made on or after 1 August 1989: the author (the 'maker') is the person or body who at the time the recording was made was the owner of the original record on which it was made.

1956 s12(8); 1988 (CDPA) Sch 1 para 11(2)

2.5.7 Author: 1989–1994

Sound recordings made between 1 August 1989 and 30 June 1994: the author is the person or body who made the (normally financial) arrangements necessary for the making of the recording (that is, the producer).

1988 (CDPA) s9(2)(a); *A&M Records v Video Collection International*, 1995

2.5.8 Author: after 1994

Sound recordings made on or after 1 July 1994: the author is the producer (who may be a company). The producer is the person who instigated the recording and made the necessary (normally financial) arrangements.

1988 (CDPA) ss9(2)(aa), 178 'producer'; SI 1996/2967 regs 18, 36; *A&M Records v Video Collection International*, 1995; *Bamgboye v Reed*, 2004

2.5.9   Author: recording and work recorded

Where no recording, in any form, of a literary, dramatic or musical work previously existed, and a sound recording is made, the author of the literary, dramatic or musical work so recorded is the creator of the words or music recorded, who will normally be the speaker or player (see 2.2.9). However, the person making the recording will have a right in the recording as the author of the recorded version itself. Thus, the composer or player of a new musical work first recorded as a sound recording would be the author of that musical work while the person who made a sound recording of it would be the author of the sound recording.

1988 (CDPA) ss3(3), 9(1)

2.5.10 Author: Crown and Parliamentary copyright

The identity of the author of a Crown or Parliamentary copyright sound recording determines the copyright status of the work, and is decided as for other recordings. However, Parliamentary copyright may only subsist in a sound recording made on or after 1 August 1989, so the authorship of an earlier recording made by an employee of Parliament will determine its first ownership in accordance with the normal provisions (see Chapter 3).

1988 (CDPA) ss163, 165, Sch 1 para 43(1)

2.5.11 Duration: standard term

Copyright in a sound recording expires at the end of the calendar year 50 years after it was made, or, if it is published or made available to the public during that time, 50 years after the end of the calendar year in which it was published or made available (see 4.1.2, 4.1.10, 4.1.12), except as noted below (see 2.5.12–13).

1988 (CDPA) s13A; SI 1995/3297 reg 6(1); SI 2003/2498 reg 29

2.5.12 Duration: unpublished 1957–1989

Copyright in an unpublished sound recording made between 1 June 1957 and 31 July 1989 expires on 31 December 2039, unless it was made available to the public (see 4.1.10) after 31 December 1989 but within 50 years of creation, in which case it expires 50 years after the sound recording was made available to the public.

1988 (CDPA) s13A, Sch 1 para 12(5)(a); SI 1995/3297 reg 15; SI 2003/2498 regs 29, 39

2.5.13 Duration: Crown copyright

Duration is as for other sound recordings (see 2.5.11–12) except in the case of unpublished sound recordings made between 1 June 1957 and 31 July 1989. In these, copyright expires on 31 December 2039 unless they are published before that date, in which case copyright expires 50 years after the end of the calendar year of publication.

1988 (CDPA) Sch 1 para 41(5)

2.5.14 Duration: Parliamentary copyright

Duration in recordings made since 1 August 1989 is as for other sound recordings (see 2.5.11–12).

1988 (CDPA) s165(6)

2.6   Other works

2.6.1   Broadcasts: definition before 1957

Broadcasts made before 1 June 1957 had no copyright protection, but:

- any work included in such a broadcast could be protected, for example as a literary, dramatic or musical work (see 2.2); and
- any broadcast made before 1 June 1957 but repeated on or after that date could have copyright protection as from the date of the re-broadcast.

1956 Sch 7 para 18; 1988 (CDPA) Sch 1 paras 5(1), 9(a)

2.6.2   Broadcasts: definition after 1957

The definition of a broadcast in the 1956 and 1988 Acts has been superseded by the definition in the 2003 Regulations. Only the latest definition is thus of any practical relevance.

A broadcast is an electronic transmission of visual images, sounds or other information which is transmitted for simultaneous and lawful reception by members of the public or is transmitted at a time determined by the broadcaster for presentation to members of the public (for instance, big screen relays of operas from Covent Garden). The definition thus includes:

- conventional terrestrial television and radio broadcasts;
- satellite broadcasts;
- cable programmes; and

- material made available by means of the internet which is also being simultaneously broadcast by other means; is showing a live event; or is transmitted at scheduled times set by the broadcaster.

The important elements in the definition are that the broadcaster controls the start and stop times, and the broadcast is ultimately received or seen by the public.

A re-transmission is now regarded as a distinct broadcast from the original one which is being re-transmitted, although authorship remains with the author of the original work (see 2.6.8).

It is important to remember that while a 'broadcast' is a type of copyright work, 'broadcasting' is no longer a distinct right belonging to the copyright owner. Broadcasting is now a part of 'communication to the public' (see 5.1.6).

1988 (CDPA) s6; SI 2003/2498 regs 4, 5, 31

2.6.3 Internet

The definition of a broadcast does not cover any internet service or website unless what the user receives is equivalent to a conventional broadcast (see 2.6.2). A website is thus not of itself a copyright work, although it will consist of copyright works including, for instance, computer programs (see 6.6), databases (see 8.2), literary and musical works (see 2.2) and artistic works (see 2.3). Judgments which found that internet websites were cable programme services are thus no longer relevant.

1988 (CDPA) s6; SI 2003/2498 reg 4

2.6.4 Cable programmes

Cable programmes and cable programme services are no longer a separate category of copyright work, but have been subsumed in the definition of broadcasts (see 2.6.2). There is no copyright in a broadcast made by cable before 1 January 1985.

1988 (CDPA) Sch 1 para 9(b); SI 2003/2498 reg 5(1)

2.6.5 Protection for the signal

In all broadcasts, it is the actual signal that is protected by the copyright. There may be a separate copyright in the content (for example a dramatic copyright in a play being broadcast). The copying down by hand of the words of the play might be an infringement of the dramatic copyright but not of the broadcast copyright, since the actual signal has not been copied.

2.6.6   Person making the broadcast before 1957

Broadcasts made before 1 June 1957 have no author as they were not recognized as works in themselves.

1988 (CDPA) Sch 1 para 9(a)

2.6.7   Body or person making the broadcast 1957–1989

A broadcast made between 1 June 1957 and 31 July 1989 was made by the body which broadcast the visual images or sounds, or both together, which comprised the broadcast. This body could be either the British Broadcasting Corporation or the Independent Television (later Broadcasting) Authority, but no other. The IBA was dissolved and its assets divided between the Independent Television Commission, the Radio Authority and National Transcommunications Ltd. The first two of these have now been absorbed into the Office of Communications (Ofcom). Copyright in recordings of original broadcasts presumably passed with the rights to the use of the broadcasts.

1956 s14(1) and (10); 1988 (CDPA) Sch 1 para 9(a); 1990 (Broadcasting) s127; 2003 (Communications) ss1, 405; SI 1990/2540

2.6.8   Person making the broadcast after 1989

Broadcasts made on or after 1 August 1989: the author is the person making the broadcast, who is:

- the person transmitting the broadcast, if he or she has responsibility to any extent for its contents; and /or
- any person providing the programme, who makes with the person transmitting it the necessary arrangements for its transmission; or
- in the case of a broadcast which relays another broadcast, the person making the original broadcast.

Many original broadcasts will be the joint authorship of the person transmitting and the person providing the programme, but some may be the sole authorship of the second.

1988 (CDPA) ss6(3), 9(2)(b), 10(2)

2.6.9   Place of broadcasting and person making a satellite broadcast since 1996

In the case of broadcasts made on or after 1 December 1996:

- if a satellite broadcast is made from outside the UK and the EEA (see 1.2.8), and from a country that does not provide adequate protection (so that the broadcast would not qualify for protection under UK law, see 3.1.1), the definition of the place of broadcasting is re-defined so as to give it qualification under certain circumstances;
- if the programme-carrying signal is transmitted to the satellite from a place ('the uplink station') within an EEA state, that place is the place from which the broadcast is made, and the person operating that station is the person making the broadcast;
- if the uplink station is not within an EEA state, but the broadcast has been commissioned by a person established in an EEA state, the place where he or she is established is the place from which the broadcast is made, and that person is the person making the broadcast.

1988 (CDPA) s6A; SI 1996/2967 reg 6

2.6.10 Broadcasts: place of broadcasting

Broadcasts made on or after 1 December 1996: the place from which a broadcast is made is the place where, under the control and responsibility of the person making the broadcast, the programme-carrying signals are introduced into an uninterrupted chain of communication. In the case of satellite broadcasts, this chain of communication includes the parts between the ground and the satellite in both directions.

1988 (CDPA) s6(4); SI 1996/2967 reg 5

2.6.11 Place of satellite broadcasting

Broadcasts made between 1 August 1989 and 30 November 1996: the place from which a satellite broadcast is made is the place from which the signals carrying the broadcast are transmitted to the satellite.

1988 (CDPA) s6(4)

2.6.12 Place of broadcasting and person making the broadcast: satellite broadcasts 1984–1996

Broadcasts made on or after 1 January 1985 but before 1 December 1996: a satellite broadcast was made by the body by whom and at the place from which the visual images and/or sounds were transmitted to the satellite.

1984 Sch 5 para 6(7)

2.6.13 Broadcasts: duration

Copyright expires 50 years from the end of the calendar year in which the broadcast was made. However, where the author is not a national of an EEA state (see 1.2.8), the duration is determined by the country of which the author is a national, provided it is not longer than the duration set out above.

1988 (CDPA) s14, Sch 1 para 12(6); SI 1995/3297 reg 7

2.6.14 Author and duration of Crown and Parliamentary copyright broadcasts

Crown and Parliamentary copyright broadcasts have authors and durations as other broadcasts (see 2.6.7–8, 2.6.13).

1988 (CDPA) ss163(5), 165(6)

2.6.15 Typographical arrangement: definition

There is a distinct copyright in the typographical arrangement of a published edition of the whole or part of one or more literary, dramatic or musical works. In this context 'published edition' means the item protected by this type of copyright as described below. Note the following:

- There can be no copyright in the typographical arrangement of a published edition of an artistic work.
- There can be no copyright in the typographical arrangement of a published edition if, or to the extent that, it reproduces the typographical arrangement of a previous edition.
- It is possible to have copyright in the typographical arrangement of a work which is itself out of copyright, but this does not create a new copyright in the work itself.
- The copyright relates to the whole of the edition as published, whether the edition consists of a single literary, dramatic or musical work, part of such a work, or several such works. The published edition is what the publisher issues to the public, and the courts do not appear to believe that the typographical arrangement of a published edition can refer to anything less than a whole page.
- The copyright protects the skill and labour involved in designing the edition: the appearance of an individual page (use of elements such as pictures, fonts, margins, columns, and the relationship between the various elements) and the distinctions between different parts of a published edition (such as the front page and the leader page of a newspaper).

1956 s15; 1988 (CDPA) ss1(1)(c), 8; *Newspaper Licensing Agency v Marks and Spencer*, 2001

2.6.16 Typographical arrangement: author

The author of the typographical arrangement of a published edition is the publisher. In the case of a Crown copyright edition, the publisher is the Crown, and of a Parliamentary work the publisher is the relevant House or both Houses together as joint publishers.

1956 s15; 1988 (CDPA) s9(2)(d)

2.6.17 Typographical arrangement: duration

Copyright in the typographical arrangement of a published edition expires 25 years after the end of the calendar year in which the edition was published.

1956 s15(2); 1988 (CDPA) s15

3   Ownership

3.1   Qualification

3.1.1   Definition

Although a work might otherwise be eligible for copyright protection, by reason of such things as its originality, the date of its creation or publication, or the date of the author's death, it only 'qualifies' for protection under UK law if particular conditions are fulfilled at the time of creation or publication. In practice, most works in UK archives that are eligible for copyright will also fulfil the qualification requirements and will therefore be protected by the terms of UK law. There are two grounds for qualification of all works except broadcasts, only one of which needs to be satisfied for the work to qualify, and both relate to the 'country of origin'. They are the status of the author of the work and the place of publication. By definition, an unpublished work can qualify only under the former.

A broadcast qualifies if the place of transmission is a qualifying country (defined as for publication, see 3.1.3, but see also 2.6.9–12).

1988 (CDPA) ss153–162

3.1.2   Author of the work

A work qualifies for protection under UK copyright law if, at the time the work was made or published, the author was: a British citizen, a British Dependent Territories citizen, a British National (Overseas), a British Overseas citizen, a British subject or a British protected person, an individual living in the UK or in one of the countries currently recognized as providing qualification (see 3.1.4) or a body incorporated under UK law or the law of one of the countries currently recognized as providing qualification (see 3.1.4). However, if a literary, dramatic, musical or artistic work was published before 1 June 1957 in one of the countries not then recognized as providing qualification, it cannot qualify on grounds of authorship even if the author is from a qualifying country now.

1988 (CDPA) s154; SI 2005/852 para 2(2)

3.1.3   Place of publication

UK copyright law protects literary, dramatic, musical and artistic works, films and typographical arrangements that were published in countries that provide copyright protection to a similar standard to that provided in the UK. For the most part this means countries that are members of the Berne Union or signatories of the Universal Copyright Convention, the WIPO Copyright Treaty or the TRIPS Agreement, or (for sound and broadcast works) the Rome Convention (see 1.2.5–8). The latest order in council has a table listing all these countries, and may be seen online (see 3.2.28). It also provides that if a work was published in a country which is now a qualifying country it qualifies for protection even if it did not qualify at the date of publication.

1956 Sch 1 para 45(1); 1988 (CDPA) s155, Sch 1 para 35; SI 2005/852 para 2, Sch

3.1.4 International copyright

Qualifying material held in a UK archive is protected by UK copyright law: the copyright laws of other countries may apply only in strictly limited ways (notably for the duration of copyright, see 1.2.10). If a work does not qualify it has no copyright protection in the UK at all, regardless of the law of the country where it was made. Conversely, since UK law does not apply outside the UK (except in some Commonwealth countries), protection and even ownership overseas might be entirely different (see 1.2.9, 6.2.6).

The application of the qualification rules may be summarized as follows:

- There is reciprocal protection, using the local law with few exceptions, between the UK and countries that are signatories (see 1.2.5–7) of the Berne Convention, the WIPO Copyright Treaty or the TRIPS Agreement (most countries of the world, except notably Afghanistan, Iran, Iraq, San Marino, Somalia and Turkmenistan).
- There are no longer any countries which are members of the Universal Copyright Convention but not at least one of the Berne Convention, the WIPO Copyright Treaty or the TRIPS Agreement, so the specific provisions of the Universal Copyright Convention are no longer of much practical application. Even so, the © symbol introduced by the Universal Copyright Convention remains useful as a means of asserting a claim to copyright (see 3.4).
- If a literary, dramatic, musical or artistic work was first published before 1 June 1957 it qualifies in the UK only if the country is now a qualifying country, even if the author was or is a qualifying author.
- Unpublished works by a qualifying author qualify for protection in the UK regardless of their date of creation, but the duration of the copyright is likely to be shorter (see 1.2.10 and compare 2.2.17).

On the internet, up-to-date texts and lists of signatories of treaties and conventions are available:

Berne Convention and WIPO treaties: www.wipo.int/
UCC: www.unesco.org/
TRIPS: www.wto.org/

1988 (CDPA) ss12(6), 153ff.; SI 2005/852; *Peer International Corporation v Termidor Music Publishers*, 2003

3.1.5 International performers', record producers' and broadcasters' rights

Membership of the Rome Convention (see 1.2.6–7) is not as widespread internationally as membership of the Berne Convention, and countries that are parties to the TRIPS Agreement are not obliged to apply it. Significant countries that are not members include the USA and Russia. The TRIPS Agreement itself specifies only a limited range of rights for performers, record producers and broadcasters. The texts and current membership of the Rome Convention is available from WIPO and of the TRIPS Agreement from the WTO (see 3.1.4).

The UK gives protection under its domestic legislation to performers, record producers and broadcasters from countries listed in the 2005 order in council (see 3.1.3). The list of countries is much less extensive than that for literary, dramatic, musical and artistic works, films and typographical arrangements. By definition, the countries listed give reciprocal protection to equivalent creators, or equivalent creations, from the UK.

SI 2005/852, Sch

3.2 First owner

3.2.1 Author

Laurence Sterne wrote in *Tristram Shandy* (1760), 'the sweat of a man's brows and the exsudations [sic] of a man's brains, are as much a man's own property, as the breeches upon his backside'. The law agrees, so in the majority of cases, but with important exceptions, the author of the work is the first owner of the copyright in it (see also 2.1.16–17). The copyright will pass, unless it is explicitly bequeathed or assigned otherwise, to the author's legal heirs. The author may be unknown if it is not possible, by reasonable enquiry, to ascertain his or her identity, in which case the work is of 'unknown authorship', but that unknown author is still normally the first owner. To deal with some cases of uncertainty, the law makes certain assumptions about authorship, which apply unless they are shown to be wrong (see 3.2.37).

In some circumstances when copyright has been revived (see 2.1.22–25), ownership reverts to the author or his or her heirs even if someone else (for instance an employer, see 3.2.12, or a person commissioning an artistic work, see 3.2.19) was first owner (see 2.1.23).

Care is needed with photographs: the definition of the author has varied significantly (see 2.3.7).

1988 (CDPA) ss9(4) and (5), 11; Laurence Sterne, *Tristram Shandy* III c34

3.2.2 Applicable law

The first owner of the copyright in a work is determined by the law in force at the time when the work was made or completed, except in some cases of revived copyright (see 2.1.23).

1988 (CDPA) Sch 1 para 11(1)

3.2.3 Ownership of the original documents

The owner of an original document is not necessarily the owner of the copyright in it. The law recognizes a clear distinction between the common law ownership of the physical object containing the work (the 'chattel') and the statutory ownership of the copyright in the work. As one judge said in 1907, the law 'contemplated a property in a composition independently of the property in the manuscript in which that composition was to be found'. However, there are special presumptions about the ownership of both chattel and copyright when a work has been bequeathed by the copyright owner (see 3.3.1–6). An author may sell or give the manuscripts of his or her work to one person but may assign the copyrights to quite a different person, or retain them him or herself, and may bequeath them separately in his or her will in which case the presumptions do not apply.

The sending of the manuscript of a book to a publisher for publication does not in itself transfer ownership of the manuscript, even if the copyright is assigned to the publisher, though if the manuscript of a published work is left with the publisher without being reclaimed the ownership of it could be found to have been abandoned. The owner of the physical object has rights in that object that have nothing to do with copyright: he or she may allow or refuse access to it (subject to the law of freedom of information, see 5.3.3–4), may refuse to allow it to be reproduced, may charge a fee for its reproduction, and may destroy it, for instance.

Fletcher-Moulton J in *Macmillan v Dent*, 1907, at 120; *Dickens v Hawksley*, 1935; *Moorhouse v Angus & Robertson*, 1980

3.2.4 Original letters and ownership

Letters raise special problems because they are treated differently by their authors from other manuscript materials. The author of a letter will normally be the owner of the copyright, while, since the purpose of a letter is to send it to someone else, the recipient will normally be the owner of the original document. The courts have decided, in a succession of cases starting with one brought by Alexander Pope, that although the recipient may sell, give away or even destroy the original letter, because he or she is not the copyright owner he or she may not reproduce it or do any of the other acts restricted by copyright (see 5.1). There may be an implied licence to the recipient (see 3.3.15–16) or the copyright may have been assigned to the recipient or someone else, though assignments are more likely of copyrights owned by companies and other bodies than by private individuals (see 3.3.8). The presumptions about the ownership of copyright in works bequeathed (see 3.3.1–6) are unlikely to apply to collections of letters since the testator is rarely the copyright owner.

Pope v Curl, 1741; *Perceval (Lord and Lady) v Phipps*, 1813; *Gee v Pritchard*, 1818; *Macmillan v Dent*, 1907

3.2.5 Original documents

There are major implications in this for archivists and records managers. They might find themselves responsible for four different categories of material, even within a single collection or file series:

- material owned by the archive or authority (as creators or by gift or sale), in which the archive or authority also owns the copyright (as employers of the author (see 3.2.12) or by bequest (see 3.3.2ff.) or assignment (see 3.3.8)). In such cases, the archivist, records manager or authority may do anything with the material, so long as moral rights are not infringed (see 8.1);
- material owned by the archive or authority (for example by gift or sale, or as a result of a commission), in which the copyright is owned by someone else. In such cases, the archivist, records manager or authority may care for (or destroy), make available to the public and exhibit the original material, but may not make copies except within the prescribed limits (see 5.3). The archivist, records manager or other authorized officer may also give (or refuse) permission for reproduction of the documents (they being the institution's property), so long as it is made clear that permission is also required from the copyright owner and so long as moral rights are not infringed (see 8.1). If the artefact were something like a photograph, there would be nothing to prevent a person obtaining a copy, with the copyright owner's and relevant custodian's permission, from another original print held elsewhere;

- material owned by someone else (such as a depositor) in which copyright is owned by the same or another person. In such cases, the archivist, records manager or authority may do nothing with the material without permission, save care for it under the terms of the deposit or return it to the depositor. Even the copyright exceptions for libraries and archives (see 5.3) do not apply if the owner of the artefacts or of the copyright has refused permission to copy;
- material supplied by a person or body, the ownership of which is uncertain, for example exhibits found among court records or items lent to a company but not reclaimed. Even if the copyright position is clear, the freedom to do things with the work might be limited.

1988 (CDPA) s43(2)(b)

3.2.6 Original documents: checklist

To summarize, an archivist or records manager might like to consider the following in respect of materials in his or her care:

- Does the archive (authority) own these records, or have permission from the owner to control their use, copy them and give permission for their reproduction?
- Does the archive (authority) own all or any of the copyright in these records?
- Does the archive (authority) have a licence from the owner of the copyright in all or any of these records to give permission for their reproduction?

It is worth remembering that, even without owning the copyright, an archivist or records manager with the appropriate rights of control over artefacts in his or her custody may still refuse to allow the copying of the documents on preservation grounds, and may if desired impose conditions on their use, such as the payment of fees for publication. Such conditions have nothing to do with copyright; they would normally be stated on any order form completed by the purchaser of copies and thus would be enforceable as a contract (see 5.4.34), though freedom of information legislation (see 5.3.3–4) and legislation regulating use of public sector information (see 5.4.32) will of course need to be taken into account.

3.2.7 Joint authorship

A work is in joint authorship if it was produced by the collaboration of two or more authors and either the contribution of each author is not distinct from that of the other author or authors (see also 2.2.14, 3.2.17) or the second author's contribution could not stand alone (as for example with a violin part to a song, which was meaningless alone). However, there must be 'joint labouring in the furtherance of a common design' by all authors, and each must make a genuinely significant and original contribution of skill and/or labour (see 2.1.5ff.). Although it is not necessary for each contributor to make a contribution that is equal in terms of quantity, quality or originality to that of the others, a slight contribution, the suggestion of a few general ideas, the specification of the results to be achieved, or proof-reading and correction of the text would not be enough.

The author of a work used by someone else as the basis for a new derivative work (see 2.1.6), such as a translation, is not a joint author of the new work since the contribution of each author is quite distinct. However, if the author of the source work was actively involved in the process of adaptation (see 5.1.7) there is collaboration and thus joint authorship.

1988 (CDPA) s10; Keating J in *Levy v Rutley*, 1871, at 529; *Cala Homes (South) v Alfred McAlpine Homes East*, 1995; *Creation Records v News Group Newspapers*, 1997; *Fylde Microsystems v Key Radio Systems*, 1998; *Hadley v Kemp*, 1999; *Beckingham v Hodgens*, 2003; *Gabrin v Universal Music Operations*, 2004

3.2.8   Joint ownership

Each joint author will normally also be a joint first owner of the copyright (but the normal rules apply: for employees for instance, see 3.2.12). Joint owners, whether or not they are also joint authors, have the legal status of tenants in common. This means that:

- each joint owner's share is separate from the other shares, and may be owned, assigned, bequeathed or inherited under the normal rules;
- the action of any one joint owner (for instance, the giving of permission to reproduce the work) is likely to infringe the copyright of the others if their permission was not also obtained, because it authorizes an infringement (see 5.2.30); and
- any one joint owner may sue for infringement without involving the others, but is likely only to be able to obtain the appropriate proportion of any damages awarded.

1988 (CDPA) ss10, 173(2); *Prior v Landsdown Press*, 1977; *Mail Newspapers v Express Newspapers*, 1987; *Robin Ray v Classic FM*, 1998

3.2.9   Joint authorship: Crown and Parliamentary copyright

If a work is in joint authorship, and one or more but not all of the authors is an officer or servant of the Crown acting in the course of his or her duties or is acting under the direction or control of either House of Parliament, the work will be partly Crown (see 3.2.28) or Parliamentary (see 3.2.32) copyright, as appropriate and in accordance with their contribution to the whole.

1988 (CDPA) ss163(4), 165(5)

3.2.10 Anonymous and pseudonymous works, and works of unknown authorship

If the first owner of an anonymous or pseudonymous work (see 2.1.17) is not the author (but is for example the employer, see 3.2.12) then that owner will normally be identifiable. If however the first owner of an anonymous or pseudonymous work is the author, there will be considerable difficulties securing permission to do anything with it (see also 3.3.20). There are some special provisions allowing the publication of such works (see 5.4.23–24). There are also some assumptions about the expiry of copyright that may be made about older works (see 5.4.25–26).

3.2.11 Collective works

The expression 'collective works' comes from the Copyright Act 1911, summarizing some lengthy drafting in the Literary Copyright Act 1842, which gave a right to the publisher of a literary work such as an encyclopedia, magazine or periodical to exploit the whole work, regardless of the various copyrights in the component parts (see also 3.2.25). The term has been replaced by 'compilation' (a type of literary work, see 2.2.3), so it now applies only to works created before 1 July 1912. It appears in the 1988 Act only in connection with reversionary rights (see 3.3.12).

1842 s18; 1911 ss24(1)(a)(ii), 35(1); 1988 (CDPA) Sch 1 para 27

3.2.12 Employer (contract of service)

The employer is the first owner of the copyright in a literary, dramatic, musical or artistic work made on or after 1 July 1912, or a film (including its sound track) made on or after 1 July 1994, when made by an employee in the course of his or her employment under a contract of service or apprenticeship (which is different from a contract for services, see 3.2.17).

However, for artistic works to which the provisions giving ownership to the person who commissioned the work (see 3.2.19) applied:

- when the work was commissioned between 1 July 1912 and 31 May 1957 the title of the person who commissioned it took precedence over the claims of both author and employer under all circumstances; and
- when the work was commissioned between 1 June 1957 and 31 July 1989, the title of the person who commissioned it took precedence over the claims of the author and the employer except when the work was made for publication in a newspaper (see 3.2.27).

In some circumstances, ownership of revived copyright can revert to the author (see 2.1.23).

1911 s5(1); 1956 s4(2–4); 1988 (CDPA) ss11(2), 178 'employed'; SI 1996/2967 regs 18(3), 36(1); *Massine v De Basil*, 1938

3.2.13 Employer (contract of service): general exceptions

The express statutory provisions seem clear enough and in the majority of cases they can be applied without problems, but there are circumstances in which the copyright in a work produced by an employee but outside the terms of his or her contract (even if the work was produced in working time) could belong to the author. It seems that an employee will be deemed to be acting in the course of employment when:

- what he or she does is subject to the supervision and control of the employer;
- the work is an integral part of the business of the employer;
- the employer provides all of the materials; or
- the employer has the opportunity for gain but also bears the costs and the risk of loss.

Judges have said that the author (not the employer) was the copyright owner when the author was:

- a doctor on a hospital's staff who wrote a book in his or her own time but using skills and specialist knowledge gained as a result of the work he or she did at the hospital;
- a teacher or lecturer who made written notes for the series of lectures or oral lessons he or she was employed to give; the notes were made for the teacher's own convenience though it would have been different if they were explicitly required by the contract of employment (but see 3.2.22–23);
- an accountant who was asked to give a series of lectures in his or her employer's time, a duty outside their normal area of work, even though the lectures were prepared in the employer's time and using the employer's facilities (such as a library and typing);
- the director of a company (in some cases, see 7.9.2).

Montreal v Montreal Locomotive Works, 1947; *Stephenson, Jordan and Harrison v MacDonald and Evans*, 1952; *Beloff v Pressdram*, 1973; *Noah v Shuba*, 1991

3.2.14 Employer (contract of service): casual staff

A decision on whether a contract of service exists at all will depend on the evidence in each case. The question can be particularly awkward with casual staff, the evidence for whose conditions of employment may be both written and oral, contained in such things as a letter of appointment, letters offering and accepting or declining particular jobs, and the conduct of the parties. Criteria for deciding whether casual work is being performed under a contract of service appear to include whether:

- there is some obligation on the employer to provide work and on the employee to take it when offered;

- regular payments are made for services performed; and
- the employee is in business on his or her own account.

In the absence of cases specifically looking at the issue from a copyright point of view, though, it is not possible to be certain how a contract of service for casual staff might be defined (see also 3.2.21).

O'Kelly v Trusthouse Forte, 1983; *Carmichael and Leese v National Power*, 1999; *Eastbourne Borough Council v Foster*, 2001

3.2.15 Employer (contract of service): joint authorship

In some circumstances joint authorship and thus joint ownership might be found by a court to apply (see 3.2.8–9), so the employer might be part owner, even if not sole owner, of the copyright.

1911 s5(1)(b); 1956 s4(4); 1988 (CDPA) ss11(2), 178 'employed'; SI 1996/2967 regs 18(3), 36(1); *Stephenson, Jordan and Harrison v MacDonald and Evans*, 1952

3.2.16 Employer (contract of service): before 1912

There was no general provision for employers to own the copyright in their employees' works in legislation before the 1911 Act and the employment provisions in that Act were not retrospective. Under the common law, the normal position was that the author was owner of an unpublished work he or she had created (see 1.2.2). Unfortunately, various 19th-century judgments came to differing conclusions. In one, the judge did not reach a decision but he 'entertained the strong impression' that a work written by an agent or servant would be copyright of the employer. However, two senior judges both seem to have concluded, rather earlier, that an employer was 'author and proprietor' only if he or she had taken a significant part in specifying what was to be created. This means that in many cases the employed author might have been the first owner of copyright in a work created before 1 July 1912. It is especially important for archivists to understand this since it applies to unpublished literary works created by employees, and many published ones. It could have unexpected consequences for, for instance, poor law and estates' records where a large proportion of the documents created was produced by employed clerks, stewards and bailiffs (see 3.3.18, 7.1.2, 7.10.2). The circumstances in which the employer certainly owned the copyright prior to 1912 include:

- employment of the author to write literary works for publication in encyclopedias, magazines, periodicals and part-works, but in most cases the employer's copyright extended only to publication in that form and the author was entitled to retain the right to publish the work separately; and

- production of a graphic artistic work (painting, drawing or photograph) made for or on behalf of another for a good or a valuable consideration, which certainly included creation in return for a salary (see 3.2.19).

1842 ss3, 18; 1862 s1; 1911 s24, Sch 1; *Harfield v Nicolson*, 1824–6; *Shepherd v Conquest*, 1856; *Nottage v Jackson*, 1883; Kekewich J in *Hildesheimer and Faulkner v Dunn*, 1891, at 454

3.2.17 Commission (contract for services)

Where a literary, dramatic or musical work of any date was created under an implied or express (that is, written down) contract for services (not to be confused with a contract of service, see 3.2.12) or commission, the author is normally the first owner of the copyright in it, unless there is written agreement (normally in the original contract) to the contrary. One obvious type of commissioned material is produced by consultants (see also 6.6.1). An archivist or records manager entering into a contract with a consultant should ensure that it contains clear clauses covering all possible uses to which the material might be put, besides simple implementation of the recommendations, including such things as sharing the products with partners and publicity and publications. If appropriate it should also contain a confidentiality clause, to prevent unauthorized disclosure by the consultant to others (see 5.4.1, 8.7).

Ownership will normally lie with the author of any artistic work commissioned after 1 August 1989, but only of some commissioned earlier (see 3.2.19). In the case of a film made on or after 1 July 1994, the principal director is co-author and thus first owner of the copyright jointly with the producer, so there is no question of one being commissioned by the other. There are other contexts too where a court might decide that joint authorship rather than a straight commission applies (see 3.2.7–9). Although in most cases it is fairly clear when a work has been commissioned and who is the author, there can be difficulties.

3.2.18 Commission (contract for services): possible variations

A contract for services is generally regarded as being one in which the work is performed by someone who is acting in a material sense on his or her own account so that the way the work is carried out is not controlled by the person who commissioned it. It may be too that the work is to some extent incidental to the normal functions of the business commissioning it. A self-employed person such as an architect, lawyer, doctor, management consultant or newspaper contributor (as distinct from staff reporter) would normally be thought to be self-employed and thus working on commission. However, much depends on how a judge will apply the principles laid down in earlier cases. Under some circumstances, for instance, the person commissioning the work might have equitable rights in the copyright, such that the copyright owner is regarded as being merely the trustee for him or her (see 3.3.15–18).

Almost whatever happens, the person who commissioned the work, or his or her heirs and assigns, will have the right to use the work for purposes falling within the contract (whether implied or written), regardless of copyright, so it is up to the person giving the commission to ensure that the contract covers all uses for which the work might be required (and see 3.3.17). It is worth noting that a work commissioned by the Crown before 1 August 1989 might be Crown copyright, not the copyright of the author (see 3.2.28).

If the person giving the commission needs to prevent the author, as well as other people, from using the work, an assignment or exclusive licence will be needed, preferably as part of the original contract (see 3.3.8, 5.4.1). For a contract to be enforceable it must be in return for a consideration (such as payment in money). If no assignment was made in the commissioning contract (see 3.3.9), any assignment made later should be in return for a new consideration; the original fee for the work itself is not enough.

Byrne v Statist, 1914; *Stephenson, Jordan and Harrison v MacDonald and Evans*, 1952; *Blair v Osborne and Tomkins*, 1971; *Robin Ray v Classic FM*, 1998

3.2.19 Artistic works commissioned before 1989

Where an artistic work was produced to commission and was created after the commission was agreed, the person commissioning it was the first owner of the copyright in:

- an engraving made between 1766 and 30 June 1912, if the design was originated by the person who commissioned it and his or her name and the date were put on the engraving;
- a painting, drawing or photograph made between 29 July 1862 and 30 June 1912 for or on behalf of the person giving the commission for a good or valuable consideration. A good or valuable consideration could include payment (or an intention to pay) or for instance the granting of access to private premises to take photographs, but not merely allowing portraits to be taken;
- an engraving, photograph or portrait (in any medium) made in pursuance of an order (that is, made after the order had been received) for valuable consideration (that is, in return for payment), if the work was commissioned between 1 July 1912 and 31 May 1957, even if the work was created after the latter date;

- an engraving, photograph or portrait (painted or drawn) for which the person giving the commission paid or agreed to pay money or money's worth, if the work was commissioned between 1 June 1957 and 31 July 1989, even if the work was created after the latter date.

An engraving includes an etching, lithograph, woodcut, print or similar work that is not a photograph (see 7.12.1, 7.12.5).

The ownership by the person giving the commission may have reverted to the author and his or her heirs in some circumstances if the copyright has been revived (see 2.1.23).

1766 s1; 1862 s1; 1911 s5(1)(a); 1956 s4(3), Sch 7 para 3; 1988 (CDPA) Sch 1 para 11; *Jefferys v Baldwin*, 1753; *Ellis v Horace Marshall*, 1895; *Ellis v Ogden*, 1895; *Boucas v Cooke*, 1903; *Davis v Baird*, 1904; *Stackemann v Paton*, 1906; *Sasha v Stoenesco*, 1929; *Leah v Two Worlds Publishing*, 1951

3.2.20 Commissioned sound recordings

Where a sound recording was produced to a commission made between 1 June 1957 and 31 July 1989 for which the person giving the commission paid or agreed to pay money or money's worth and the recording was created after the commission was agreed, the person who commissioned it is the first owner of the copyright, even if the work was created after the latter date. However, the 1988 Act did not make much practical difference because a person who is commissioned since 1 August 1989 to make a sound recording is unlikely to be the author or the owner of the copyright in the recording unless he or she can show that he or she is also the producer, that is the person who made the arrangements for the recording (see 2.5.7–8). Doing all the work of arranging the musicians and the recording session is not enough for this purpose; it is the person or body that provides the money that is the producer.

1956 s12(4); 1988 (CDPA) ss9(2)(aa), 178 'producer', Sch 1 para 11(2)(b); *A&M Records v Video Collection International*, 1995

3.2.21 Voluntary or honorary service

The author is the first owner of copyright in a literary, dramatic, musical or artistic work created when working in a voluntary or honorary capacity, whether for an individual or an institution, including a statutory body or public institution (except the Crown before 1 August 1989, see 3.2.28), unless there is express written agreement to the contrary. This would cover, for instance, volunteer officers of societies and volunteer workers on an archaeological dig or in a record office (but see 7.4, and see also 3.2.14). Archivists should therefore ensure that before volunteer and casual staff start work they have signed an assignment of copyright covering anything they produce for the record office (see 3.3.8–9), otherwise there could be difficulties with, for instance, catalogues. Similarly, if work is performed for the record office by a Friends organization or similar body which is constitutionally separate from the record office:

- the Friends organization should secure assignments to it from its members before they do any work; and
- the record office should secure at least a sole licence (see 5.4.1) from the Friends organization, allowing both parties to use the material but preventing the Friends from licensing anyone else to use it.

3.2.22 Universities

The position in universities is particularly uncertain. Clearly the work of administrative staff is carried out in the course of employment, as are the administrative activities of academic staff such as professors, heads of department and chairs of committees. However, the products of research and teaching are less obviously subject to the sorts of control normally applied to an employee's work. In the past it was normal for universities tacitly to permit their academic staff to claim their own copyrights, giving them the freedom to conduct their research and to publish the results by, for instance, allowing them to assign copyrights in their articles to journal publishers. There are some universities, though, which have adopted a policy of asserting their rights to ownership of all copyrights, and some have even required students to assign their copyrights (see 3.2.23).

Now that intellectual property rights are widely recognized as valuable assets, ownership in the hands of academics is not necessarily acceptable any longer to university authorities. Such practice in the past might result though, for existing staff at least, in universities being unable to secure the rights without an agreed change in the contractual terms of employment. Each university has to come to its own conclusions on what is desirable and achievable, and to reach a settlement with its staff. The Joint Information Systems Committee (JISC) and SURF, a sister body in the Netherlands, have addressed this question and issued a statement of principles known as the Zwolle principles after the place where they were agreed. These recognize the importance of ensuring academic freedom but also recognize that different rights will require different solutions. Copyrights in research materials, articles and publications might without much difficulty be left to the academics, though collaborative materials and works in joint authorship will require care (see 3.2.7, 3.2.23). Rights in material which has a considerable potential value through commercial exploitation, such as copyrights in software (see 6.6), and rights in databases (see 8.2) and patentable inventions (see 8.6.7), raise new issues. The solution seems likely to lie in university ownership of these valuable rights coupled with shared control and enjoyment of the fruits.

For the policy of a particular university, try searching on its website for 'copyright policy' or 'intellectual property policy'. Universities in the UK, the USA and Australia that had published such policies by 2002 are listed in the bibliography to Monotti's and Ricketson's book (see 10.2), though the web addresses have often changed since.

3.2.23 Teachers and students

The copyright status of teachers' notes and publications will depend largely on the precise terms of the individual's contract with his or her employer and on the conduct of employer and employee (but for university lecturers see 3.2.22). If the individual is employed to teach, the employer will in almost all cases be the first owner of the copyright in material for the classes (but see 3.2.13). If publication is not a specified part of the contract but it is left to the initiative of the individual to write articles and books and to have them published, the individual is likely to be the first owner of copyright in them.

The work of employed research assistants would have to be assessed in the same way as that of other staff (see 3.2.22). Research students, working with but not paid by a supervisor within a university, are likely to be the first owners of the copyright in their work, except that there will in some cases be overlap between their work and that of other members of a research group and the supervisor, which could mean joint authorship (see 3.2.7). Undergraduates will normally be the first owners of the copyright in their material (but some will be under 18 and so much the same as schoolchildren, see below). Some students, though, pursue their studies as part of a period of apprenticeship or employment (for instance as engineers or army officers). Since apprentices are treated in the same way as employees for the purposes of copyright ownership, copyright in their work will belong to the person to whom or the body to which they are apprenticed or by which they are employed (see 3.2.12). Some universities require students of all kinds to assign their copyrights or have introduced policies asserting their ownership of the rights. Either approach appears unnecessary and improper, and seems unlikely to succeed if it were ever legally challenged.

Schoolchildren are the owners of copyright in their work, though their rights are administered by their parents or guardians until they reach adulthood. The work of schoolchildren should only be used in the classroom context, including the context of a record office's training room, unless permission has been obtained from the parents or guardians.

1989 ss3, 5; *Stephenson, Jordan and Harrison v MacDonald and Evans*, 1952; *Noah v Shuba*, 1991

3.2.24 Employed journalists

Before the 1988 Act, there were special provisions for the first ownership of copyright in the work of journalists who were employees. They changed with successive Acts, but the provisions of each Act still apply to works made when they were in force except in some cases of revived copyrights (see 2.1.23). There are no special provisions for journalists in the 1988 Act.

1988 (CDPA) Sch 1 para 11(1)

3.2.25 Employed journalists: before 1912

Before 1 July 1912 the publisher of a collective literary work (encyclopedia, magazine or periodical, see 3.2.11) was the owner of the copyright in the whole work, and in the component articles if they were written by his or her employees. However, the publisher had to have the consent of the authors (whether employed or not) to publish the works separately; the authors could, by express or implied contract, have the right themselves to publish the works separately, and 28 years after first publication (in whatever form) the ownership of the copyright in the works reverted to the authors. If that reversion had not happened by 1 July 1912 it could not happen at all and the publisher of the collective work retained the right to publish until copyright expired under the provisions of the 1911 Act.

1842 s18; 1911 s24(1)(a)(ii)

3.2.26 Employed journalists: 1912–1957

Between 1 July 1912 and 31 May 1957 the employer was the first owner of the copyright in a literary, dramatic, musical or artistic work produced by an employee in the course of his or her employment, but where the work was a contribution to a newspaper or periodical the author had the right to prevent its publication in any other form, unless the terms of his or her contract said otherwise. However, see 3.2.12 for the exclusion of the employer in the case of a commissioned artistic work.

1911 s5(1)(b)

3.2.27 Employed journalists: 1957–1988

Between 1 June 1957 and 31 July 1988 the publisher was the first owner of the copyright in a newspaper or periodical published by him or her, and in works produced by his or her employees in the course of their employment so long as they were published in a newspaper or periodical. However, the journalist employee-author was the first owner of the copyright in his or her individual literary, dramatic and artistic (but not musical) works for all other purposes, unless his or her contract said otherwise. The employee's (but not the employer's) rights were over-ridden by the rights of a person who commissioned an artistic work (see 3.2.12).

1956 s4(2), (5)

3.2.28 Crown copyright

The Crown is the owner of the copyright in any work made on or after 1 August 1989 by an officer or servant of the Crown, including civil servants, diplomats, members of the armed forces and government ministers, in the course of his or her duties (so not in the person's own time and for his or her own purposes). This is much narrower than earlier definitions (see below), and might not cover a work produced by a non-departmental public body. All Acts of Parliament (including local and personal Acts) and Measures of the General Synod of the Church of England, after they have received Royal Assent, are also Crown copyright.

The Crown is also the owner of the copyright in:

- any work prepared or published by or under the direction or control of His/Her Majesty or any government department before 1 June 1957, subject to any agreement to the contrary; and
- any work made or first published by or under the direction or control of Her Majesty or a government department between 1 June 1957 and 31 July 1989, subject to any agreement to the contrary.

These provisions can be difficult to apply, and an Australian judge described the pre-1957 one as a 'legislative monstrosity', but it survives with little change in Australian law. In both, the publication provision gave to the Crown the copyright in a work that it published (after 1957, only that it first published), apparently in both its manuscript and printed forms, regardless of who the author was.

'Under the direction or control' has a fairly broad meaning. When applied to a publication it included works issued for publication subject to an embargo as well as works actually published by the Crown. When applied to creation it covered works produced not only by such people as civil servants, diplomats, members of the armed forces and government ministers, but also by the officers and members of bodies over which the Crown exercised some direction or control of what work was done and how, including many advisory or executive non-departmental public bodies (NDPBs or quangos) and royal commissions. Evidence submitted to a royal commission was not covered unless there was power to compel the giving of evidence. Works commissioned by the Crown over which the Crown exercised direction or control are Crown copyright but a work commissioned by the Crown and prepared thereafter independently of supervision would be the copyright of the author, unless the form of publication gave copyright to the Crown. A body, such as the BBC, which was merely licensed by the Crown was not acting under its direction or control.

Crown copyright is, except in Scotland (see 3.2.30), administered on behalf of the Crown by the Queen's Printer and Controller of Her Majesty's Stationery Office (HMSO), who is now at The National Archives. The Controller publishes all statutes and statutory instruments together with guidance on Crown copyright and public sector information licensing issues (see 5.4.32) online at www.opsi.gov.uk/.

1911 s18; 1956 s39; 1988 (CDPA) ss163(1), 164, Sch 1(40)(1)(a), (42); *BBC v Wireless League Gazette Publishing*, 1926; Long Innes CJ in *Attorney General for New South Wales v Butterworth*, 1938, at 258; *Ironside v Attorney General*, 1988; *HRH the Prince of Wales v Associated Newspapers*, 2006; TNA: STAT 14/44

3.2.29 Crown copyright: Welsh Assembly Government

Records of the Welsh Assembly Government and Acts and Measures of the Welsh Assembly are Crown copyright. Crown copyright in Wales is administered by the Controller (see 3.2.28).

1988 (CDPA) ss164, 178 'Crown'; 2006 Sch 10 paras 27, 31

3.2.30 Crown copyright: Scotland

Records and publications of the Scottish Administration and Acts and subordinate legislation of the Scottish Parliament are Crown copyright. Crown copyright in Scotland is administered by the Queen's Printer for Scotland (who is also, at present, the Queen's Printer and Controller of HMSO, see 3.2.28).

1988 (CDPA) ss164, 178 'Crown'; 1998 (Scotland) s92, Sch 8 para 25(5) and (7)

3.2.31 Crown copyright: Northern Ireland

Records and publications of Northern Ireland departments are Crown copyright, as are any Acts of the Northern Ireland Assembly. The copyright is administered by the Controller (see 3.2.28).

1988 (CDPA) ss164, 178 'Crown'; 1998 (Northern Ireland) s23, Sch 13 para 8(5)

3.2.32 Parliamentary copyright

Parliament, that is the House of Lords and the House of Commons jointly or severally as appropriate, is the first owner of copyright in works made by or under the direction or control (see 3.2.28) of either House, including:

- all Bills until they receive Royal Assent (when they become Crown copyright Acts, see 3.2.28) or are withdrawn (when copyright expires);
- any literary, dramatic, musical or artistic work or any sound recording, film or broadcast, or any typographical arrangement made by an officer or employee of

either House in the course of his or her duties, including, for instance, *Hansard*; and

• any sound recording, film or live broadcast of the proceedings of either House.

However, 'under the direction or control' does not necessarily include works which were merely commissioned by either House.

Parliamentary copyright is the responsibility of the Speaker for the House of Commons, and the Clerk of the Parliaments for the House of Lords, but is administered on their behalf by the Controller of HMSO (see 3.2.28).

1988 (CDPA) ss165–6

3.2.33 Parliamentary copyright: limitations

Parliamentary copyright extends only to:

• any work created on or after 1 August 1989 which falls within the definition; and
• any literary, dramatic, musical or artistic work created and unpublished before that date which falls within the appropriate part of the definition.

Bills introduced and some works published before 1 August 1989 are subject to the normal rules for authorship, ownership and duration. *Hansard* published before the same date is Crown copyright (see 3.2.28).

1988 (CDPA) Sch 1 para 43(1)

3.2.34 Parliamentary copyright: Welsh Assembly

Proposed Bills and Measures of the Welsh Assembly until they receive Royal Assent, are approved by the Queen in Council or are withdrawn, and proceedings and records of the Assembly are copyright of the National Assembly for Wales Commission.

1988 (CDPA) ss164(1), 165(7), 166C–D; 2006 s27(7), Sch 10 paras 27–28

3.2.35 Parliamentary copyright: Scottish Parliament

Bills of the Scottish Parliament, until they receive Royal Assent or are withdrawn, and proceedings and records of the Parliament, are the copyright of the Scottish Parliamentary Corporate Body. Much the same considerations apply as to Parliamentary copyright (see 3.2.32), save that anything made before 6 May 1999 qualifies for protection instead under the normal rules. Copyright in at least some of the material of the Scottish Parliament is administered on its behalf by the Queen's Printer for Scotland (see 3.2.30).

1988 (CDPA) ss165(7), 166A; 1998 (Scotland) Sch 8 para 25(6); SI 1999/676

3.2.36 Parliamentary copyright: Northern Ireland Assembly

Bills of the Northern Ireland Assembly (when it is in existence), until they receive Royal Assent or are withdrawn, and the official report of the Assembly are the copyright of the Northern Ireland Assembly Commission.

1988 (CDPA) s166B; 1998 (Northern Ireland) Sch 13 para 8(6)

3.2.37 Presumptions about subsistence and ownership

Successive Acts have allowed certain presumptions to be made by the courts about the subsistence and ownership of copyright. Those in the 1911 and 1956 Acts have now been replaced by those in the 1988 Act, regardless of the date when the work in question was created, unless the infringement itself occurred before 1 August 1989. Some key points of these presumptions are given below.

Unless the contrary is proved:

- If a name of an author is on copies of a published work or on the original of a work, that person is presumed to be the first owner of the copyright;
- If there is no author's name but the name of the publisher is on copies of a published work, the publisher is presumed to have been the copyright owner at the time of publication;
- If the author of an unpublished work is unknown, and there is evidence that the author was a qualifying person (see 3.1.2), the work is presumed to qualify for protection;
- Statements on sound recordings and films as to such things as ownership, the identity of the producer or 'persons connected with the film' (see 2.4.9), or about publication are presumed to be correct.

1911 s6(3); 1956 s20; 1988 (CDPA) ss104, 105(1, 2, 5, 6), 169(1), Sch 1 para 31(1, 4)

3.3   Acquisition of copyright

3.3.1 Inheritance

Unless otherwise assigned or bequeathed, copyright in most works descends to the residuary beneficiary (the one who receives 'everything else') or beneficiaries under the will of the owner or to the next of kin if he or she died intestate. Intestacy rules are complex, specifying the categories of beneficiary, starting with a surviving spouse and children and ending with any surviving cousins. Where there is more than one beneficiary in a category, all assets are divided equally between them (see 3.2.8). If there was no survivor in any of the categories the assets, including copyright, of an intestate person become *bona vacantia* (see 3.3.19).

For copyright in the will itself see 7.3.9.

The standard rule is varied by successive statutes, which have set out presumptions about copyright when copyright works have been bequeathed by will, as explained below (see 3.3.2–6). However, if the testator explicitly bequeaths his or her copyright in any work or works, that bequest takes precedence over the presumptions.

1925 ss45–52; 1952 (Intestates); 1988 (CDPA) s90(1); *Dickens v Hawksley*, 1935

3.3.2 Bequest

The following provisions apply where artefacts embodying copyright works have been left by bequest in a will; they do not apply in cases of intestacy (see 3.3.1). Since the testator will not own the copyright, the provisions do not apply to letters received by him or her (see 3.2.4). In each case, the significant date is the date of death of the testator, not the date of creation of the work.

3.3.3 Bequest: until 1957

If a testator who died before 1 June 1957, and who was the author of a work, bequeathed to a particular person or institution (for instance, a record office or company) a manuscript of that work and it had neither been published nor performed in public at the time of his or her death (or, if he or she died before 1 July 1912, it had not been published before that date), the ownership of the manuscript as a result of the bequest was taken to be prima facie proof of ownership of the copyright in it. A manuscript was taken to mean only a literary, dramatic or musical work on paper or similar material. Since under this provision the testator had to be also the author of the work bequeathed, the presumption cannot apply to works of which the testator was merely the assignee of the copyright, or which the testator had him or herself received by bequest.

1911 s17(2); 1988 (CDPA) Sch 1 para 30(2); *Dickens v Hawksley*, 1935

3.3.4 Bequest: 1957–1989

If a testator who died between 1 June 1957 and 31 July 1989 bequeathed to a particular person or institution (such as a record office or company) an original document embodying the manuscript of a literary, dramatic or musical work, or an artistic work, that had not been published at the time of his or her death, the bequest was taken to include any copyright which the testator owned in the work. An original document was taken to mean most literary, dramatic, musical or artistic works, but not those recorded in non-documentary forms such as computer disks. This is a wider provision than that under the 1911 Act and applies to any bequest, including one of works bequeathed to the testator or whose copyright had been assigned to him or her, or whose copyright he or she owned as (for instance) the employer of the author.

1956 s38; 1988 (CDPA) Sch 1 paras 25(1), 30(1)(b)

3.3.5 Bequest: since 1989

If a testator who dies on or after 1 August 1989 bequeathes to a particular person or institution (for example, a record office) an original document or other material thing (such as a computer disk) recording or embodying a literary, dramatic, musical or artistic work, or an original material thing containing a sound recording or film, that had not been published at the time of his or her death, the bequest shall be taken to include any copyright which the testator owned in the work.

1988 (CDPA) s93

3.3.6 Bequest: to more than one person

Where assets (including copyright) are bequeathed to more than one beneficiary under a will (whether the bequest is explicit or to the residuary legatees), they are divided equally between the beneficiaries (see 3.2.8).

It appears that if an author made several bequests covering various identical, or substantially identical, versions of the same work, the copyright in these variant versions or recensions would pass to different owners, but it is not clear how this would work in practice. The most likely outcome is joint ownership (see 3.2.8). In some contexts, such a distribution of more than one copy might constitute publication of the work.

3.3.7 Succession

If the first owner of copyright is a corporate body, and the body is taken over or purchased, ownership will pass with other rights and assets to the successor body unless otherwise assigned.

3.3.8 Assignment

Copyright is a property right and so may be assigned, provided the assignment (assignation in Scotland) is made in writing and is signed by or on behalf of the owner of the copyright, and (where appropriate) provided the person making the assignment has the necessary authority within the organization. An assignment by someone without the necessary authority could be worthless to the recipient, but on the other hand could be damaging to the organization apparently making it if the recipient takes action and spends money in reliance on it, especially if it was reasonable to assume that the assignor did have the necessary authority. In the case of an assignment made by a corporate body after 1 August 1989, it may be signed by two directors or a director and the company secretary, or by the fixing of the body's seal.

Once an assignment is made, it is possible for the person making it to infringe copyright in his or her own work, except that the author of an artistic work may copy that work in making a new artistic work, so long as he or she does not repeat or imitate the main design of the earlier work.

An assignment should preferably take the form of a binding and enforceable contract, which requires the making and acceptance of an offer and an intention to create a legal relationship. It must also be in return for a consideration, so a contractual assignment cannot be a gift. The consideration could be a payment of money or some non-financial return such as a benefit in kind like free membership. The consideration (even if only £1) must actually be given, and receipt of it should be acknowledged (see also 3.2.18). The assignment may be of all of the copyright owned by the person making the assignment or of only part of it, and may be for the whole of the term of copyright or for only a specified period.

Assignments made before 1 July 1912 of copyright in some kinds of work had to be registered at Stationers' Hall (see 2.1.17); there is no official registry of assignments made since that date. Assignments made by an author between 1 July 1912 and 1 June 1957 reverted to the author's heirs 25 years after his or her death; see 3.3.12. For the effect of an assignment on licences see 5.4.1. See also 9.4.

1911 ss2(1)(ii), 5(2); 1956 ss9(9), 36(3); 1985 (Companies) s36A; 1988 (CDPA) ss64, 90, 176(1), Sch 1 paras 25(1), 27; *Gross v Seligman*, 1914; *Beloff v Pressdram*, 1973; *Hadley v Kemp*, 1999

3.3.9 Assignment of future copyright

Copyright in a work created after 1 June 1957 may be assigned prospectively, before the work is created. As soon as the work is created (if it is), the person receiving the assignment becomes the copyright owner. An example of such an assignment would be one included in a contract commissioning someone to do some work, when the person commissioning the work needs to own the copyright in the results (see 3.2.17–18).

1956 s37(1); 1988 (CDPA) s91

3.3.10 Crown and Parliamentary copyright

Although copyright previously owned by another person or institution may be acquired by the Crown, other than by publication, or by Parliament (such as by assignment, inheritance or bequest, see above), such copyright does not become 'Crown copyright' or 'Parliamentary copyright' as a result, and the expiry of copyright is determined by the appropriate general provisions for duration. Similarly, Crown or Parliamentary copyright in a work may be assigned by the Controller or Parliament to another person or body, but it continues to be called 'Crown copyright' or 'Parliamentary copyright', and its expiry is still determined on that basis.

1988 (CDPA) ss163(2), 165

3.3.11 Substituted rights under the 1911 Act

The 1911 Copyright Act changed the duration of copyright for some existing works. If copyright in a work had been assigned for the whole of its term by the author before 1 July 1912, the Act said that the assignment was to have effect only for the period of copyright that applied at the time of the assignment. The rights for any extended period created by the new Act were given to the author, with only limited rights remaining to the assignee, unless the author made a new assignment after the passing of the Act.

1911 s24; 1956 Sch 7 para 34; 1988 (CDPA) Sch 1 para 28

3.3.12 Reversionary interests

The 1911 Copyright Act tried to protect the interests of the heirs of 'improvident' authors who had made 'imprudent dispositions' of their copyrights. Any assignment (other than one made by will) made between 16 December 1911 (the date the 1911 Act was passed) and 31 May 1957, by the author as first copyright owner, of the copyright in any work other than a collective work (see 3.2.11), ceased to be effective 25 years after the death of the author, and the rights (the 'reversionary interests') reverted to his or her heirs. The author could not override this provision by any additional agreement. Since 1 June 1957 the author, if he or she was still alive, has been able to assign the reversionary interests. There could of course be no reversionary interests in a work produced during the course of employment (see 3.2.12) or as a result of some types of commission (see 3.2.20) since the author was not then the owner and had no rights to assign.

1911 s5(2); 1956 Sch 7 para 28(3); 1988 (CDPA) Sch 1 para 27; Greene MR in *Coleridge-Taylor v Novello*, 1938, at 514; *Redwood Music v B Feldman*, 1979; Lord Salmon in *Chappell v Redwood Music*, 1981, at 344; *Novello v Keith Prowse Publishing*, 2005

3.3.13 Bankruptcy of individuals

When an individual is declared bankrupt, the copyrights in all his or her works, including unpublished works, pass to the trustee as soon as one is appointed. The trustee may then either sell the copyrights or exploit them, in order to secure the best return for the creditors.

1986 s306

3.3.14 Insolvency and winding-up of companies

When a company becomes insolvent, the administrator or administrative receiver may take possession of all its copyrights, and exploit, sell or otherwise dispose of them, in order to secure the best return for the creditors. When a company is wound up, the liquidator has the power to sell the copyrights.

1986 Sch 1 paras 1, 2, Sch 4 para 6

3.3.15 Equity and implied licences

Although the statute is quite clear about the identification of the first owner of copyright at law, the courts have recognized that there are cases where someone else is entitled to ownership, part ownership or the means to exploit the work. Their solution has been to decide either that the legal owner has implied a licence to the other person or is the owner in trust for the equitable owner. This could have implications for some works held in archives, as discussed below.

3.3.16 Implied licences

The person who commissioned a work will almost always be entitled to use it for the intended, or a closely related, purpose (see 3.2.18) if the contract does not set out the position precisely. Where the intended use is prevented as a result of the copyright belonging to the author, a court may decide that a licence is implied simply as a result of the author's actions or behaviour. A licence to publish is, for example, always implied when a person writes a letter to the editor of a newspaper, unless the letter is clearly marked 'not for publication'. One case has found an implied licence for the use of a computer catalogue of a company's material prepared by someone on commission, where the contract failed to mention copyright. The company had an implied licence to use the catalogue for its internal purposes, but not to license others' use of it.

Archivists and records managers should note that implied licences are only of limited extent. They are given to the person commissioning a work for the purpose of the commission, and to their agents acting for the same purpose. For instance, if an archivist commissions a photographer to take pictures of a new record office for the purpose of publicity, there will be an implied licence (if the contract does not mention one) to use the images for relevant purposes such as in advertisements and the annual report, so long as (normally) the photographer is acknowledged (see 8.1.5). The archivist's printer will be covered by the same licence. However, the implied licence would probably not extend to the use of the images in a history of archival services in the county. An implied licence to a person who commissioned a work is also unlikely to extend to the records manager or archivist after the person who commissioned it has deposited it in the registry or record office. If an archivist finds him or herself in a position where there is any doubt as to whether a licence to use a work has been implied, it would be sensible to seek legal advice (see 5.5).

Perceval (Lord and Lady) v Phipps, 1813; *Blair v Osborne and Tomkins*, 1971; *Solar Thompson Engineering v Barton*, 1977; *Robin Ray v Classic FM*, 1998; *Durand v Molino*, 2000; *Brighton v Jones*, 2004

3.3.17 Equity

There are also cases where the courts have found that the author holds the copyright in trust for the equitable owner (that is, the person or body who, in fairness, should be the owner of the copyright), and the latter is entitled to call for an assignment if necessary. A finding of equitable ownership depends on the particular circumstances, but cases include works created by partnerships and by the director of a company, where the partnership or company was found to be the equitable owner of works created by people doing work for the company but not as employees. Other cases concern individuals commissioned and paid to produce specified products. The distinction from other commissioned works (see 3.2.17–18) appears to arise from a range of possible circumstances:

- The equitable owner has specified the contents of the work quite precisely or has supplied the materials for the work's preparation.
- The author has no intention or expectation of owning the copyright.
- The legal owner has received 'valuable consideration' from the equitable owner.
- The equitable owner needs to own the copyright in order to be able to exploit rights in other related material (such as the owner of a ballet company who needed the rights in all aspects of a ballet he had commissioned in order to stage it) or to prevent others using the work.

Equitable owners may use the material, may seek an injunction to prevent infringement, and perhaps may give permission to others to use it (at least non-commercially), but may not sue for infringement without making the legal owner a party to the suit or obtaining an assignment from him or her. An equitable owner would be well advised to seek an assigment of the copyright (to acquire the 'legal' as well as the 'equitable' title) as soon as possible (see 3.3.8). If the legal owner sells his or her title to someone else who does not know of the equitable owner's interest, the equitable title is likely to disappear.

Massine v De Basil, 1938; *Antocks Lairn v I Bloohn*, 1972; *Roban Jig and Tool Co v Taylor*, 1979; *Acorn v MCS Microcomputer Systems*, 1983–5; *Robin Ray v Classic FM*, 1998; *Griggs v Evans and Raben Footwear*, 2005

3.3.18 The application of equitable ownership to archives

The concept of equitable ownership could be of particular value to archivists, and perhaps to records managers, but it is important to remember that equitable solutions are available to the court and are not rights granted by statute. In applying equity's principles as suggested, archivists should be aware that others might disagree that it applies. However, the types of circumstance considered below involve relatively obscure authorship and ownership, in relatively old material, so that any claimant would have grave difficulty in proving a case.

For archivists, equitable ownership might be applicable in works created by unpaid office-holders (for instance, an honorary secretary of a society or a parochial church council) and in works created on behalf of a body or group by office-holders who, while perhaps paid, are not strictly employees (for instance, parochial material by an incumbent clergyman) (see 7.2). It might also apply to some works created by employees before the coming into force of the 1911 Act (see 3.2.16), such as estate, poor law union and workhouse records (see 7.1.2, 7.10.2). Such people are likely to be working under instruction from the body they represent or in accordance with the law, and are unlikely to expect to be owners of the copyright or to have asserted their ownership of it. Unless, therefore, it is known that an author has explicitly asserted his or her rights to the copyright in material produced, archivists will not go far wrong if they take the practical approach and regard the executive committee (or equivalent), the current national or local officers of the body (or a successor body), the current office-holder, or the modern local authority as the equitable owners of the copyright and the people to whom to refer enquiries (see 7.4). Any such referral should be unspecific: 'it appears likely that you are the person to whom enquiries should be made'. It will then be up to those people to decide whether they have authority to give permission for use of the material. Equity also appears to be relevant in the cases of wills (see 7.3.9) and of some business records (see 7.9).

Merchant Adventurers v M Grew, 1973

3.3.19 Bona vacantia

Sometimes there will be no one left to own the copyright in a work, and in certain limited circumstances the Crown may step in to claim it as *bona vacantia*. Copyrights may become the property of the Crown as *bona vacantia* when:

- an individual dies intestate with no known kin;
- a company is dissolved with all debts discharged and the copyrights are among the remaining assets;
- a corporation is dissolved;
- a friendly society or club that is not a charity becomes defunct because it has no members; or
- a trust fails and there are no remaining beneficiaries.

This is not a common outcome: a solvent company will not often be dissolved with no successors interested in the assets. Copyrights that are *bona vacantia* pass to the Crown, which may sell the rights or retain them to receive royalty payments.

Enquiries as to whether the rights of a particular owner have passed to the Crown as *bona vacantia* should be addressed, for England and Wales (except the Duchies of Cornwall and Lancaster), to the Treasury Solicitor (BV), 1 Kemble Street, London WC2B 4TS. *Bona vacantia* for the two duchies is handled by the solicitors Farrer and Co at 66 Lincoln's Inn Fields, London WC2A 3LH. In Scotland it is handled by the Queen's and Lord Treasurer's Remembrancer, Crown Office, 25 Chambers Street, Edinburgh EH1 1LA, and in Northern Ireland by the Crown Solicitor's Office, Royal Courts of Justice, Chichester Street, Belfast BT1 3JY. It will be necessary to name the last owner, whether an individual or a body of some sort.

3.3.20 Orphan works

Almost all archives and registries will contain many 'orphan works', a term used to describe works which are, or may be, still in copyright but whose owner is impossible to identify. Examples include many letters and especially many documentary photographs. Anonymous and pseudonymous works, particularly unpublished ones from earlier centuries, are very likely to be orphans (see 2.1.17); consider, for instance, the copyright in the writings of Jack the Ripper. If the author was the first owner, proof of the descent of the title to the current owner will only be possible if the author is identified. The work then ceases to be anonymous, and, in the case of most artistic works and published literary, dramatic and musical works, if the author died more than 70 years ago the copyright will immediately terminate.

The Act provides some help, by allowing certain assumptions to be made about the termination of copyright (see 5.4.23–26), but a large part of the problem remains. There is nothing in the Act providing a defence against an infringement action on the basis that 'reasonable efforts' were taken to identify and trace the copyright owner and secure permission. Instead a decision to use an orphan work must be taken after an assessment of the risks (though in practical terms these might be very small) (see 5.4.21).

3.4 Assertion of ownership

Copyright subsists automatically as soon as the work is created, but it is helpful nevertheless to make some statement about it and about related rights. This is normal when a work is published, but it is definitely advisable also with unpublished material when it is leaving the control of the author or being made available to the public, in order to remind the user and to establish ownership. This can most conveniently be done by using the © symbol, together with the year and the name of the copyright owner. Nothing more is needed for copyright. However, the addition of the statement 'all rights reserved' makes sure that the owner is also claiming any other intellectual property rights that might subsist. Finally, if the author has the moral right of attribution in the work and has asserted it in writing (see 8.1.5), some statement to that effect is also needed, such as 'X has asserted her moral right to be identified as the author of this work' (but this does not apply to works in Crown or Parliamentary copyright, see 8.1.6).

4 Publication, exhibition and performance

4.1 Publication

4.1.1 Significance

The definition of publication was altered by regulations made in 1996 in response to EU directives, and the new definition applies to all copyright works, whether they were made under earlier legislation or not. Previous definitions of publication no longer, therefore, have any practical relevance. An archivist or records manager needs to be able to distinguish between published and unpublished works for three reasons:

- The act of publication, which is irrevocable, may have consequences for the duration of copyright (so long as publication was authorized by the copyright owner).
- The legal provisions concerning the copying of literary, dramatic, musical and artistic works by libraries and archives differ between published and unpublished material, which affects how much of a work may be copied, by whom and for what purposes (see 5.3).
- The publication of a literary, dramatic, musical or artistic work or a film which is still in copyright means that publication right can never be applied to it, but the publication for the first time of such a work which is no longer in copyright gives publication right to its publisher (see 8.3).

Directives 1992, 1993 (Term); 1988 (CDPA) s175(6); SI 1996/2967 regs 16–17, 26(1)

4.1.2 Issue to the public

Publication of a work, in the context of copyright, means the issue of copies to the public (by sale or otherwise), including (in the case of a literary, dramatic, musical and artistic work) making it available to the public by means of an electronic retrieval system (including one containing, say, archival databases in a record office). This means that any archivist wishing to include digitized images of original documents in a publicly available electronic catalogue must ensure either that those works are out of copyright or that he or she has permission to publish them. The internet involves use of a computer (an electronic retrieval system), so placing a work on a website publishes it as well as communicates it to the public (see 4.1.7, 5.1.6). For the effect of providing copies of documents to records users see 4.1.8.

One significant change made by the 1996 Regulations means that the issue of copies now (apparently) includes the issue of the original, of any date, though there are differences of opinion as to whether this change affects publication. There is no direct impact on most material in archives since allowing public access to an original work does not constitute 'issuing' it to the public, which is taken to mean putting the work into circulation or transferring possession of it from one person to another. It could possibly mean, though, that a manuscript offered for sale by auction and bought by an archive has been published in the process, and there might be an impact on electoral registers (see 7.8.5). It is now clear, as has always been accepted in practice, that the issue of letters patent has the effect of publishing them.

For the nature of 'the public' see 4.1.11. For means of making works available to the public which do not involve publishing them, see 4.1.10.

1988 (CDPA) ss18(4), 175(1), Sch 1 para 3; SI 1996/2967 regs 9(3), 26(1)

4.1.3 Publication right

There is a different definition of publication for the purposes of publication right (see 8.3), and care must be taken to ensure that they are not confused.

4.1.4 Commercial publication

Commercial publication, in relation to literary, dramatic, musical and artistic works only, means:

* issuing copies of a work to the public at a time when copies made in advance of the receipt of orders are generally available to the public; or
* making the work available to the public by means of an electronic retrieval system.

The first part of this definition means that a work is not a commercial publication if it is published only after subscriptions have been received for it, which is an arrangement often used for academic or limited-edition works. The second part of the definition is the same as for publication generally. This means that any electronic publication, such as on the internet (see 4.1.7), qualifies as commercial publication even if no charge is made for use. Commercial publication is a concept that is directly relevant to Crown copyright (see 2.2.24, 2.2.25, 2.2.27, 2.3.28) and to moral rights (see 8.1.5, 8.1.7), rather than to copyright generally, but there are significant implications in the categorization of internet publication as inherently commercial which are reflected in the approach of picture libraries and others in granting reproduction rights (see 5.4.34).

1988 (CDPA) s175(2)

4.1.5 Exceptions

The following acts do not constitute publication or commercial publication:

- for literary, dramatic and musical works, performance in public or communication to the public (unless it is by an electronic retrieval system);
- for artistic works, public exhibition or communication to the public;
- for sound recordings and films, being shown in public or communication to the public;
- issue to the public which is what the law calls 'colourable': inadequate to satisfy 'the reasonable requirements of the public', perhaps because too few copies are made available (though there would have to be very few) or because the means of distribution is inadequate. This might be done as a tactical ploy, or might include, say, the issue of underground ('samizdat') copies which most members of the public would not be able to obtain; and
- the issuing of copies to readers by archivists (see 4.1.8).

The fact that these acts do not constitute publication, though, does not necessarily mean that doing them is not an infringement of copyright (see 5.1).

1988 (CDPA) s175(4 and 5); *Francis, Day and Hunter v Feldman*, 1914; *Bodley Head v Flegon*, 1972

4.1.6 Exceptions: announcements

In some legal contexts the terms 'publish' and 'publication' are used to mean the announcement or supply of information to members of the public, whether or not in written form and whether or not copies are issued. This applies, for example, to banns of marriage and to electoral registers. Banns of marriage are published only in this sense so would not normally be published for copyright purposes, but electoral registers are published in both senses (see 7.8.5).

4.1.7 Internet

The act of placing a literary, dramatic, musical or artistic work on an internet website appears certain to publish it (although the courts in the UK have not yet had to decide the issue definitively) (see 6.2.1–2). The making available to the public of a literary, dramatic, musical or artistic work by means of an electronic retrieval system is publication, and a website must be an electronic retrieval system. Placing one of these types of work on a website also communicates it to the public (see 5.1.6), but while sound recordings and films are communicated to the public they are not published by these means. This question of publication on the internet is distinct from the question of whether the act is an infringement (see 5.1.6). For internet publication as a commercial act see 4.1.4.

1988 (CDPA) ss175(1)(b), 175(4)(a)(ii), 175(4)(b)(iv), 175(4)(c)(ii); *Shetland Times v Wills*, 1997

4.1.8 Authorized

In all references to publication, it should be understood that the action was lawful and authorized. Pirate editions and other infringing copies, or the theft and subsequent sale, of an original work do not have the effect of publishing it.

More to the point for an archivist, the issuing of copies of documents to readers under the library and archive provisions or the provisions for public records (see 5.3) does not cause the original documents to be published. Publication cannot occur as a result of an unauthorized act, and the issuing of copies by archivists, while legitimate, is not 'authorized' for this purpose.

1988 (CDPA) ss175(6), 178 'unauthorized'

4.1.9 Published works: versions

Successive UK copyright statutes have made the tacit assumption that a work as published differs only in typography from its manuscript form (or in the case of a film, say, an unedited take is merely a step leading to the final film) and have not tackled directly the problem of variant versions and recensions, whether published or not. Some doubt will always exist as to the degree of variation which is possible between a manuscript (or other draft) version and a published or final version of ostensibly the same work before they can be regarded as distinct original works for copyright purposes, since each case will have to be decided on its merits (see also 2.1.6). It is clear, though, from several court cases that such a distinction can be made. For separate copyrights to subsist, one of two things must have happened.

- The published or final version has been edited or altered using sufficient independent skill and effort to give it some quality or character (apart from mere typography) which distinguishes it from the original. An edition of a manuscript, where great skill and labour were required to interpret and transcribe the text and skill has been used in the process of selection and editing, might well be counted as a new work with a new copyright in the edition (but not in the original manuscript itself, see 2.1.8). Similarly, an edition of a musical work, involving skill in creating a usable performing edition, is a new copyright work, though a performance which does not use the editor's material will not infringe. However, the change of a single word in a poem by Sir Walter Scott, even though this altered the meaning, was not found (admittedly as long ago as 1870) to be enough. In many cases, the published text of a new book might be little different from the author's draft, but it certainly can be. Every one of James Joyce's corrected drafts, including printer's proofs, for *Ulysses* has been found to be a separate copyright work. Only the final proof was found to be the same work as the text published from it. In the case of a film, the differences between takes and the changes made during the editing of the selected takes to assemble the edited film may often be enough to leave distinct copyrights in the finished film and each take. In the case of artistic works, successive revised versions of drawings may be sufficiently different to be distinct original works, but the revisions must be 'visually significant' (not, for instance, new textual annotations).

- The manuscript or first version has been amended substantially after the published or final version was taken from it, so that it is materially different from the published version.

The publication of unamended manuscripts prior to their deposit in an archive may cause problems where copying by archivists is concerned (see 5.3.16).

Black v Murray, 1870; *Evans v Tout*, 1905–10; *Hyperion v Warner*, 1991; *Drayton Controls v Honeywell Control Systems*, 1992; *Biotrading and Financing v Biohit*, 1998; *Robin Ray v Classic FM*, 1998; *Norowzian v Arks (No 2)*, 2000; *Sweeney v Macmillan Publishers*, 2002; *Sawkins v Hyperion Records*, 2005

4.1.10 Available to the public

Making available to the public is a term that is confusingly used in the Act, being employed in different contexts with slightly different meanings. No work has been made available to the public for any of the purposes set out below if the act concerned was an act restricted by copyright (such as copying or the issue of copies to the public) and it was done without the permission of the owner of the copyright.

The term is defined by examples in the context of anonymous literary, dramatic, musical and artistic works and films, and of sound recordings, where it seems there was a need for a concept with a wider scope than that given to publication in order to fix the starting point for the calculation of the duration of copyright. A work is made available to the public for this purpose when it is:

- communicated to the public (see 5.1.6);
- performed in public (literary, dramatic and musical works only);
- exhibited in public (artistic works only);
- included in a film shown to the public (artistic works only);
- shown in public (films only); or
- played in public (sound recordings only).

This list is not comprehensive, since the Act gives only examples not a definition. To the list may be added publication (i.e. the issue of copies to the public, see 5.1.3). A rather different list of acts gave a starting point for the commencement of copyright in posthumous literary, dramatic and musical works created before 1 August 1989 (see 2.2.17–18).

The term has a similar but broader meaning when applied as a condition for fair dealing for the purposes of criticism or review (see 5.2.10). Here it includes all the acts listed above plus:

- making available to the public by means of an electronic retrieval system (see 4.1.2); and
- rental and lending (see 5.1.4).

For fair dealing purposes all the acts listed apply to all types of work, including broadcasts (see 2.6.2) and typographical arrangements (see 2.6.15), and to performances (see 8.5.6). This same extended list of acts also applies to manual copying for educational purposes of literary, dramatic, musical and artistic works (see 5.2.15), and to publication right in any type of work (see 8.3.2). In publication right, though, the term 'making available to the public' is prefaced by the word 'any', which appears to mean that it should be interpreted as widely as possible, perhaps even to encompass an act such as making available to the public in a record office, though there are doubts about this. In database right (see 8.2.9) there is no definition but the term 'available to the public' is followed by 'in any manner', which again suggests a very wide interpretation that might include availability in a record office.

In communication to the public (see 5.1.6) and in the 'making available right' of performers (see 8.5.3) the term is limited to meaning by electronic transmission to members of the public where and when they choose. In the definition of publication (see 4.1.2), making available applies only to making available to the public by means of an electronic retrieval system; all other meanings of making available are explicitly excluded.

1956 s2(3); 1988 (CDPA) ss12(5), 13A(2)(c), 13B(6), 20(2)(b), 30(1A), 32(2B), 175, 182CA, Sch 1 para 12(2)(a), Sch 2 para 2; SI 1995/3297 regs 5, 6; SI 1996/2967 reg 16(2); SI 1997/3032 regs 12(1), 19, 20; SI 2003/2498 regs 10, 29, Sch 1 para 27

4.1.11 Available to the public: application to archives

Although it is important to archivists, making available to the public is not a term that has attracted much judicial or academic attention in relation to copyright, but some parallels can usefully be drawn from rights in performances and patents. The 'public' has tended to be given quite a wide meaning, and could probably be taken to include a restricted group of people so long as it was possible in principle for anyone to join the group (for instance the members of a club or the staff of an office, or the staff and students given access to a university library). It may be (though there is no authority for interpretation of the term beyond what the statute says) that making available to the public in an archival context encompasses allowing the public access to documents, whether original or surrogates, and whether or not subject to specified conditions (such as the signing of an undertaking of confidentiality concerning specified categories of information). It would not include:

- the making available of descriptions of documents that are themselves not available to the public, for instance in a file list included in a freedom of information publication scheme or an archival catalogue;
- the preservation in a registry or archive of documents that are not producible, whether because they are as yet uncatalogued or because they are subject to confidentiality restrictions or closure (as under a Freedom of Information Act); or
- the allowing of privileged and discretionary access for certain individuals, particularly if the individuals are subject to conditions of confidentiality.

Harms and Chappell v Martans Club, 1926; *Jennings v Stephens*, 1936; *Ernest Turner Electrical Instruments v Performing Right Society*, 1943

4.1.12 Release, publication and availability to the public of sound recordings and films

Under the 1911 and 1956 Acts, the concept of 'publication' was thought sufficient to cover sound recordings and films. It was not used in the original text of the 1988 Act, where originally the term 'release' was applied to both. Subsequently, the term 'made available' has been used for films and the terms 'publication' and 'made available' have been used for sound recordings, but the duration of copyright in some films made between 1989 and 1995 may still be dependent on their 'release'. The definition of 'release' is wider than that of 'publication', and was widened further after the 1988 Act was passed. A film made between 1989 and 1995 was 'released' when it was first published, played in public or broadcast.

SI 1995/3297 regs 6, 9

4.1.13 Transmission: broadcasts

The concept of publication is not applied to broadcasts. Instead they may be transmitted.

1988 (CDPA) ss6, 6A, 7, 14(2); SI 1995/3297 reg 7; SI 1996/2967 regs 5, 6

4.2   Exhibition and performance

4.2.1   Importance to archives

Archivists will on occasion wish to place originals or copies of documents in their care on temporary or permanent display on the institution's own premises or elsewhere. They might also wish to quote a copyright work in a speech, show a film or video, play a sound recording, or show a broadcast, as a part of an exhibition or conference, or as a separate event. Similarly, members of staff may ask records managers about such uses and other organizations may wish to make use of material for these purposes. In some cases, if what is planned would infringe copyright it should be possible to obtain a licence from the appropriate body (see 5.4.29).

4.2.2   Exhibition of originals: literary, dramatic and musical works

The unauthorized public exhibition of copyright literary, dramatic and musical works is an infringement of copyright, but does not count as publication (see 4.1.2). The work may not, of course, be reproduced in a catalogue of an exhibition without permission, since that involves issue to the public (see 4.1.2). The Government of Ireland had to make hasty provision to ensure that the organizers of an exhibition to celebrate the centenary of Bloomsday (the day in 1904 when the events in James Joyce's *Ulysses* occurred) did not infringe. Oddly, though, they made provision only for literary works; the exhibition in Ireland of dramatic and musical works would still infringe.

1988 (CDPA) s19(1, 2(b)); 2000 (Ireland) s40(7A); 2004 (Ireland) s1

4.2.3   Exhibition of originals: artistic works

The public exhibition of copyright artistic works of any sort is not an infringement of copyright, and does not count as publication (see 4.1.2). However, if the author was alive on or after 1 August 1989, he or she has a moral right to be identified as the author of an artistic work on public exhibition (see 8.1.5). This is normally simply accomplished on the caption to the work, but infringement of the right could be just as serious as infringement of copyright. The work may not be reproduced in a catalogue of the exhibition without permission, except in the case of a work being exhibited for sale when it may be reproduced in the sale catalogue.

1988 (CDPA) s19(1), 63

4.2.4   Exhibition of originals: photographs

In the case of a photograph taken on or after 1 August 1989 in response to a commission for private and domestic purposes (such as wedding photographs and family portraits), the person who commissioned it (not necessarily the person portrayed) has the moral right not to have the work exhibited in public (see 8.1.10). A similar right existed prior to 1989, but it was common rather than statutory law.

1988 (CDPA) s85, Sch 1 para 24; *Pollard v Photographic Co*, 1889; *Stedall v Houghton*, 1901

4.2.5 Exhibition of originals: buildings, models and sculptures

It is not an infringement of the copyright in any building or in a model of a building, a sculpture or a work of artistic craftsmanship (such as stained glass, perhaps) that is on permanent display in a public place or in premises open to the public, to paint, draw, photograph or film it, or include it in a broadcast. The resulting image would almost certainly be a new copyright work, and may be reproduced and sold, still without infringement of the original copyright. This provision would thus apply to an archive building, and to any relevant works permanently displayed inside it, but not to works in a temporary exhibition. If access to the building were on the basis that such copying was not permitted, any copies nevertheless made would be covered by the provision but the person making them might be in breach of contract.

1988 (CDPA) ss28(1), 62

4.2.6 Exhibition of copies: literary, dramatic, musical and artistic works

If the public exhibition of literary, dramatic and musical copyright works is in itself an infringement of copyright, the making of copies for that purpose must also be. It may be that the making of copies of artistic works for this purpose would infringe too. Public exhibition cannot reasonably be considered to be covered by any of the categories of fair dealing (see 5.2.7–12), nor by the general library and archive copying provisions (see 5.3.5ff.). In Ireland, the exhibition of copies of literary and artistic works does not infringe, so presumably there would be no infringement by the making of copies for that purpose.

2000 (Ireland) s40(7A); 2004 (Ireland) s1

4.2.7 Performance of literary, dramatic and musical works

The performance in public of a copyright literary, dramatic or musical work is an infringement. This includes the reading of a lecture, speech or sermon, the performance of a dramatic or musical work, and the presentation of such a work in a sound recording, film or broadcast (including by communicating it to the public on an internet website). However, it is permissible for one person to read in public a reasonable extract from a published literary or dramatic copyright work, so long as the source is acknowledged (by giving the title and the name of the author), and such a reading may be recorded in a sound recording (including the soundtrack to a film) or included in a broadcast so long as it forms only a small part of the whole recording. A 'reasonable extract' is not defined, but it would seem that it would depend not only on the size and nature of the extract but also on the circumstances of the reading and the effect on the copyright owner (whether, for instance, the use would be in competition with the copyright owner).

1988 (CDPA) ss5A and B, 19, 59(1), 178 'sufficient acknowledgement'

4.2.8   Films and sound recordings

The showing or playing in public of a copyright sound recording, or a film made on or after 1 June 1957, is an infringement. It is, however, permissible to play a sound recording as part of the activities or for the benefit of a club, society or other organization that is not established or run for profit and that is mainly charitable or exists for quasi-charitable religious, educational or social welfare purposes, so long as any income from admission charges or the sale of goods and services is used for the purposes of the organization. Also, the person playing the recordings must be acting for the organization and not for gain (so the exception would not cover the activities of a professional disc jockey unless he was giving his services free and with no advertising). This permission might apply to a few archival institutions, but not to any that are run by a local authority or the government.

The showing of a fiction film made before 1 June 1957 is an infringement in the film as a dramatic work, but the showing of a non-fiction film from the same period is not an infringement since it is protected as a sequence of photographs which, being artistic works, may be shown without infringement (see 2.4.1, 4.2.3).

1988 (CDPA) ss16(1)(c), 19(3), 67; SI 2003/2498 reg 18; *Phonographic Performance v South Tyneside Metropolitan Borough Council*, 2002

4.2.9   Broadcasts

The showing or playing in public of a copyright broadcast is not an infringement of the copyright in the broadcast or in any film included in it, if the audience has not paid for admission. However, the making of a copy of a broadcast would be an infringement, as would any subsequent playing of the recording. The exception covers a sound recording included in the broadcast only if:

• the author of the broadcast and the sound recording are the same and it is not a recording of music; or

- the playing or showing of the broadcast forms part of the activities of an organization that is not established or run for profit, or was necessary for demonstrating or repairing equipment.

There are special new provisions for licensing schemes to license the playing of sound recordings not covered by this exception. For details contact one of the relevant licensing bodies (see 5.4.29). Also, while the exception covers the broadcast, film and sound recording, it does not cover any other work, such as a piece of music, being performed so permission might still be required in some cases.

1988 (CDPA) ss16(1)(a), 17(1), 19(3), 72, 128A, 128B; SI 2003/2498 reg 21

4.2.10 Rights in performances

For performers' rights see 8.5.

5 Use

5.1 The copyright owner's rights

5.1.1 Introduction

The law of copyright gives certain rights to the owner of the copyright in a work. It must be remembered that in using the copyright work, other people do not themselves have rights. Rather, in accordance with the common law practice of giving liberties rather than rights, they are exercising certain freedoms granted to them by the law which limit the rights of the copyright owner in various ways.

The copyright owner has the exclusive right to do the things set out below with his or her copyright work, and to allow other people to do them (see 5.4.1), subject to the exceptions and limitations (see 5.2 and 5.3) and subject also to the rights of others (see 1.1.3). Some of these rights, known as 'acts restricted by copyright', are dealt with in more detail elsewhere, as shown. The doing of any of these acts without permission and outside the scope of the exceptions and limitations is an infringement (see 5.2.28ff.).

5.1.2 Copying

The copyright owner has the exclusive right (see 5.1.1) to copy or authorize the copying of a work of any type (but see 5.3). This includes any form of copying including, for instance, transcription, tracing, photocopying, digitization and the saving of a copy within a computer (see also 5.1.10). A transient copy made by a computer simply in order to display a work on screen does not infringe, nor does a copy made by an internet service provider in innocently transmitting a work (see 6.2.5). There is no infringement by making a similar, or even identical, work independently, but if the author of the new work had access to the earlier one he or she will be assumed to have copied in the absence of evidence to the contrary (see 2.1.7, 2.1.11).

The unauthorized copying of a three-dimensional work in two dimensions (and vice versa) is certainly an infringement only if it is an artistic work. It would therefore be an infringement to make a topographical model from a map. In the case of three-dimensional copying of a literary work, there could be infringement by making an object using precise dimensions contained in, say, a computer data file or by making a circuit from a circuit diagram (each of which can be both a literary work and an artistic one, see 2.1.2, 6.2.1). There is no infringement by simply following instructions, for instance a cookery recipe or a knitting pattern, since the finished article does not reproduce the instructions, it merely carries them out.

Copying does not have to be directly from the copyright work for there to be infringement. Indirect copying of, say, a drawing may be from other copies of the drawing, from a three-dimensional object made using it, or of the salient features of several drawings (such as cartoons of Popeye). The copying of a typographical arrangement of a published edition is an infringement only if it is a facsimile copy (even if reduced or enlarged in scale).

1911 s35(1) 'infringing'; 1956 s48(1) 'reproduction'; 1988 (CDPA) ss16(1)(a), 17, 28A, 178 'facsimile copy'; SI 2002/2013 regs 17–19; SI 2003/2498 reg 8; *King Features Syndicate v O and M Kleeman*, 1941; *LB (Plastics) v Swish Products*, 1979; *Brigid Foley v Elliott*, 1982; *Interlego v Tyco*, 1988; *Ibcos Computers v Barclays Mercantile Highland Finance*, 1994; *Autospin v Beehive Spinning*, 1995; *Cala Homes (South) v Alfred McAlpine Homes East*, 1995; *Canon Kabushiki Kaisha v Green Cartridge (Hong Kong)*, 1997; *Aubrey Max Sandman v Panasonic UK*, 1998; *Lambretta Clothing v Teddy Smith (UK)*, 2005

5.1.3 Issue of copies to the public

The copyright owner has the exclusive right (see 5.1.1) to issue or authorize the issuing of copies of a work of any type to the public (see 4.1). It is noteworthy that the statute does not mention 'publication' in the definition of this right, although earlier statutes did. The definition of publication (see 4.1.2) is such that unauthorized publication could be infringement by communication to the public instead (see 5.1.6).

1988 (CDPA) ss16(1)(b), 18

5.1.4 Rental and lending: definition

The copyright owner has the exclusive right (see 5.1.1) to rent or lend, or authorize the rental or lending of, certain types of work to the public. This right applies to:

- all literary, dramatic and musical works;
- any artistic work except a building or model for a building or a work of applied art; and
- all films and sound recordings (including, for example, videos and CDs).

In summary, rental means making the original or a copy of the work available for borrowing on a commercial basis. Lending means making the original or a copy available for borrowing on a non-commercial basis through an establishment that is open to the public. There are explicit exceptions and exclusions to the right (see 5.2.14).

1988 (CDPA) ss16(1)(ba), 18A, 36A, 40A; SI 1996/2967 regs 10, 11, 35

5.1.5 Performance

The copyright owner has the exclusive right (see 5.1.1) to perform or authorize the performance of a literary, dramatic or musical work, or to play or show, or to authorize the playing or showing of a sound recording, film or broadcast in public (see 4.2.7–10).

1988 (CDPA) ss16(1)(c), 19

5.1.6 Communication to the public

The copyright owner has the exclusive right (see 5.1.1) to communicate to the public, or to authorize the communication to the public, of a literary, dramatic, musical or artistic work, a sound recording or film or a broadcast. This right was introduced following an EU directive of 2001, and it replaced the right to broadcast a work. A communication to the public in this sense is an electronic transmission, including one by broadcasting (by terrestrial or satellite television, wireless or cable) or one by which users may access the work when and where they wish. It includes a communication by means of the internet (see 6.2.2). There is no infringement if the relevant members of the public are all present at the place where the communication originates. Display from a local server on screens in a record office should therefore not infringe this right.

It is important to remember that communication to the public is a right belonging to the copyright owner; it is not a type of copyright work. On the other hand, a broadcast (see 2.6.2) is a type of work, but 'broadcasting' is not a distinct right. Instead it is a part of communication to the public.

Directive 2001 (Information Society) recital 23; 1988 (CDPA) ss16(1)(d), 20; SI 2003/2498 reg 6

5.1.7 Adaptation

The copyright owner has the exclusive right (see 5.1.1) to make or authorize the making of an adaptation of a literary, dramatic or musical work, or to do or authorize the doing of any of the other acts restricted by copyright in connection with such an adaptation.

- For most literary works and for dramatic works, adaptation means a translation, a conversion of a literary work to a dramatic work (for instance, into a screenplay for a film) or vice versa, and a conversion of a work into pictorial form, such as a strip cartoon (with or without words).
- For a computer program it means an arrangement or altered version, or a translation into a different computer language.
- For a database it means an arrangement or altered version or a translation.
- For a musical work it means an arrangement or transcription.

Clearly the definition of an adaptation is quite narrow. Many uses of a work that might in general be thought of as adaptations, such as abridgements, will instead be infringements by copying (see 5.1.2, 5.1.10).

If an adaptation of a work exists, any non-infringing use of the adaptation does not infringe the copyright in the original. In order to infringe the copyright in an original work, an unauthorized adaptation must be fixed in some material form (see 2.1.3), but something like the public performance of even an unfixed adaptation, such as the ad-libbed performance of a spoof version of a play, or the translation during a speech of a quotation from a text, could infringe the copyright in the original work (but see 4.2.7). The resulting adaptations will normally qualify as new copyright works if they are fixed (see 2.1.6).

1988 (CDPA) ss16(1)(e), 21, 76; *Wood v Boosey*, 1868; *Byrne v Statist*, 1914

5.1.8   Education

The copyright owner has the exclusive right (see 5.1.1) to make or authorize the making of a reprographic copy or copies of a literary, dramatic, musical or artistic work for use in the course of instruction or preparation for instruction (see 5.2.15–16).

1988 (CDPA) s32(1)(b)

5.1.9   Music examination

The copyright owner has the exclusive right (see 5.1.1) to make or authorize the making of a reprographic copy or copies of a musical work for use by an examination candidate in performing the work.

1988 (CDPA) s32(4)

5.1.10 Indexes, translations, tracings, summaries and transcripts

The making of indexes, translations, summaries and transcripts of copyright literary, dramatic and musical works is or may be an infringement by copying (see 5.1.2) unless prior approval is obtained.

- An index will probably not constitute an infringement if it merely reproduces single words or short passages and provides an indication of where to find the relevant text or passage in the original work. If, however, it reproduces the whole or a substantial part of the content, but in a different order, it will count as a copy of the original work and thus will be an infringement.

- A translation into another language counts as an adaptation and thus is an infringement (see 5.1.7).
- A transcript of a literary or dramatic work or a tracing of an artistic work (such as a map) is a manual copy and, unless it is of an insubstantial part of the work, will be an infringement (see 5.1.2). A transcription of a musical work is an adaptation, and thus will again be an infringement (see 5.1.7).
- A precis of a literary or dramatic work, using a selection of the author's own words, will almost always be an infringement. A paraphrase or abridgement, summarizing the work in the paraphraser's own words, would raise more difficult issues. To be an infringement it would have to be shown that the paraphrase used a substantial part (see 5.2.3) of the author's skill and labour in creating the source work, rather than merely using his or her general ideas (see 2.1.4).

In some cases, the resulting indexes, translations, summaries and transcripts will themselves qualify as new copyright works (see 2.1.5ff.), but use of them could indirectly infringe any copyright still subsisting in the original works (see 2.1.6, 5.1.2).

1988 (CDPA) ss17, 21; *Anon*, 1774; *Valcarenghi v Gramophone*, 1928–35

5.2 Exceptions and infringements

5.2.1 Introduction

As noted above, there are some limits on the copyright owner's exercise of his or her rights, which allow the use of copyright works for particular purposes, in particular circumstances or in particular quantities. Where these do not apply there is infringement.

The Berne Convention, the WIPO Copyright Treaty (see 1.2.7) and the Information Society Directive (see 1.2.8) all contain a test to assist in deciding on the scope of an exception. While not written into UK law, the 'three-step test' can be helpful in deciding whether an exception applies in particular circumstances. The test specifies that exceptions may only apply:

- in certain special cases (that is, as defined in statute);
- when the use does not conflict with the normal exploitation of the work by the rights owner; and
- when the use does not unreasonably prejudice the legitimate interests of the author or other rights owner.

Berne Convention art 9(2); WIPO Copyright Treaty art 10(1); Directive 2001 (Information Society) art 5(5)

5.2.2   Out of copyright

If copyright no longer subsists in a work (see especially 2.2.16ff., 2.3.12ff., 2.4.9ff., 2.5.11ff.) it is commonly said to be in the 'public domain'. No permission on copyright grounds is then needed to use it in any way, although care should be taken to ensure that there is no new copyright that might be infringed, for instance in the typography of a recent published edition or in a skilfully executed photograph of a medieval seal (see 2.1.5ff.). It is important to be careful about this, because it is rarely a defence to a claim of copyright infringement to say that you thought that copyright no longer subsisted, although this might affect the size of any damages awarded. However, if a literary, dramatic, musical or artistic work is anonymous (see 2.1.17) and it is reasonable to assume that the author or authors died more than 70 years earlier, it may be possible in some limited circumstances to use it without infringement (see 5.4.25–26).

1988 (CDPA) s57

5.2.3   Substantial

Copyright protects only the whole or a substantial part of a work, so an insubstantial part may be reproduced. Successive Acts have not defined substantial, and the Government's Stationery Office sought legal advice on the subject when the concept appeared in the Copyright Act 1911. It was told that 'it is impossible to define what a substantial part is. The words exclude mere trivial extracts, but anything of serious value would no doubt fall within it.' The judges have taken a similar line, so case law has made clear over the years that substantiality must be considered primarily in a qualitative sense and only secondarily in a quantitative one. Also, in some cases the purpose and circumstances must be taken into account. Use in one context might be regarded as unimportant to the interests of the copyright owner, but use of the same material in another might justify the payment of fees; a music student quoting from a musical work in a new piece of music would be rather different, for instance, from a major composer using the same quotation. It must be remembered that the test of what is substantial relates to the source work: it does not matter whether the new work attracts copyright, nor whether the extract forms an insubstantial part of the user's work or (for instance) the final visual effect is different.

Ladbroke (Football) v William Hill (Football), 1964; *Waterlow Publishers v Rose*, 1995; *Designers Guild v Russell Williams (Textiles)*, 2000; *Scottish and Universal Newspapers v Paul Mack*, 2003; TNA: OS 1/6/2

5.2.4   Substantial: quantity

The proportion of a copyright work that would be regarded as substantial varies with the work and the nature of the extract, which is why quality is the more important test.

What is certain, though, is that what is measured is the proportion that is taken from the source work; the proportion that the extract makes up in the copier's work is irrelevant. Four lines out of 32 from Kipling's poem *If* were found to be substantial, but the quality of what was taken, and the use to which it was put, were probably more decisive. Each separate entry in a diary is a distinct copyright work, so an extract using an entry for one day must be a substantial part.

A substantial part of the typographical arrangement of a published edition is likely to be a whole page (see 5.2.6). A substantial part of a film means a substantial part of any image forming part of the film. The reproduction of a whole still from a film is thus always a reproduction of a substantial part of the film.

1956 s13(10) 'copy'; 1988 (CDPA) s17(4); *Kipling v Genatosan*, 1917–23; *Spelling Goldberg Productions v BPC Publishing*, 1981; *Bleiman v News Media (Auckland)*, 1994; *A v B*, 2000; *Newspaper Licensing Agency v Marks and Spencer*, 2001

5.2.5 Substantial: quantity: suggested limits

It is worth bearing in mind guidance published respectively by the Society of Authors and the Chartered Institute of Library and Information Professionals (CILIP) as to the quantities they consider appropriate for fair dealing and library copying (see 5.2.7 and 5.3.12). For purposes of quotation in another publication these are up to 400 words in a single quotation and up to 800 words in shorter quotations none of which is longer than 300 words. For the purposes of copying for private study or non-commercial research they are a single article in a journal or a single chapter in a book, up to a maximum of 5% of the whole. If these are accepted as sensible limits, as they have been for many years, an insubstantial part must be smaller.

5.2.6 Substantial: quality

The quality of an extract used has links with the question of originality (see 2.1.5ff.) since it is that which is the basis of copyright protection in a literary, dramatic, musical or artistic work. To take the essence or the words embodying the central idea of the original creation is likely to be to take a substantial part, even if few words are involved, since that is likely to be much of what made the source work original in the first place. Further, if an extract that has been taken is original in itself or has required considerable skill and effort on the part of the author to create, it is likely to be considered to be a substantial part of the whole work. Ultimately, though, substantiality can only be decided in the particular circumstances.

• A quotation of a couple of sentences from a book would certainly be substantial if it contained one of the book's main themes or showed how the author was thinking.

Scattered lines taken from an early manuscript version of James Joyce's *Ulysses* were found to be a substantial part of that version because of their significance as passages omitted from the published text; four lines from Kipling's *If* 'formed an essential part of the crescendo of the poem'; and a few lines from the lyrics of a song used in another song were found to be substantial because they embodied the source song's central idea.

- The playing of a short extract from the march *Colonel Bogey* was substantial because the extract included the principal theme.

- A quotation of a few words from a commonplace letter could become substantial if, say, those words constituted evidence of a relationship between the writer and the recipient.

- The taking of a single name and address from a directory (or, say, from census records) would be the use of unprotected information (see 2.1.4), but the taking of a larger number, especially for the purpose of creating a rival product, is likely to be use of a substantial part (but see 8.2 for databases).

- If Leonardo's painting *Mona Lisa* were in copyright, an area of a few square inches of background would probably not be substantial but the same area including her smile certainly would be, because a substantial part of an artistic work is that which is 'visually significant'.

- The use of a photograph to create a much simplified version might not be use of a substantial part if the simplification is such that none of what made the source photograph original remains.

- If the author has quoted from an earlier work which is out of copyright, an extract taken by someone else which consists of just this quotation will not be a substantial part of the author's work (no matter how large the quotation) because there is no originality in it (that is, it did not originate with the author, so he or she cannot claim copyright in it, see 2.1.5, 2.1.8).

- Since every part of a computer program might be essential for its operation, greater weight than usual might have to be given to the quantity taken and the level of skill required to create it. However, to take the architecture of a program is likely to be akin to taking the plot of a novel and thus a substantial part.

- A facsimile copy (see 5.1.2) of a whole page of a published edition is likely to be a substantial part of the typographical arrangement, since the skill and labour involved in creating that arrangement is in the design of the whole page through the relationships between its parts (fonts, layout, use of columns, margins, use of pictures and so on). An extract which does not show how the part taken relates to the rest of the page cannot be a substantial part.

1988 (CDPA) s16(3)(a); Peterson J in *Kipling v Genatosan*, 1917–23, at 205; *Hawkes v Paramount Film Service*, 1934; *Warwick Film Productions v Eisinger*, 1969; Lord Oliver in *Interlego v Tyco*, 1988, at 367; Whitford J in *Rose Plastics v William Beckett (Plastics)*, 1989, at 123; *Waterlow Publishers v Rose*, 1995; *Cantor Fitzgerald v Tradition*, 2000; *Newspaper Licensing Agency v Marks and Spencer*, 2001; *Sweeney v Macmillan Publishers*, 2002

5.2.7   Fair dealing

Once it has been decided that a substantial part of a copyright work is being used, the question which most commonly then arises is whether the use of it is 'fair dealing': is the use 'fair' and is it for a permitted purpose? It is not impossible for the use of even the whole of certain types of work (for example a short poem) or of several very significant extracts to be fair depending on the purpose for which the material is used. Although the American term 'fair use' actually first appeared in an English case in 1839 it has no meaning in UK law, and it is important to note that fair dealing has a much narrower scope. Fair dealing first appeared explicitly in UK law in 1911, but has never actually been defined by a statute. Instead, each individual use has to be looked at in the specific circumstances, bearing in mind that it is otherwise an infringement.

There appear to be some general factors to consider:

- Is the quantity being used excessive in the circumstances? What proportion of the work being quoted has been used? The Society of Authors continues to stand by the suggested quantities once agreed with the Publishers' Association. They considered that extracts could be fair dealing if they amounted to no more than:
  — up to 400 words in a single quotation; or
  — up to a total of 800 words in a series of short quotations, none of which is longer than 300 words.
- What is the motive for the use? Does the use compete with the copyright owner's exploitation, for instance by evading purchase of a legitimate copy? Is the motive really simply to save effort by the user?
- Does the use fit within one of the three categories of fair dealing (see 5.2.8–12)? If not, no matter how 'fair' the use is, it will not be fair dealing. Moreover, if the use changes (for instance a copy was made for private study but is then deposited in a record office for access and inevitably copying by others), fair dealing might no longer apply so that the copy becomes an infringing copy and mere possession of it could be an infringement (see 5.2.31).
- Has a 'sufficient acknowledgement' been given? A sufficient acknowledgement is one which identifies the work by its title or some other description and identifies the author (unless the work is anonymous and the author cannot be identified by reasonable enquiry, see 2.1.17). No acknowledgement is required for the purposes of private study or non-commercial research if an acknowledgement is impossible for reasons of practicality or otherwise, which are unlikely often to occur. Members of the public using self-service copiers should therefore be encouraged to record the title and author on their copies.

Other important factors might be:

- Has the copyright owner made the work freely available to the public (see 4.1.10, 5.2.10–11), or could the use be seen as a breach of confidence (see 8.7)?
- Is this use necessary in the circumstances? For instance, is direct quotation of the author's own words necessary or would use of the information but not the actual form of expression be enough? Freedom of speech is not a sufficient justification.

1911 s2(1)(i); 1956 s6; 1988 (CDPA) ss29–30, 178 'sufficient acknowledgement'; SI 2003/2498 reg 9; *Lewis v Fullarton*, 1839; *Hubbard v Vosper*, 1972; *Beloff v Pressdram*, 1973; *Associated Newspapers Group v News Group Newspapers*, 1986; *Ashdown v Telegraph Group*, 2001

5.2.8   Fair dealing: non-commercial research or private study

Fair dealing for the purposes of private study or research for a non-commercial purpose does not infringe copyright in:

- most literary works (except as mentioned below);
- a database;
- a computer program, except in order to convert it from a low- to a high-level language (but see 6.6), but the fairness of any use might be difficult to prove since it would almost certainly damage the interests of the copyright owner;
- any dramatic, musical or artistic work;
- the typographical arrangement of a published edition.

There is no fair dealing for these purposes in films, sound recordings or broadcasts.

Until the law had to be amended to conform to a European directive, research could be of any kind. It is now limited to research for a non-commercial purpose, but no definition of 'commercial' is offered. It is important to remember, though, that it is the purpose at the time that the possibly infringing act was done that matters. If the facts show that the motive was non-commercial but the purpose was in fact commercial (for instance because a person making a copy did not realize that the research was commercial), fair dealing will not apply. Thus commercial research will probably include:

- research for a book for which payment of any kind will be received;
- research for paying clients of any sort (e.g. by a record agent, a consultant);
- research which is intended to assist the creation of any commercial product or directly assist the operation of a commercial service, including one by, for instance, a charity;
- research for a television or radio programme (including the BBC);

- study which might also assist personal development but which is prompted immediately by, for instance, the needs of paying clients; and
- research for training materials to be used in a commercial training course.

Private study must be solely for the benefit of the individual concerned; it is not fair dealing to publish material so that others may use it for private study. No use which is for a commercial purpose will qualify, since private study cannot by definition be commercial. There is little point in seeking to distinguish private study from non-commercial research, since they are much the same and both qualify as fair dealing. Non-commercial research or private study might thus include:

- study by a student for an educational course, or by an archivist or other professional for personal development with no other specific aim in mind;
- background research even if it might later be used for a commercial purpose, though such later use would not be fair dealing and could itself be an infringement;
- research for charitable purposes, even if the funding comes from a commercial source; and
- personal or family history research which will result at most in distribution of the results (but not of copies of the copyright work) free of charge to a limited circle.

For databases see 8.2.14.

1988 (CDPA) ss29, 178 'private study'; SI 2003/2498 reg 9, Sch 1 para 15(3); *University of London Press v University Tutorial Press*, 1916; *Sillitoe v McGraw Hill Book Co*, 1983

5.2.9   Fair dealing: non-commercial research or private study: copying on behalf of others

For the first time, the 1988 Act accepted that some copying by a person acting on behalf of the user, as well as by the user him or herself, may be fair dealing for the purposes of research or private study. This would cover, for instance, a professional researcher or record agent making a self-service copy for a client, but he or she must be satisfied that multiple copies will not be supplied for similar purposes to the same client or anyone else. However, there are special provisions for copying on behalf of a researcher by an archivist or librarian (see 5.3.5ff.). Because of this, it seems that the defence of fair dealing would not for the most part be available to a librarian or archivist who supplied copies outside the terms of those special provisions. The principal effect of this is that an archivist should not normally supply a copy of an artistic work unless it is an illustration to a literary, dramatic or musical work that is also being copied (but see 5.3.18). Librarians, however, are explicitly allowed to make copies under fair dealing so long as they are satisfied that multiple copies will not be supplied for similar purposes to the same person or anyone else, and it may be (but this is far from clear) that the effect of this is that a librarian may supply a copy of a published edition of an artistic work.

1988 (CDPA) ss29(3), 37–43

5.2.10 Fair dealing: criticism and review

Fair dealing with any type of work for the purpose of criticism or review of that work or another work is not an infringement, provided sufficient acknowledgement is made by giving the title and author. However, it has long been the case in the UK, and is now also across the European Union, that this form of fair dealing does not apply to works that have never been made available to the public (see 4.1.10–12), on the grounds that it would be unfair to the author.

The criticism or review must be of the same or another work or works (that is, something falling within one of the statutory categories of works, see 2.1.1, whether actually protected by copyright or not) and the thoughts or themes underlying it or them, including the social and moral implications. It is not fair dealing to use extracts from a copyright work to criticize, say, the general conduct of the author. However, the Court of Appeal has said that criticism and review are of wide scope and the expression should be interpreted liberally. It is therefore worth considering whether an act which is excluded from fair dealing for non-commercial research or private study on the grounds that it is for a commercial purpose is instead covered by criticism or review.

In deciding whether the use is fair, a court will consider what proportion of the user's work consists of quotation, and what proportion consists of comment and analysis. There must be a preponderance of comment and analysis. It will not consider, though, whether the criticism itself is fair: 'What is in issue is not whether the criticism is fair . . . but whether the extent of copying is fair in all the circumstances so as to support or illustrate the criticisms being made.' A work that is the subject of the criticism or review may be copied for that purpose.

Directive 2001 (Information Society) art 5(3)(d); 1988 (CDPA) ss30(1), 178 'sufficient acknowledgement'; SI 2003/2498 reg 10; *British Oxygen v Liquid Air*, 1925, at 393; *Hubbard v Vosper*, 1972; *Beloff v Pressdram*, 1973; *Time Warner Entertainment v Channel 4 Television*, 1994; *Pro Sieben Media v Carlton UK Television*, 1998 (Laddie J at 52) and 1999 (Robert Walker LJ at 620); *Fraser-Woodward v BBC and Brighter Pictures*, 2005

5.2.11 Fair dealing: news reporting

Fair dealing with any type of work other than a photograph (but including a still from a film made since 1 June 1957, since that is not classified as a photograph, see 2.3.3) for the purpose of reporting current events is not an infringement, provided sufficient acknowledgement is made by giving the title and author (unless such acknowledgement is impractical). The work itself need not be current (for example it may be 30 years old but newly released under freedom of information, see 5.3.3–4) but the news must be of current concern to the public, and the use of the quotation from the work must be reasonably necessary to the reporting of the current events. The reporting involved must be reporting to the public, not reporting to, for instance, the board of directors of a company. Thus, it was found not to be for the purpose of reporting current events to use extracts from the private letters of the Duchess of Windsor in reporting her death, nor to copy newspaper cuttings in order to make senior staff aware of current events. Unlike with fair dealing for criticism and review there is no statutory authority for the principle that the exception does not apply to works which have never been made available to the public (see 5.2.10). The judges have decided, though, that there must be an over-riding public interest in disclosure (see 5.2.25) or alternatively that a work must have been published or at least communicated to a wide audience with the approval of the copyright owner before it may legitimately be used for current news reporting.

1988 (CDPA) ss30(2 and 3), 58, 178 'sufficient acknowledgement'; *Distillers (Biochemicals) v Times Newspapers*, 1975; *Associated Newspapers Group v News Group Newspapers*, 1986; *Pro Sieben Media v Carlton UK TV*, 1999; *Hyde Park Residence v Yelland*, 2000; *Ashdown v Telegraph Group*, 2001

5.2.12 Fair dealing: news reporting: recordings

The making and use of written notes or a tape or other recording of spoken words for the purposes of reporting current events or broadcasting is not an infringement, provided:

* the record is a direct record of the words spoken, not a copy from an earlier record;
* the speaker did not forbid the making of the record, and the record did not infringe any existing copyright in the words spoken (that is, if the words came from another copyright work);
* the use made of the record was not forbidden by the speaker or other copyright owner before the record was made; and
* the use is approved by the person who is lawfully in possession of the record.

This exception could help oral history projects which are aimed at the making of broadcasts. It might also apply, for instance, to interviews which are connected with the reporting of the release of historical material relating to the same topic.

1988 (CDPA) s58

5.2.13 Incidental inclusion

Copyright in almost any work is not infringed by its incidental inclusion (whether deliberately or not) in an artistic work, sound recording, film or broadcast, and the resulting work may be published, shown or broadcast also without infringement. However, this exception does not apply to the deliberate inclusion, no matter how incidental, of a musical work or words spoken or sung with music. If the use of the work is essential to the purpose of the work in which it appears the use cannot be incidental, so that for instance because the showing of authentic team kit including the Football Association logo (an artistic work) in photographs of footballers sold to collectors was essential to the purpose of the images, copyright in the logo was infringed.

1988 (CDPA) s31; *Hawkes & Son v Paramount Film Service*, 1934; *Football Association Premier League v Panini*, 2003

5.2.14 Rental and lending

For the purposes of rental and lending right (see 5.1.4), neither rental nor lending includes public performance, playing or showing in public or broadcasting, exhibiting in public or reference use in the institution. Archivists may therefore make documents available on-site without infringing. Rental and lending right is not infringed by:

- lending by an institution that is open to the public to another institution that is open to the public, for instance for an exhibition;
- the lending of a book by a public library under the public lending right scheme (see 8.4); or
- the lending of originals or copies of works (such as books or indeed manuscripts) by a prescribed archive, or a prescribed library that is not a public library (including, for instance, a manuscripts collection in a university library, see 5.3.6), provided that either the institution is not conducted for profit or it is part of an educational establishment. The work may be lent for use anywhere off-site and it may be lent whether or not it is accessible to the public.

In any other circumstances, lending is permitted only so long as reasonable royalties are paid or the lending is under licence.

1988 (CDPA) ss16(1)(ba), 18A, 36A, 40A; SI 1996/2967 regs 10, 11, 35

5.2.15 Education

The use of copyright works by educational establishments for non-commercial educational purposes is covered by a range of exceptions. The following is a summary of them; an archivist involved with education should consult the Act itself. The exceptions apply in all cases to teachers and pupils, and in some also to other staff of the establishment, but not for instance to parents. Copying for all these purposes must be accompanied by a sufficient acknowledgement (see 5.2.7). The main exceptions are:

- unlimited manual (but not reprographic) copies of literary, dramatic, musical or artistic works that have been made available to the public (see 4.1.10) may be made for the purposes of instruction (such as by writing on the blackboard or by using quotations in school work);
- the multiple copying and use of any work (except for the performance of a musical one, see 5.1.9) is permitted for an examination; 'examination' in this context is interpreted broadly to cover, for instance, the preparation of a dissertation or thesis which is to be submitted for examination;
- performances of literary, dramatic and musical works may be given, and sound recordings, films and broadcasts may be played or shown, to the pupils and staff on the premises;
- copies of sound recordings, films or broadcasts may be made for the purposes of instruction in the making of films or film sound tracks;
- recordings of broadcasts may be made unless there is a licensing scheme available which would cover the activity (see 5.4.28), but they may be shown within the establishment only and thus not to off-site students even if they have restricted access; and
- very limited reprographic copies of published literary, dramatic and musical works may be made (see 5.2.16), unless there is a licensing scheme available which would cover the activity (see 5.4.28). Such copies do not infringe any copyright in the typographical arrangement. There are licensing schemes covering all educational sectors, so in practice this exception is of no effect in the UK. For details of schemes affecting particular sectors contact the relevant licensing body (see 5.4.29).

The term 'reprographic' as used in these exceptions is quite wide, and covers the making of facsimile and multiple copies by any means including electronic ones, and the making of copies from a work held in electronic form.

If a copy made under one of these exceptions is sold or hired out, it becomes an infringing copy.

It is important to appreciate that it is the educational purpose that must be non-commercial, not the institution. Thus the teaching of project management skills to the staff of a company would probably be commercial but the teaching of English to foreign-language students by a commercial college might not.

1988 (CDPA) ss32–36, 178 'reprographic copy', 'reprographic process', 'sufficient acknowledgement'; SI 2003/2498 regs 11–13

5.2.16 Education: archivists' obligations

If an archivist receives a request for copies from someone who wishes to use them for educational purposes, therefore, he or she must note the following:

- Any reprographic copying of unpublished literary, dramatic and musical works must fall within the provisions for copying for other members of the public (see 5.3.10). This means that only single copies may be supplied, and none should be supplied if the archivist has reason to believe that the teacher is intending to make further copies from the copies by a reprographic process. There is no problem if the teacher intends to make further copies by hand.
- Any copying of published literary, dramatic and musical works must fall within the provisions for copying for other members of the public (see 5.3.12–14), or be covered by the special provisions for education. For this purpose, the educational establishment must fall within the definition given in the Act or Regulations (all schools, universities (including component colleges), further education establishments under specified acts and theological colleges). The archivist must also discover whether the establishment is covered by a licensing agreement (see 5.2.15), and if so what are its terms (see 5.4.28). If there were no licensing agreement, no more than 1% of any work could be copied within any quarter of the year, which is not very much.
- The educational copying exceptions do not all apply to artistic works. The only way that artistic works may be copied, other than manually, for educational purposes is under a licence from DACS (see 5.4.29). Similarly, musical works may be copied for use in an examination only under a licence from the MPA.

1988 (CDPA) ss32(1), 36, 174; SI 1989/1067–8

5.2.17 Judicial, parliamentary and public proceedings

Any work, of any date, and whether published or unpublished, may be copied and used for the purposes of parliamentary or judicial proceedings (including for instance an inquest, and including proceedings of the Scottish Parliament and the Assemblies of Wales and Northern Ireland) or the proceedings of a royal commission or statutory inquiry (such as a public inquiry for planning or into a right of way), without infringement of copyright. Copies of documents, including multiple copies, may therefore be supplied for use in such proceedings. Archivists need not require the completion of a declaration form, but they should ask to be provided with evidence that the purpose is as stated. It is not at all clear when 'judicial proceedings' can be said to start, but it appears that preparation for proceedings that have been announced, such as when someone has said that he or she intends to obtain a divorce, would be covered. For a limitation on the use of such copies see 5.2.21.

If for some purpose an unpublished literary, dramatic, musical or artistic work has been communicated to the Crown or to a National Health Service body with the approval of the copyright owner, so that a document or object (such as a CD-ROM or a network server) on which it is recorded is now owned by the Crown or an NHS body, it may be copied and copies may be issued to the public for the same or a related purpose which could reasonably have been anticipated by the copyright owner. One purpose that a copyright owner should nowadays expect is the supply of copies under a Freedom of Information Act (see 5.3.3–4). This provision would not affect archivists holding NHS records unless the archive is actually part of a Crown or NHS body, but it would certainly apply to NHS records managers. Note though that the copyright owner must have consented to the supply in the first place, so an e-mail from an individual would be covered but not necessarily one forwarded by someone else or from an employee (see 3.2.4, 3.2.12), or an attachment.

1988 (CDPA) ss45, 46, 48, 178 'parliamentary proceedings'; 1998 (Scotland) Sch 8 para 25(7); 2006 Sch 10 para 29; *A v B*, 2000

5.2.18 Open to public inspection

If copyright material is open to public inspection for statutory purposes (such as the register of local planning applications) copyright is not infringed if, with the authority of the person responsible for making it open to public inspection, copies are made and issued to the public to facilitate the statutory purposes. For a limitation on the use of such copies see 5.2.21.

1988 (CDPA) s47(2); 1990 (Planning) s69(5)

5.2.19 Statutory registers

If copyright material is open to public inspection for statutory purposes or is on a statutory register that is open to the public, copyright is not infringed if, with the authority of the person responsible for the register or for making the material open to public inspection:

- it is a literary work, and factual information is copied from it, so long as copies are not issued to the public; this means, for instance, that a local authority archivist may supply copies from any such statutory register in his or her custody, whether open to the public or not, to officers of the authority for their official use;
- it contains information of general scientific, technical, commercial or economic interest, and copies are made and issued to the public to disseminate that information.

For a limitation on the use of such copies see 5.2.21.

1988 (CDPA) s47(1),(3)

5.2.20 Maps, plans and drawings

Where copies are issued to the public of maps that are open to public inspection for statutory purposes or are on a statutory register (see 5.2.18–19), the copies must bear the following note:

> This copy has been made by or with the authority of [the name of the responsible person] pursuant to section 47 of the Copyright, Designs and Patents Act 1988 ('the Act'). Unless the Act provides a relevant exception to copyright, the copy must not be copied without the prior permission of the copyright owner.

Where copies are issued to the public of plans and drawings that are open to public inspection for statutory purposes (see 5.2.18), the copies must bear the following note:

> This copy has been made by or with the authority of [the name of the responsible person] pursuant to section 47 of the Copyright, Designs and Patents Act 1988. Unless that Act provides a relevant exception to copyright, the copy must not be copied without the prior permission of the copyright owner.

For a limitation on the use of such copies see 5.2.21.

1988 (CDPA) s47(2 and 3); SI 1989/1099; SI 1990/1427

5.2.21 Public administration

These public administration provisions (5.2.17–20) will apply only so long as the circumstances that gave rise to them continue. Thus, once court proceedings or a public inquiry have ended, it will no longer be possible to make copies for their use, and once a statutory register has been superseded the provisions will apply to the replacement, but not to the earlier version.

5.2.22 Works being exported

A copy may be made of any work of cultural or historical importance and deposited in an appropriate library or archive, without infringement of copyright, if such a copy is required by law before the original work may be exported from the UK. The Act makes no provision for how the resulting copy may be used, and there is no reason to suppose that it may be treated as an item in the permanent collection of the library or archive for the purposes of making further copies (see 5.3.5ff.). An archivist would be well advised, therefore, not to allow copies to be made from such a copy without the permission of the owner of the copyright in the original work.

1988 (CDPA) s44

5.2.23 Visually impaired persons

There is a special exception to enable visually impaired people to make or obtain for their personal use 'accessible copies' of all or part of copyright works in a form that allows them to have improved access to the contents, so long as suitable versions are not made commercially available by the copyright owner. The accessible copy may include special navigation facilities so long as these are required to counter the visual or physical impairment, but must not contain changes that amount to derogatory treatment (see 8.1.7).

A visually impaired person is one who is blind; has an impairment of vision so that he or she cannot read without special lighting; has a physical disability which prevents him or her holding a book; or cannot focus or move his or her eyes so as to be able to read. An 'accessible copy' may be made by or for the visually impaired person so long as that person legitimately owns a copy of the work or has legitimate access to it, for instance through a library or record office. Accessible copies may be made of literary, dramatic, musical and artistic works (see 2.2–2.3), whether published or unpublished, and of published editions (see 2.6.15), but may not consist of a recording of a performance of music nor a copy of a database if the making of the copy would infringe copyright in the database (see 8.2.3ff.).

1988 (CDPA) ss31A(1–3), 31F(3–4, 9); 2002 (Visually Impaired) ss1, 6

5.2.24 Visually impaired persons: copying

An archivist or records manager may make, or arrange for others to make, an accessible copy of a work that he or she holds in the record office or registry, and may pass the copy to a person whom he or she has reasonable grounds for believing is visually impaired. Any charge made for making the copy must not exceed the cost of making and supplying it, with no allowance for overheads. The copy must carry an acknowledgement identifying the author (if known) and the work, and must state that it was made under s31A of the 1988 Act. A declaration form (see 5.3.10, 5.3.15) should not be used.

There are special arrangements for educational establishments and other bodies not conducted for profit to make multiple accessible copies of published works for supply to visually impaired people for their personal use. Such copies may not be made if there is a licensing scheme covering the activity or there are accessible copies commercially available. It is to be expected that such multiple copying would mostly be by specialist organizations working in the field, including special schools. Licensing schemes are available from the CLA and the MPA (see 5.4.29) and should for the most part be more beneficial to users than the terms of the Act itself.

1988 (CDPA) ss31A(1, 5–8), 31B–D, 178 'sufficient acknowledgement'; 2002 (Visually Impaired) ss2–4

5.2.25 Public interest

In some instances, a court will decline to enforce a copyright in a work if an unauthorized use made of it has been in the public interest. In making such a decision, the court has to balance the public interest and the right to freedom of speech on the one hand against the property rights of the copyright owner and perhaps also any duty of confidence (see 8.7.3) owed by the alleged infringer on the other. It also has to distinguish between the public interest and things in which the public is interested, or perhaps the narrow interest of the alleged infringer (which might be, say, a newspaper wishing to enlarge its market share). Factors that appear to be important are:

- the nature of the material disclosed;
- whether the same result could have been achieved without infringing copyright; and
- whether there is another public interest (such as the protection of national security) that ought to have precedence.

The Court of Appeal has decided that the public interest itself cannot be rigidly defined and can be assessed only in the circumstances of the particular case. It has concluded, though, that the public interest in freedom of speech, as set out in the Human Rights Act, will rarely require unauthorized use of a copyright work, since it will not normally be a restraint on freedom of speech to require the user to employ his or her own words, except perhaps by the use of short extracts to demonstrate the authenticity of the material.

1988 (CDPA) s171(3); *Shelley Films v Rex Features*, 1994; *Hyde Park Residence v Yelland*, 2000; *Ashdown v Telegraph Group*, 2001

5.2.26 Public interest: successful defences

Examples of successful public interest defences are:

- publication by an ex-employee of confidential documents revealing price fixing (contrary to a statute) and excessive profit taking by a company;

- publication by ex-employees of confidential memoranda that cast doubt on the accuracy of breathalysers used to provide the sole evidence to convict motorists of drink driving;
- publication of extracts from Peter Wright's book *Spycatcher* about his experiences in the Security Service, since 'his action reeked of turpitude' so he did not deserve copyright protection; national security would not be damaged since the material had already been widely published overseas;
- the broadcasting by the BBC of a programme about the dangers of a low-calorie diet at a time chosen by the BBC in line with its duty to broadcast on matters of public interest and concern.

Initial Services v Putterill, 1968; *Lion Laboratories v Evans*, 1985; Lord Jauncey in *Attorney General v Guardian Newspapers*, 1988, at 668; *Cambridge Nutrition v BBC*, 1990

5.2.27 Public interest: failed defences

The courts have not accepted a public interest defence:

- for the publication, in an attack on a politician, of an internal memorandum of one newspaper leaked to a competing one where the memorandum revealed no misdeeds of a serious nature;
- for the publication of material copied from another newspaper, since the information was already available to the public;
- for the publication of stills from security videos showing the length of time that Diana, Princess of Wales and Dodi al Fayed had spent at the Villa Windsor in Paris the night before they died; the information could have been made available without infringing copyright and while of interest to the public the publication of the stills was not necessary in the public interest; and
- for the use of lengthy extracts from a politician's diary, when only short extracts were needed to show the authenticity of the material and the remaining information could have been expressed without infringing copyright.

Beloff v Pressdram, 1973; *Express Newspapers v News UK*, 1991; *Hyde Park Residence v Yelland*, 2000; *Ashdown v Telegraph Group*, 2001

5.2.28 Primary infringement

It is an infringement of copyright to do, or to authorize someone else to do (see 5.2.30), any of the acts restricted by copyright (see 5.1) without the permission of the copyright owner, unless one of the exceptions applies. If copyright is infringed the copyright owner may sue to prevent any further infringement (by securing an 'injunction'; 'interdict' in Scotland), to seize copies of offending works and to seek civil damages (discounting any loss arising from, say, legitimate competition or use only of ideas, see 2.1.4). The rights owner has unconditional rights and so can take action against infringing use, for instance to protect privacy, even if he or she has no intention of exploiting the work.

There is strict liability for a copyright infringement, which means that an infringer's motives are irrelevant. It is, for instance, possible to infringe after obtaining permission or a licence from the wrong person; it is up to the user to ensure that the permission or licence is valid by requesting proof of the other person's rights. It is also possible to infringe unconsciously, for instance by using material from a work previously studied but not consciously remembered, but the rights owner will first have to show that the infringer had access to the work.

The Act does not allow damages to be awarded if the defendant was unaware that the work was protected, but ignorance of the law is no defence so it might be quite difficult to satisfy the court that a belief that there was no copyright was genuine. Further, following a European directive, damages are only to be awarded against a defendant who had actual or constructive knowledge (see 5.2.33) that he or she was infringing. Note though that even without any knowledge the defendant can still be sued and found liable for other remedies and costs. Damages must be appropriate to the actual prejudice suffered by the rights owner, including loss of profit, unfair profits of the infringer, moral prejudice (such as damage to reputation) and loss of royalty fees. There is also the possibility of additional damages if the court decides that a penalty is needed, for instance if the infringement was blatant.

It is no defence for a defendant to claim that he or she intended to obtain a licence after the event. One judge was forthright about a newspaper in such a case, quoting the Duke of Wellington: 'with its eyes wide open to the risk of proceedings for infringement it decided to publish and be damned. In the circumstances it can have no basis for complaint that it is now damned.'

If an infringement has occurred in the course of business (including a trade or profession, such as that of archivist or records manager), the infringer may also be liable to criminal prosecution. This could result, for instance, from the making of an infringing copy for sale, which could possibly cover the supply of copies by an archivist who wilfully disregards the special provisions for copying (see 5.3), and causes actual damage to the copyright owner's interests (an unlikely result for most archival materials but not an impossible one for more recent files). The EU is preparing further legislation to extend the criminal sanctions, but they are not expected to apply to people acting in good faith.

This book does not attempt to deal with the complexities of civil and criminal legal action; if an archivist or records manager finds him or herself in need of advice in this area a visit to a solicitor is called for (see 5.5).

Directive 2004; 1988 (CDPA) ss16(2), 96, 97(1), 99–100, 107, 178 'business'; SI 2003/2498 reg 26; SI 2006/1028 reg 3; *Mansell v Valley Printing*, 1908; *Hawkes and Son v Paramount Film Service*, 1934; *Francis Day and Hunter v Bron*, 1963; *Lady Anne Tennant v Associated Newspaper Group*, 1979; *Work Model Enterprises v Ecosystem*, 1996; Lightman J in *Banier v News Group Newspapers*, 1997, at 816; *HRH the Prince of Wales v Associated Newspapers*, 2006; *USP v London General Holdings*, 2006

5.2.29 Primary infringement: archivists

An archivist who, in good faith, provides a copy of a copyright work to a user on the basis of the exceptions for librarians and archivists (see 5.3) is safe from primary infringement. Therefore, if the user has made a false statement in the declaration, and there is no reason for the archivist to know that it is false, the user is liable for any infringement as if he or she had made the copy him or herself. However, if an archivist fails to obtain a declaration from the user before making a copy of most copyright works, or if an archivist is aware that such a declaration is false, he or she will be liable for primary infringement.

1988 (CDPA) ss23–24, 37(2)(a), 37(3)

5.2.30 Primary infringement: authorizing infringement

It is also a primary infringement of copyright, without the permission of the copyright owner to authorize someone else to do any of the acts restricted by copyright, and the same penalties apply to the person giving the authority as to the actual infringer. It is not necessary to know that the act authorized is an infringement, and it is no defence to plead that it was believed not to be. However, the House of Lords has made plain that authorize means 'sanction, approve or countenance', so authorization must be deliberate or at least involve some awareness of what is happening.

This is quite a risky area. It is almost certain, for instance, to be taken as authorizing infringement in an architect's drawings for an archivist to instruct a builder to use the plans for one record office in order to construct another. Archivists and records managers must be very careful about giving, or even appearing to give, authority for copyright works to be used by someone else. Advice given on copyright should thus be in general terms, and where appropriate qualified by a comment that it is not legal advice and does not constitute authority to do anything.

Self-service copiers (see 5.3.20–21) should carry very obvious notices about the limits of permitted copying, with a warning that the institution accepts no responsibility for copying of copyright material beyond those limits. An Australian university suffered severely for its failure to do this, but more recently a Canadian law library's notices were found to be sufficient. This is particularly important in archives holding little but unpublished material, since that will largely be in copyright. The risk will be much less if users are free to copy out of copyright works or works in their own copyright, because the mere provision of equipment which might (rather than will inevitably) be used to infringe is legitimate.

The taking of photographs of works displayed in exhibitions is likely to infringe. The organizers of exhibitions would therefore do well to be seen to be discouraging photography so as to make plain that they are not authorizing any infringement by those means.

It is possible that merely making available copyright works on the internet could infringe under this heading (as well as by a communication to the public, see 5.1.6) because the person making the material available is effectively giving the user authority to copy the work: it is impossible to view a document on the internet without making a copy of it (see also 6.2).

1988 (CDPA) s16(2); *Moorhouse v University of New South Wales*, 1976; Lord Templeman in *CBS Songs v Amstrad*, 1988, at 604; *Durand v Molino*, 2000; *Pensher Security Doors v Sunderland City Council*, 2000; *CCH Canadian v Law Society of Upper Canada*, 2004

5.2.31 Secondary infringement

It is possible to infringe copyright without doing or authorizing any of the acts restricted by copyright: it is called secondary infringement. A person committing a secondary infringement must have 'knowledge' (see 5.2.33), but may then be liable to civil and criminal action in the same way as a person committing a primary infringement. Secondary infringement includes:

- importing an infringing copy into the UK for purposes other than private and domestic use;
- possessing, exhibiting or distributing an infringing copy in the course of business or in such a way as to prejudice the interests of the copyright owner;
- providing equipment specifically designed or adapted for making infringing copies
- providing the means for giving an infringing public performance; and
- permitting the use of premises for an infringing public performance.

1988 (CDPA) ss22ff., 107ff.

5.2.32 Secondary infringement: archivists and records managers

If an archive or document registry holds infringing copies of copyright works the copies would almost certainly be considered to be in the possession of the archivist or records manager in the course of his or her business, which would amount to a secondary infringement if there is also the necessary knowledge (see 5.2.33). Business, in the context of the 1988 Act, includes a trade or profession. Secondary infringement could also occur if an archive accepted work to repair or bind infringing copies not actually deposited (the conservator or bookbinder is a professional), or put infringing copies on display in an exhibition, again if the necessary knowledge existed.

An archivist should thus be careful about accepting the deposit or loan of copies of copyright works, and would be well advised to require clear assurances from the depositor that the copies have been legitimately made (see 5.3.23). It seems clear, for instance, that normal copies made under the library and archive copying provisions are for the use of the individual researcher and should not be deposited in another record office or library (see 5.3.15). Records managers should check that their parent body has policies in place to ensure that material obtained in the course of business is obtained legitimately. If an archivist or records manager is unfortunate enough to receive notice from a copyright owner that material held or displayed in the archive consists of infringing copies, no time should be lost before:

- assessing the evidence supplied to ensure that it identifies the particular items that are said to be infringing and gives reasonable grounds for belief that there has been infringement;
- removing the items from display and/or public access; and
- seeking legal advice (see 5.5).

1988 (CDPA) ss23, 178 'business'; *Van Dusen v Kritz*, 1936

5.2.33 Knowledge

In each case, to prove secondary infringement it has to be shown that the infringer knew ('actual knowledge', see also 6.2.5), or had reason to believe ('constructive knowledge'), that the copies or the acts concerned were infringements or that the equipment was to be used for infringing purposes. It has been said in a judgment in 1997, citing another of five years earlier, that 'reason to believe' 'involves the concept of knowledge of facts from which a reasonable man would arrive at the relevant belief'. Merely suspecting that a copy might be an infringing one is not knowledge, and nor is knowing that the question of infringement is in dispute but so far undecided between two other parties. If, though, it is apparent from comparison of two works that one has been copied from the other, or if the copyright owner has provided evidence that the copies or activities are infringing, it would be difficult to justify a claim of lack of the necessary knowledge. In the face of such facts, simply thinking that a copy or act is not infringing, relying on a licence without checking that the licensor is entitled to grant the rights or relying on advice (including legal advice from a lawyer), will be of no help. Once a secondary infringer has been served with reason to suspect, for example in a letter from the copyright owner which identifies the particular copies that are infringing, he or she must then investigate the source of the materials at issue to see whether they are likely to be infringing copies. Failure to investigate would mean that it would be very difficult to resist a claim of infringement. The secondary infringer then has a period of grace (likely to be a maximum of 14 days, but possibly much less) to assess the evidence and arrive at the necessary belief, and to take action so as to avoid liability.

Knowledge is also necessary before damages can be awarded for a primary infringement, but lack of knowledge will not remove the liability in other respects (see 5.2.28).

1988 (CDPA) ss22ff., 107ff.; *Lady Anne Tennant v Associated Newspaper Group*, 1979; *Sillitoe v McGraw Hill Book Co*, 1983; *LA Gear v High Tech Sports*, 1992; *ZYX Music v King*, 1997; *Nouveau Fabrics v Voyage Decoration and Dunelm Soft Furnishings*, 2004

5.2.34 Copies of broadcasts

It is not an infringement of copyright in a broadcast, or in any work included in it, to record the broadcast for private and domestic use in order to enable the broadcast to be watched or listened to at a more convenient time, so long as the recording is made at home. This 'time-shifting' exception does not, therefore, cover the making of a recording for sale to a person who will then use it for private or domestic use, nor the making by an archivist of a recording for home viewing by readers (and see 5.3.25), nor the building up of a library of recordings. Also, there is no infringement of a broadcast or of a film being shown by photographing an image on the television screen, so long as the photograph is for private and domestic use and was taken at home.

1988 (CDPA) ss70–71; SI 2003/2498 regs 19–20; *Sony Music Entertainment v Easyinternetcafé*, 2003

5.3   Copying in libraries and archives

5.3.1   Public records

Any public record, whether published or unpublished, that is available to the public may be copied by an officer appointed under the relevant Act, or with the authority of such an officer, and supplied to any person, without infringement of copyright, irrespective of the permission or prohibition of the copyright owner. This affects all public records in what the Controller (see 3.2.28) terms 'public record repositories':

- The National Archives, Kew, and places of deposit of public records under the Public Records Act 1958;
- the National Archives of Scotland under the Public Records (Scotland) Act 1937;
- the Public Record Office of Northern Ireland under the Public Records Act (Northern Ireland) 1923; and
- all Welsh public records in The National Archives or places of deposit pending creation of a Welsh national archive, under the Government of Wales Act 2006.

The terms of this exception permit the copying of public records by a member of staff for internal use or on behalf of a member of the public, or by a member of the public so long as copying is authorized by an officer. They impose no requirement on the institution to determine the purpose for which the person obtaining the copy will use it. The exception does not mean, however, that use of the copy thereafter will not be an infringement; it is the responsibility of the individual or body obtaining the copy to ensure that their use of it is not an infringement.

1958 s4(1); 1988 (CDPA) s49; 2006 ss146, 148

5.3.2 Public records not selected

The provision for the copying of public records does not apply to records not selected for permanent preservation under one of the Acts but which have been presented to repositories under the statutory provisions for disposal other than by destruction. Such records cease, on presentation, to be public records but the copyright in them is unaffected, so that Crown copyright material, for instance, is still Crown copyright. Because they are no longer public records, copyright works in them may be copied only in accordance with general provisions such as fair dealing or, as appropriate, in accordance with the general regulations for libraries and archives (see 5.3.6ff.).

1923 s8; 1937 s12(1); 1958 s3(6)

5.3.3 Freedom of information: England, Wales and Northern Ireland

Where an archive or registry is, is part of, or holds the records of a public authority as defined in the Freedom of Information Act 2000 it must supply information from relevant records unless one of the exceptions set out in the Act applies. Archivists and records managers should bear the following in mind:

- Applications for information must be in writing (including electronically), giving a name and address and describing the information requested.
- The application may request a copy of the information. The Government has advised that such a copy may be supplied without infringement of copyright under a general exception for acts done under statutory authority. The special exceptions for librarians and archivists do not apply so there is no need for the applicant to complete a declaration form (see 5.3.10).
- It is worth making clear, in any covering letter, that the use of the copies or of the information supplied, and any infringement of copyright that may result, is the responsibility of the applicant.
- FoI applications, and a record of the copies supplied, should be preserved for at least seven years or such other period as legal advisers recommend.

- All archives other than The National Archives and the Public Record Office of Northern Ireland may claim the exemptions for works which are available to the public by means other than the Freedom of Information Act (that is, they are freely open for consultation) or works which are to be published (by for instance being opened for consultation once cataloguing is complete). If copies are made and supplied from documents which are made available to the public outside the terms of the Freedom of Information Act the normal copyright rules for copying apply (see 5.3.10ff.).

Public authorities under the Freedom of Information Act include:

- government departments, legislative bodies in England, Northern Ireland and Wales and the armed forces;
- local authorities and related bodies including magistrates' court committees;
- National Health Service bodies;
- some schools, universities and colleges;
- police authorities;
- non-departmental public bodies (NDPBs) and quangos (quasi-autonomous non-governmental organizations); and
- publicly owned companies.

Archivists and records managers for authorities, or of record offices which hold records of authorities, that fall under any of these categories should obtain a copy of the Freedom of Information Act, the codes of practice under it and any other guidance available, and study it all carefully. Archivists should also remember that records that were gifts or deposits might also be subject to the Act, depending on the precise circumstances in each case (see 5.4.8).

1988 (CDPA) s50; 2000 (FoI) ss1, 5, 6, 8, 11, 13, 21, 22, 77, 80(3), Sch 1; SI 2004/3089 reg 3(3)

5.3.4 Freedom of information: Scotland

The Freedom of Information (Scotland) Act is very similar to the Act for the remainder of the UK but differs in some ways that are relevant here:

- It covers public authorities in Scotland only, along the same lines.
- Applications must be in writing (including by electronic means) or some other permanent form such as a sound or video recording.
- Records in the National Archives of Scotland are exempt, since they are already accessible under public records legislation which has not been amended or repealed, but records in all other archives are subject to the Freedom of Information access

provisions unless it can be shown that the same information is more accessible to the applicant elsewhere.

- A statutory instrument has made clear that the supply of copies under the Scottish Freedom of Information Act is not an infringement of copyright.
- Scottish authorities would be well advised, like those elsewhere in the UK, to make clear to applicants their responsibility for any infringement arising from their use of copies or information supplied.
- Archivists and records managers in Scotland should carefully study their Act and any advice and guidance provided by the Scottish Information Commissioner.

2002 (Scotland) ss1, 3–8, 11, 25, Sch 1; SI 2004/3089 reg 3(3)

5.3.5 Special copying provisions for libraries and archives

The 1988 Act contains special provisions which allow the supply by libraries and archives of copies of published and unpublished material, as exceptions to the rights of copyright owners. These provisions are elaborated in the supplementary Copyright (Librarians and Archivists) (Copying of Copyright Material) Regulations 1989, the full text of which is given in the Appendix (see 9.2). The statutory provisions and the Regulations have both been amended in line with the Information Society Directive, and archivists should take note of the further limitations imposed on copying for commercial research and changes to the requirements for fees. The terms 'library' and 'archive' are left to their dictionary definitions, but they are refined by definitions of 'prescribed' libraries and archives, to which alone the Regulations apply. The nature of a prescribed library or archive varies with the different provisions, but is determined first by whether or not it (or its parent body) is run for profit, and secondly, in the case of libraries, either by the nature of a library's parent body or by its purpose.

Where a service to provide access to records and/or copies is provided electronically and on a commercial basis ('for remuneration') archivists are providing an 'information society service' which must conform to the requirements of the Electronic Commerce Directive. In particular these cover the information to be given to users and the way in which users enter into contracts with the service provider. Archivists providing this sort of service should consult the Electronic Commerce Regulations.

1988 (CDPA) s37; SI 1989/1212 para 3, Sch 1; SI 2002/2013 regs 6, 9, 11, 15; SI 2003/2500 reg 2, Sch 1

5.3.6 Prescribed libraries and archives

All archives in the UK are prescribed archives under the 1989 Regulations (see 9.2), except that an archive that is run for profit (or administered by a body that is run for profit) is not prescribed for the purpose of receiving replacement copies of material (see 5.3.8).

All libraries in the UK are prescribed libraries for the purpose of supplying copies to another library (see 5.3.8), but for all other purposes prescribed libraries are libraries that are not conducted for profit, and that are not administered by a body that is conducted for profit, and that fall into one of the following categories:

- a library administered by a library authority;
- the five copyright libraries in the UK;
- a library of a school or most other educational establishments;
- a Parliamentary library, a library administered by a government department or a library administered by any agency administered by a minister of the Crown (including, for example, an NHS hospital library);
- a local authority library;
- a library for the study of bibliography, education, fine arts, history, languages, law, literature, medicine, music, philosophy, religion, science or technology, or which is administered by an organization which is conducted for one of those purposes.

In addition, libraries (but not archives) outside the UK that exist for the study of these subjects are also prescribed for the purpose of receiving copies (see 5.3.8).

This is a summary only; for full details consult the Regulations (see 9.2).

1988 (CDPA) s37; SI 1989/1212 para 3, Sch 1

5.3.7 Material that is copiable

The provisions of the 1988 Act and the 1989 Regulations (see 9.2) provide for different categories of material. Confusingly, the range of material in a library or archive that is covered varies from one exception to the next. Thus:

- Copying for preservation purposes (see 5.3.8–9) is allowed only of items in the permanent collection or to replace items in the permanent collection. The term 'permanent collection' is not defined, but it may be taken to include material on indefinite or permanent deposit. It will probably not include material on loan at the whim of the depositor, and will certainly not include material on temporary deposit, for instance for conservation or exhibition purposes.
- Copying of unpublished works for users (see 5.3.10–11, and see also 4.1.8) is allowed of all such works that are in the library or archive (though remember that the manuscript of a published work normally counts as published, see below and 4.1.9, 5.3.16). There is no requirement for deposit to be on any particular terms, so the provision presumably covers material even on short-term deposit for any reason.
- Copying of published works (see 5.3.12–14) is allowed of the published edition of any published work, regardless of whether it is held in the collection of the library

making the copy. Note that this does not cover manuscripts of works published before deposit in the archive (see 5.3.16).

1988 (CDPA) ss37–43

5.3.8   Preservation

Under the 1989 Regulations (see 9.2), all archives and libraries in the UK, including those run for profit, may, without infringement of copyright, make preservation copies of items in their permanent collections. Material that may be copied must be preserved for reference on the premises or for reference in another library or archive and may not be available for loan to the public; it does not apparently actually have to be available to the public. A copy may be made of a literary, dramatic or musical work, including any illustrations (see 5.3.18), in order to:

- preserve or replace that item in the collection, by adding the copy to the collection in addition to or in place of the original; or
- replace an item that has been lost, destroyed or damaged in the permanent collection of a prescribed archive or library that is neither run for profit nor run by an organization that is run for profit.

Provided that:

- it was not reasonably practicable to purchase a replacement;
- where appropriate, the other archive or library gives a written statement that the item has been lost, destroyed or damaged, that the copy will be used only to replace it, and that it was not reasonably practicable for it to purchase a replacement; and
- where appropriate, that the other archive or library pays for the copy at a level to cover the cost of production but no more.

1988 (CDPA) s42; SI 1989/1212 para 6

5.3.9   Preservation: purpose and use

Any copy made for preservation purposes within the same institution should be treated, for copyright purposes, as if it were the original: the fact that it is a copy does not reduce any other limitations on copying from it. Preservation copying would cover microfilming or digitization* in order to avoid excessive handling of popular or fragile originals. That part of the exception which allows copying for preservation purposes for another institution will rarely be applicable to unpublished works (but see 5.3.23).

1988 (CDPA) s42; SI 1989/1212 para 6

* only onto CD-Rom not onto a network
(see LISCopyseek)

5.3.10 Unpublished works: libraries and archives regulations

Under the 1989 Regulations (see 9.2), all archives and libraries in the UK, including those run for profit, may make and supply single copies of literary, dramatic or musical works, including any illustrations, that have been deposited in the library or archive and that were unpublished prior to deposit, without permission and without infringement of copyright, provided that:

- the copyright owner has not prohibited copying. If he or she has prohibited copying, it is an infringement to make copies if the archivist or librarian is aware, or ought to be aware (see 5.2.33), of the prohibition;
- the purchaser will use the copies only for private study or non-commercial research (see 5.2.8). If the archivist knows, or has reason to know, that the copies will be used for other purposes, including for research for a commercial purpose, it is an infringement to make them;
- the purchaser has completed a declaration form (see 5.3.15, 9.2 schedule 2 form B); and
- the purchaser pays for the copies at a level which at least covers the cost of production, including a contribution to the general expenses of the library or archive.

These provisions mean that a manuscript of a work that was published before deposit may not be copied, unless it is significantly different from the published version (see 4.1.9, 5.3.16). A manuscript that is published after deposit, however, may be copied as long as the other conditions apply. There is no restriction on the proportion of the work, including the whole of it, that may be copied. This exception does not cover independent artistic works, though it does cover artistic works that are illustrations to a literary, dramatic or musical work provided they are intrinsic to the understanding of the text, are copied as part of the main work and are not reproduced independently (see 5.3.18).

The limitation to non-commercial research (see 5.2.8) is a significant problem not only for users but for archivists and librarians trying to provide a public service. For librarians dealing with published works, and for librarians and archivists dealing with artistic works, there is the possibility of obtaining (or of the user obtaining) a licence to copy, either from the copyright owner or more likely from a collecting society (see 5.4.29). For archivists dealing with unpublished literary works the solution is not so simple. The duration of copyright in unpublished works can be very long (see 2.2.17); the identification of copyright owners can be difficult or impossible (see 5.4.20); and there are no licensing bodies or schemes available. The apparent, and unhappy, solution is for archivists to ensure that no one in their institution knows the purpose of the user's research, so that a declaration form may be accepted unless some other aspect of it is known to be false (see 5.3.15). This solution would not be available if the user revealed to a member of staff the purpose of his or her research, whether in conversation or on an application form for admission, because an archivist ought then to be aware that a declaration form was completed falsely. However, see also 5.3.11, 5.3.18.

1988 (CDPA) ss37, 43; SI 1989/1212 para 7; SI 2003/2498 reg 14(2), Sch 1 para 26; *Norowzian v Arks (No 2)*, 2000; *Sweeney v Macmillan Publishers*, 2002

5.3.11 Unpublished works: older works

Under the terms of the 1956 Act, the relevant part of which remains in force, copies may be made, without infringement of copyright, of unpublished literary, dramatic or musical works, including any illustrations, that are open to public inspection (subject to the rules of the institution) in any library, museum or other institution (including an archive) in the UK, including those run for profit, provided that:

- the work was created before 1 August 1989;
- the author has been dead for more than 50 years;
- the work is more than 100 years old; and
- the copy is obtained for the purposes of research (including, in this case, commercial research) or private study, or with a view to publication (see 5.4.23).

Once the work has been published this exception is no longer available, but if only part of it is published, the remaining part is still eligible. This exception does not cover independent artistic works, though it does cover artistic works that are illustrations to a literary, dramatic or musical work provided they are intrinsic to the understanding of the text, are copied as part of the main work and are not reproduced independently (see 5.3.18). It is not clear whether this exception allows the copying of a work of which the author is unknown. It seems probable that if the work is of a sufficient age that the author must have died at least 50 years earlier, that would be enough.

The benefits of this exception as an alternative to the more familiar one in the 1988 Act, if the work to be copied is old enough, are;

- the declaration form is not used;
- copying may be for commercial research; and
- copies may be published (see 5.4.23).

1956 ss7(6), 7(9)(d); 1988 (CDPA) Sch 1, para 16

5.3.12 Libraries: published works

Under the 1989 Regulations (see 9.2), all prescribed libraries in the UK may, without infringement of copyright, make and supply a copy of:

- a single article from a periodical, including any illustrations; and
- a reasonable proportion of a published edition of a literary, dramatic or musical work, including any illustrations.

Such copies may be made provided that:

- the copy is purely for private study or non-commercial research (see 5.2.8);
- the purchaser has completed a declaration form (see 5.3.15, 9.2 schedule 2 form A);
- the purchaser and another person are not obtaining copies of substantially the same material for substantially the same purpose and at substantially the same time, and are not working together;
- the purchaser receives only a single copy of the material; and
- the purchaser pays a reasonable price to cover at least the production costs of the copy.

This exclusion does not cover independent artistic works, though it does cover artistic works that are illustrations to a literary, dramatic or musical work provided they are intrinsic to the understanding of the text, are copied as part of the main work and are not reproduced independently (see 5.3.18).

It is worth noting that the term 'a reasonable proportion' as used in this exception is not the same as an 'insubstantial part' (see 5.2.3–6). Indeed 'a reasonable proportion' must be substantial, since if an insubstantial part is copied there is no infringement at all and the exception is not needed. No definition is given of what is a 'reasonable proportion', so librarians must use their judgment. The general advice is to restrict copying to a single article from a periodical or a chapter from a book, to a maximum of 5% of the whole (see 5.2.5).

Elaborate licensing schemes have been designed to deal with copying of published works for commercial purposes. Librarians and archivists wishing to be able to supply such copies should contact the relevant licensing body (see 5.4.29); the Chartered Institute of Library and Information Professionals (CILIP) may be contacted for advice at 7 Ridgmount Street, London WC1E 7AE. Under certain circumstances, a librarian may also rely on fair dealing to supply copies (see 5.2.9), though this will not get around the commercial purpose problem.

1988 (CDPA) ss 29(3)(a), 38, 39; SI 1989/1212 para 4; SI 2003/2498 reg 14(1), Sch 1 para 26

5.3.13 Libraries: published works: supplying copies to other libraries

Under the 1989 Regulations (see 9.2), all prescribed libraries may make and supply to a prescribed library not conducted for profit a single copy of any article in a periodical or the whole or part of a published edition of a literary, dramatic or musical work, for any purpose. The receiving library must pay the cost of the copy, but no more, and if it is receiving the whole or part of a published edition, or more than a single article from an issue of a periodical, it must supply a written statement that it is a prescribed library and that it does not know, and could not reasonably discover, the identity of the person who could authorize the making of the copy.

1988 (CDPA) s41; SI 1989/1212 para 5

5.3.14 Archives: published works

If an archive holds a library of published editions of works for reference, whether available to the public or not, it may qualify as a prescribed library (see 5.3.6) for the purposes of making copies of those works. The fact that the employer describes the person in charge as an archivist rather than a librarian would make no difference. It is by no means clear, however, whether the same provisions could be applied to published editions of works that are held among the records in the archive, which are thus not distinguishable as part of a separate library. It must be probable that it was not intended to exclude such material, given the wide scope of the definition of a prescribed library, but neither the 1989 Regulations nor the 1988 Act is explicit, and there is (unsurprisingly) no case law. There is no provision among these regulations which allows the copying of a manuscript of a work published before deposit in the archive (see 5.3.16).

1988 (CDPA) ss38, 39; SI 1989/1212 para 4

5.3.15 Declaration form

The declaration forms to be used when supplying copies of copyright works under the 1989 Regulations (see 5.3.10, 5.3.12) are given in Schedule 2 to the Regulations (see 9.2). It must be emphasized that the person signing a declaration is responsible for its truth and is responsible for the consequences if it is false. The librarian or archivist may rely on it if he or she does not know, and has no reason to know (see 5.2.33), that it was completed falsely. The most likely reason for a false declaration is probably that the purpose of the research is commercial.

A declaration form should not be used when, for instance, supplying copies under another exception such as the special provisions for visually impaired people (see 5.2.23–24), under freedom of information (see 5.3.3–4) or when the work is not pro-tected by copyright (see for example 7.2.4). When it is required, the person completing it must be the person who will use the copy; that person undertakes not to make a copy from the copy for anyone else. The signature of an agent is not acceptable, so a person acting for another (for example a record agent, professional researcher or research assist-ant) must obtain the client's or employer's signature on the form before the copy is made.

The signature may be an electronic signature, but the expense of a scheme for users to provide and the record office to accept electronic signatures is not likely, as yet, to be worthwhile for many. However, it seems that it is legitimate for an archive or library to accept forms which have been signed and then digitized and sent as e-mail attachments or faxed.

It is most unlikely that a person obtaining a copy may then pass it on to a library or archive, on its own or as part of a larger deposit, since such deposit cannot be described as research or private study on the part of that person. Librarians and archivists might be liable to action for secondary infringement if they accept such a copy in the knowledge that it was made under the Regulations (see 5.2.32–33, but see also 5.3.23).

The Act does not specify the period during which these forms should be preserved, but the Limitation Act 1980 provides that action for a tort (such as infringement of copyright) must begin within six years of the infringement in normal circumstances. In this context it is (one hopes) not the librarian or archivist but the purchaser of the copies who would be committing the infringement, and the purpose of keeping the forms is to demonstrate that the librarian or archivist was acting lawfully. Since no action can be taken against the librarian or archivist after six years from the making of the copy have passed, that is the minimum period for which the forms should be kept. It may be that in an infringement action against the user his or her good faith in completing the declaration form, and the archivist's or librarian's in accepting it, would be raised, but it seems that that possibility does not offer sufficient justification for keeping the forms for lengthy periods.

1980 s2; 1988 (CDPA) ss27(6), 37; 2000 (Communications) s7; SI 1989/1212 reg 7, Sch 2; SI 2003/2498 Sch 1 para 26; *Inland Revenue Commissioners v Conbeer*, 1996; *J Pereira Fernandes v Mehta*, 2006

5.3.16 Published editions

The provisions for copying for members of the public by archivists explicitly exclude the copying of any work that was published before deposit, and those for librarians apply only to 'published editions'. This means that a document that consists of the draft of a work that was published before deposit in the archive or library may not be copied without the permission of the copyright owner. This might apply, for instance, to the author's manuscript of a published novel. It may be that if there are significant differences between the manuscript and published versions they would be regarded as being distinct works, but each case would have to be considered on its merits (see 4.1.9).

Sweeney v Macmillan Publishers, 2002

5.3.17 Anonymous works

While the regulations implementing the Information Society directive largely had the effect of diminishing the freedoms available to users of archives, one change had a small liberalizing effect. It is not an infringement to do any of the restricted acts (see 5.1), including copying, to an anonymous or pseudonymous work (see 2.1.17) that is still in copyright (which it almost certainly will be if it is unpublished) if it is reasonable to assume that the author (or all of the authors) has (have) been dead for at least 70 years. Important points to note are that:

- the exception does not cover works of known authorship, even if the first or present owner of the copyright is unknown;
- the exception covers literary, dramatic, musical and artistic works and films, whether published or unpublished, and so is of wider scope than other exceptions applying to archival material; and
- the purpose of the use is unrestricted, so copying may be for purposes of commercial research or even publication (see 5.4.25–26).

1988 (CDPA) ss57, 66A, Sch 1 para 15; SI 1995/3297 reg 6(2); SI 2003/2498 Sch 2 repeal of 1988 (CDPA) Sch 1 para 15(3)

5.3.18 Artistic works

The copying, and the supply of copies, of artistic works that are illustrations to literary, dramatic or musical works is permitted by the special provisions for libraries and archives (see 5.3.10–12). This should be taken to mean artistic works that are intrinsic to the understanding of the text, are copied as part of the main work and are not reproduced independently. No other artistic works may be copied under these provisions. There is no escaping this restriction, unless:

- the records are public records (see 5.3.1);
- the records are maps, plans or drawings available to the public for statutory purposes (see 5.2.20);
- the work is of unknown authorship and it is reasonable to assume that the author has been dead for at least 70 years (see 5.3.17); or
- the archivist or librarian is confident that fair dealing will apply (see 5.2.7).

In all other cases, where copyright has not expired, archivists and records managers should be very wary of providing copies of copyright artistic works (including most maps, drawings and photographs) in their collections.

For publication of artistic works in sale catalogues see 4.2.3.

1988 (CDPA) ss37ff.

5.3.19 Recordings of folksongs

Certain not-for-profit bodies are designated as places that may, without infringement of the copyright in either the words or the music, receive deposits of recordings of folksongs made specially for the purpose, so long as the words are unpublished and of unknown authorship, the recordings do not infringe any other copyrights and the performers have not prohibited the making of the recording. The archivist of a designated body may make and supply copies of the recordings, without infringing the copyright in the recordings or the works recorded, so long as:

- the person requiring the copy satisfies the archivist that it is for private study or research for a non-commercial purpose only (see 5.2.8) and will not be used for any other purpose; and
- no person receives more than one copy of the same recording.

The designated bodies are:

- the Archive of Traditional Welsh Music, University College of North Wales;
- the Centre for English Cultural Tradition and Language;
- the Charles Parker Archive Trust (1982);
- the European Centre for Traditional and Regional Cultures;
- the Folklore Society;
- the Institute of Folklore Studies in Britain and Canada;
- the National Museum of Wales, Welsh Folk Museum;
- the National Sound Archive, British Library;
- the North West Sound Archive;
- the BBC Sound Archives;
- Ulster Folk and Transport Museum; and
- the Vaughan Williams Memorial Library, English Folk Dance and Song Society.

1988 (CDPA) s61; SI 1989/1012; SI 2003/2498 reg 16, Sch 1 para 24

5.3.20 Self-service photocopying

The user of an archive or library, including a user acting on behalf of someone else, may make copies of published or unpublished literary, dramatic, musical or artistic works without infringement of copyright, provided:

- the copies are of an insubstantial part of the work (see 5.2.3–6);
- the purpose of the copying qualifies as fair dealing or falls under some other exception (see 5.2);

- in the case of literary, dramatic and musical works only that are available to the public in a record office or similar institution, the work is at least 100 years old and its author has been dead for at least 50 years (see 5.3.11); or
- the works are public records and an officer has approved the copying (see 5.3.1).

Users of files preserved in a records management system may rely on the first and second of these.

1956 s7(6); 1988 (CDPA) ss16(3)(a), 29, 49, Sch 1 para 16

5.3.21 Self-service photocopying: precautions

An archivist, librarian or records manager should ensure that he or she is protected as far as possible from claims of negligence or of having authorized infringement (see 5.2.30) if the person making the copy goes beyond the bounds of what is permitted by the relevant exception (see 5.2). With this in mind, the following precautions should be taken:

- No member of staff should assist with the making of the copy, or seek to exercise control over what is copied or the purposes for which copies are being made, unless the provisions covering copies made by the archive or library are complied with (see 5.3.10–12).
- A notice should be displayed making clear that copying of copyright works is an infringement of copyright except under certain conditions. It should spell out that:
  — copies of a substantial part of a copyright work may be made solely for non-commercial research, private study, criticism, review or (except photographs) current news reporting;
  — only one such copy may be made;
  — further copies may not be made from such a copy for the use of anyone else; and
  — the archive gives no authority for the making of any copies of copyright works, and all responsibility for any infringement of copyright is borne by the person making the copy and the person (if different) for whom the copy is being made.

A similar notice should be displayed above copiers used by members of staff, emphasizing that management does not authorize the making of copies of copyright works and that an individual is personally responsible for any infringement.

1988 (CDPA) s29; *CCH Canadian v Law Society of Upper Canada*, 2004

5.3.22 Transcripts and tracings

The making of manual copies (such as transcripts and tracings) by users is explicitly not covered by the special exceptions for libraries and archives (which apply only to copies made by the librarian or archivist), though it would seem to be permissible under the one for public records (see 5.1.10, 5.3.1). Manual copying of insubstantial parts of a work is always permitted (see 5.2.3–6), but archivists should advise users to be careful to ensure that their copies are insubstantial in qualitative as well as quantitative terms. Beyond that, it seems likely that the limits applying to self-service photocopying would apply equally to manual copies (see 5.3.20–21).

1988 (CDPA) s17

5.3.23 Supply of copies to other archives

It is inadvisable under most circumstances for an archive to accept the deposit of copies of copyright works (see 5.2.32, 5.3.15). There appear to be three sets of circumstances in which it is possible for an archive to receive copies of unpublished documents from another archive without infringement of copyrights owned by third parties:

- to replace an item that has been lost, destroyed or damaged in the recipient repository; (but of course this would be possible only if the document is not unique) (see 5.3.8–9);
- the exception which allows public records to be copied without infringement (see 5.3.1) contains no limitations on the purpose of the copies, so there is nothing to prevent the supply of such copies to other record offices; and
- under the terms of the 1956 Act (see 5.3.11), copies may be made, for the purposes of research and private study, of documents over 100 years old whose author has been dead for more than 50 years; there is no restriction on the type of recipient or on the type of research.

The receiving institution should ensure that the copies are used solely for appropriate purposes such as non-commercial research or private study (see 5.2.7–9) or for an examination (see 5.2.15). It would also be best advised to refer requests for copies of the copies to the source institution, which can make fresh copies from the originals and will be kept aware of uses (especially commercial uses) of its material.

5.3.24 Copying from copies

There are two issues to consider in relation to the making of copies from copies: the rights of the custodian of the original document and the rights of the owner of the copyright in the original. There is unlikely to be any copyright in most copies (see 2.1.8). It is the responsibility of the custodian of the original document to decide whether and how to exercise the reproduction rights in images that they have supplied of documents in their care (see 5.4.34) where they also control the copyright (see 5.4.9ff.), and to inform any recipient record office of what it may do with the copy. For its part, the National Archives will not normally object to other record offices making limited copies from copies of Crown copyright material that it has supplied (for instance census microfilms or copy tithe maps supplied to county record offices), if they are for non-commercial research or private study. It will, however, expect that its permission will be sought for the use of such copies for other purposes, including publication or posting on the internet.

Where the documents copied are copyright, and the copyright is not controlled by the record office or other body, care must be taken to ensure that copies taken from those copies are legitimate:

- It seems that copies may be made from preservation copies as if they were the original, since they are intended to replace a lost or damaged original, under the terms of the 1989 Regulations (see 5.3.8 and 5.3.10).
- No copies may be made from copies of public records, unless they are Crown copyright (see above and 5.4.3), the copyright owner has given permission or the exception below applies.
- Copies may be made from copies of documents supplied under the terms of the 1956 Act (see 5.3.11), under the same terms.
- Under the appropriate circumstances, self-service copying might qualify as fair dealing (see 5.2.7ff.).

5.3.25 Broadcasts

It is not an infringement of copyright in a broadcast, or in any work included in it, for a recording, or a copy of a recording, to be made for deposit in an archive maintained by any of the following 'designated bodies':

- the British Film Institute (the National Film and Television Archive);
- the British Library (the National Sound Archive);
- the British Music Information Centre;
- the Imperial War Museum;
- the Music Performance Research Centre;
- the National Library of Wales; and
- the Scottish Film Council.

However, a broadcast of an encrypted transmission is excluded, which would appear to cover any pay-per-view broadcast. It should be noted that the provisions that permit copying by libraries and archives do not cover broadcasts, so copies of these deposited recordings may not be made without permission.

1988 (CDPA) s75; SI 1993/74

5.4   Permission

5.4.1   Licences

If anyone other than the copyright owner wishes to do any of the acts restricted by copyright (see 5.1) with a copyright work, he or she needs either to gain ownership of the copyright (see 3.3.8) or to obtain permission in the form of a licence. A licence does not (in most cases) have to be written, and it may be implied, for instance by an author sending a manuscript of an article to the editor of a journal (see 3.3.15–16). A licence may be for the whole term of the copyright or for a limited period. It remains in force even when the original grantor dies and so is automatically binding on the grantor's heirs (see 3.3.1) and normally on his or her assigns (see 3.3.8). However, if the copyright is sold (that is, assigned in return for payment), the licence will terminate if the purchaser of the copyright is not told about it and has no other reason to know about it, so the licence could become ineffective without warning.

The rights covered by a licence may cover the same range as those granted by assignment (see 3.3.8), and it may be 'bare' or contractual. A bare licence is one granted without payment, which is likely to include many if not all implied licences (see 3.3.16); it may be revoked by the licensor at will or after reasonable notice. A contractual licence is one for which a consideration (as little as £1) has been paid and which both parties have entered into with knowledge of the terms. Either party can then sue the other for breach and it is irrevocable except under the terms for termination set out in it. It is best that wherever possible a consideration be paid for a licence.

A licence may be non-exclusive, sole or exclusive. The non-exclusive form is the most likely to come to the attention of archivists and records managers: it gives permission to do something, but allows the copyright owner to give licences to any number of other people too. A sole licence gives the licensee permission to do something, and allows the licensor to continue to do it too, but prevents the licensor from granting a similar licence to anyone else without breach of contract (assuming that the licence is contractual). If a written licence, signed by or with the authority of a copyright owner, says that it is exclusive, the rights of the recipient while the licence is in force are very similar to the rights of an assignee of the copyright. The copyright owner may not grant similar rights to anyone else, and may not exploit the rights him or herself without being in breach of contract (assuming that the licence is contractual). The licensee can even initiate action against third parties for infringement of the copyright in order to get an injunction to stop the infringement continuing. The court would have to give consent for an action to continue beyond that without the owner being involved, since otherwise the defendant might be sued again by the owner. The licensee can only take action against the copyright owner for breach of contract, if, for example, the copyright owner continues to exploit the work or licenses someone else to do so. Any type of licence may be assigned or sub-licensed if the terms of the licence permit, and will normally say whether it applies to the licensee's agents when acting for the licensed purpose.

Because of the restrictions which are otherwise imposed on the licensor, an archivist or records manager who is in a position to grant a licence would normally be well advised to ensure that it is non-exclusive. Otherwise, licences will mostly affect archivists and records managers in three ways: controlling what they may do with documents in their care; what they say to members of the public who wish to make use of documents; and what they may do with material created for them by other people such as volunteers (see 3.2.21) and consultants (see 3.2.17).

For Creative Commons licences see 6.2.4. For model licences from a depositor to an archive and from an archive and/or depositor to a user, see 9.3.

1988 (CDPA) ss90, 92(1), 101ff.; *Blair v Osborne and Tomkins*, 1971; *Bodley Head v Flegon*, 1972; *Godfrey v Lees*, 1995; *Brighton v Jones*, 2004

5.4.2 Public records

An archivist needs no licence to make available or copy any public record in his or her care (see 5.3.1). The use of material in public records or of copies of them by members of the public is as for any other documents (see 5.1, 5.2), unless they are Crown copyright.

5.4.3 Public records: waiver of Crown copyright

Although Crown copyright continues to subsist, for most purposes the Government no longer enforces it in the contents of public records in any 'public record repository' (see 5.3.1) that are available to the public and that were unpublished, or contain material that was unpublished, at the time when they were deposited. Users are free to make copies of photocopies of Crown copyright public records for non-commercial research purposes, and to index, transcribe, publish and broadcast Crown copyright material in such public records without formal permission, payment of a copyright fee or acknowledgement of copyright. There remain, however, requirements that the appropriate record office's custody of the original document be acknowledged and the document reference given, and that a copy of any publication be supplied free to the record office if requested. It should be noted that the waiver applies to previously published public records if they contain material that was unpublished prior to deposit. This would include, for instance, an annotated map. Record offices may still control the type of copy that they supply, may still refuse to supply copies on conservation grounds, and may exercise control of the commercial exploitation of images of documents (as distinct from the information which such documents contain) (see 5.4.33–34).

The Future Management of Crown Copyright, Cm 4300; HMSO (see 3.2.28) Guidance Note 3

5.4.4   Public records: waiver of Crown copyright: exceptions

There are exceptions to the waiver as follows:

- Crown copyright material in public records may not be misused, used in a misleading context or used in a derogatory manner. Examples of where the waiver might not apply would be the publication of offensive images in a distasteful manner derogatory to the Crown, an individual or any immediate family; or the publication of a selection of material in a context which gives a false impression of the original meaning of the text.
- Crown copyright is still enforced in material published by the Crown or with the Crown's approval prior to deposit in the relevant public record repository (see 5.3.1).
- The terms of the waiver do not apply, self-evidently, to any material that is in non-Crown copyright, including all material in Parliamentary and private copyright, or that is out of copyright.
- Crown copyright continues to be enforced in material in public records that have not yet been deposited in a public record repository or that are not open to public inspection, though a licence may be obtainable from the Controller (see 3.2.28, 5.4.32).
- Crown copyright continues to be enforced in material in public record repositories in any documents that are not themselves public records.
- The terms of the waiver do not apply to certain commercially valuable information (see 5.4.5).

The Future Management of Crown Copyright, Cm 4300; HMSO (see 3.2.28) Guidance Note 3

5.4.5   Crown copyright: commercially valuable information and non-public records

The waiver of Crown copyright in public records does not apply to material which consists of commercially valuable information. This is not a fixed category of material, but includes:

- unpublished records of the Ordnance Survey, the Ordnance Survey of Northern Ireland and the UK Hydrographic Office which form the basis of current maps, charts, mapping data and other related publications; permission must be sought from the department concerned;
- copies of public records in public record repositories, but not the data which they contain. Thus while users may transcribe and publish Crown copyright text and make calendars and indexes of Crown copyright data, whether working from originals or copies, they may not reproduce, publish or place on the internet images

of Crown copyright documents without permission, and in some cases the payment of a fee (but see also 5.3.24).

The waiver does not apply to non-public records. Where there are unpublished Crown copyright works in a record office, a 'click-use' PSI licence available free online (see 3.2.28, 5.4.32) will normally be all that is required.

The Future Management of Crown Copyright, Cm 4300; HMSO Guidance Note 3

5.4.6   Gifts and deposits

Copyright is not infringed by simply making original documents (or preservation copies) available to the public, nor by displaying artistic works in an exhibition (see 4.2). The copyright owner may not impose conditions on access to the records, therefore, unless he or she is also the owner of the documents themselves and even then only in accordance with freedom of information where appropriate (see 5.3.3–4, 5.4.8). The copyright owner's control is limited to the copying and use of his or her copyright material. If an archivist wishes to publish any of the documents, he or she is in the same position as a member of the public wishing to do so. The following comments about the deposit of records apply also to gifts, unless otherwise stated.

It is important that the depositor fully understands the terms of his or her deposit, and particularly the implications of any provisions for copyright. The archivist must also be aware that any deposit agreement and any copyright licence may be a form of contract (see 5.4.1), and that legal advice should be sought if there is any doubt about the drafting or meaning of particular provisions (see 5.5).

5.4.7   Gifts and deposits: depositor's conditions

When documents are deposited in a record office, the depositor may impose conditions of deposit which are similar to, but are entirely distinct from, copyright restrictions. It may be that the donor of records could insist on the same right, but any such conditions might be unenforceable. A depositor's conditions might include, for instance, requiring written undertakings from intending readers that they will limit their use of the material to research and private study or to education. Before accepting any deposit, the archivist will presumably be satisfied that the depositor is authorized to deposit the documents. That being the case, although the depositor may not be the owner of the copyright in the documents, the conditions must be observed (even if, for instance, they prevent copyright owners making use of their own works) though freedom of information provisions might take precedence (see 5.3.3–4).

5.4.8 Gifts and deposits: freedom of information and access

Many record offices and registries are run by bodies that are authorities under the terms of the Freedom of Information Acts 2000 and 2002 (see 5.3.3–4). Some deposits and all gifts (but not short-term loans) as well as the records of the parent body are subject to the access provisions of the Acts. There are elaborate arrangements to determine whether deposited records are subject to the Acts, which archivists and records managers should study.

5.4.9 Gifts and deposits: categories of material

Any deposit of documents is likely to contain three categories of material:

- out of copyright (for instance old published works);
- copyright of the depositor; and
- copyright of someone other than the depositor.

A deposit that contains, for instance, a family's or a company's correspondence will include copies of letters sent and originals of letters received; the depositor is likely to own only the copyright in the copy letters sent. The archivist must remember this when negotiating the terms of the deposit and when advising members of the public subsequently. No licence is needed for any use of items in the first category. The depositor is unlikely to have any right to give permission for the use of items in the third category, since any copyright licence (see 5.4.1) or assignment (see 3.3.8) is valid only for works in which copyright is owned by the person signing the agreement or the person on whose behalf it is signed. The archivist would be well advised to secure a licence or assignment to cover the second category, and must make sure that he or she understands precisely what it does and does not cover. For instance, a licence may restrict the scope of copying by librarians and archivists (see 5.3), or allow the archivist to use, or authorize others to use, the material. Any licence or assignment should be in writing and signed by the licensor, and should be in return for at least a nominal payment. Even if a licence or assignment is secured, the archivist must remember that the moral rights of the author of a work (see 8.1) remain with the author and his or her heirs unless they are explicitly waived.

5.4.10 Gifts and deposits: options

It is important that the agreement for the deposit of any collection of copyright materials in an archive deals properly with the question of copyright. There are several options, as outlined below.

5.4.11 Gifts and deposits: depositor control

The first option for the treatment of copyright in gifts and deposits is for the depositor to retain all control over material in his or her copyright, and to provide details of how he or she may be contacted by the archivist or a member of the public for permission to make use of relevant material. Provision should be made for information about changes of address to be supplied, and to ask the depositor's heirs to notify the archivist of the change in ownership of the copyright after the depositor's death. The copyright owner may then issue, or refuse to issue, licences in response to specific requests for permission to use material. This is the least desirable option from the archivist's point of view.

5.4.12 Gifts and deposits: licence to archivist

The second option for the treatment of copyright in gifts and deposits is for the depositor to give a licence to the archivist and successors to deal with requests for the reproduction of his or her copyright material on his or her behalf. The licence may be for a set term, and may specify the sorts of use that are, or are not, permitted. If it does so, the archivist should ensure that the terms of any conditions are clear. For instance, the depositor might be willing to allow use in charitable or educational publications but not in commercial ones. He or she may wish to have referred to him or her applications for uses that the licence does not allow; in that case, contact arrangements will be needed as above. The licence should also specify whether the archivist may grant permission for a fee. If the depositor is retaining the right to grant licences for commercial exploitation, if at all possible the archivist should not accept any responsibility for the collection of fees on the depositor's behalf.

There is one possible disadvantage of a licence of this sort. A licence while in force is automatically binding on the depositor's heirs, but is not binding on anyone who buys, without knowledge of the licence, an assignment of the copyright (see 3.3.8) from the depositor or the heirs. The licence could therefore become ineffective without warning (see 5.4.1).

1988 (CDPA) s90

5.4.13 Gifts and deposits: sample licence

A sample licence is given in the Appendix (see 9.3.1). One possibility should be noted: the licence granted by the depositor may be exclusive, sole or non-exclusive. If a particular right is granted exclusively the effect is much the same as a partial assignment, except that the licence may be nullified by a subsequent sale of the copyright, as mentioned above (see 5.4.12). If it is sole the depositor may do the things covered by the licence but may not license anyone else to do so. If it is non-exclusive, the depositor may continue to give permission, and may license other people to do so too (see 5.4.1).

1988 (CDPA) s92

5.4.14 Gifts and deposits: partial assignment

The third option for the treatment of copyright in gifts and deposits is for the depositor to assign some of his or her rights in the material to the archivist and successors. A partial assignment may be limited to a term of years and/or may be limited by specifying to which of the copyright owner's rights it applies. It may, for instance, specify reproduction rights, or broadcasting rights, or performing rights, or publication rights, or a combination. The assignment must be in writing and signed by the copyright owner and be given in return for a consideration (see 3.3.8) and is then binding on him or her, his or her heirs and any purchaser of his or her rights. They may then be sued for infringement of the rights assigned and for breach of contract.

Once the archivist has received an assignment of some of the depositor's rights in documents deposited, he or she may give permission and issue licences for the use of material that was the copyright of the depositor, within the limits laid down, without reference to the depositor, and may charge such fees as he or she thinks fit. He or she must, however, remember that the depositor or some other assignee owns the remaining rights in the material; the scope is limited to the rights that have been assigned. This could cause difficulties if there is a risk that the copyright owner will in future become difficult or impossible to trace; some arrangement for the future is desirable (see 5.4.11). A better solution is a full assignment.

1988 (CDPA) ss90, 173(1); *Gross v Seligman*, 1914

5.4.15 Gifts and deposits: full assignment

The fourth option for the treatment of copyright in gifts and deposits is for the depositor to assign all of his or her rights in the material to the archivist and successors. A full assignment transfers all rights to the archivist or his or her employer: he or she becomes the owner of the copyright and the depositor no longer has control (except in respect of moral rights unless they are waived, see 8.1). As with a partial assignment, the assignment must be in writing and signed by the copyright owner, and should be in return for a consideration (see 3.3.8) and is binding on the copyright owner, his or her heirs and any subsequent purchaser of any remaining rights in other material so that they may be sued for infringement.

Once the archivist has received a full assignment of the depositor's copyright in documents deposited, he or she may give permission and issue licences for the use of such of the material as was the copyright of the depositor without reference to the depositor, and may charge such fees as he or she thinks fit.

1988 (CDPA) s90; *Gross v Seligman*, 1914

5.4.16 Gifts and deposits: sample assignment

A sample assignment is given in the Appendix (see 9.4). Note the following:

- The assignor may be an individual, individuals or a company. If several members of a family are depositing records, they should all be parties to the assignment and sign it. If the assignment is by a company, it may be sealed with the company seal rather than being signed, or be signed by two directors or by a director and the company secretary.
- The head of the record office as assignee should be identified by title not by the individual's name.
- The definition of the rights is complicated by the fact that few deposits will contain material all of which is in the copyright of the depositor (see 5.4.9). For this reason it is very desirable that the background paragraph gives information on the nature of the material in which the assignor owns the copyright.
- Where a depositor is assigning rights in his or her own works, moral rights become relevant (see 8.1), and the works concerned must be clearly identified. If he or she wishes to be identified as the author, that moral right must be asserted in the assignment. Alternatively, either or both of the rights to be identified as the author and to object to derogatory treatment may be waived.
- The assignment should be in return for a consideration (see 3.3.8).
- There is no requirement that an assignment be witnessed, or that it be signed by the assignee as well as the assignor, but these precautions may prevent disputes later.

5.4.17 Gifts and deposits: licence to publish

If the archivist has been licensed to give permission for the use of copyright material deposited, or has received a partial or total assignment, he or she may authorize the use of the material and should always do so in writing, keeping a copy on file. In many cases, permission will not require the formality of a further licence to the user; a simple letter giving permission for a specified use (or uses) of a specified document (or documents) will normally be sufficient. However, a complex request for permission might justify a formal licence, and it will certainly be necessary if there is to be a continuing relationship between the archive and the licensee, for instance for the payment of royalties.

Unless there are exceptional circumstances, any licence must be non-exclusive (see

5.4.1). Archivists should be very wary of granting exclusive licences, because they mean that no one else (including the archivist) may do the same thing with the same material without the archivist being in breach of contract. Archivists should also never issue blanket licences which do not specify, in some way, the material to which the licence applies.

5.4.18 Gifts and deposits: licence to publish: sample licence

A model licence is given in the Appendix (see 9.3.2). This model licence will need to be adapted to suit the circumstances. If for instance the copyright has been assigned to the archive, it is unlikely that the depositor will be a party to the agreement. In that case the preamble will need to be rewritten appropriately and there will probably need to be a definition of depositor in clause 2. Possible options for other variations are given throughout the text.

5.4.19 Gifts and deposits: waiver, abandonment and the public domain

The legal authorities are doubtful about whether it is possible entirely to abandon a copyright or to assign it into the public domain. However, instead of assigning copyright to the archivist, a depositor can waive it or declare that the copyright will not be enforced. A waiver of copyright must be in writing and be signed by the copyright owner. It could take one of the following forms:

> I declare that where I am the owner of the copyright in material in [specify the documents], I have waived all my copyright and that no permission is required for the reproduction and use of such material.

> All the copyright of which I am the owner in material in [specify the documents] is hereby assigned to [the archivist] and successors until such time as such material shall become open to public inspection, from which time my copyright in such material shall be waived and no permission shall be required for its reproduction and use.

5.4.20 Tracing the copyright owner

An archivist should never appear to give permission for the use of copyright material unless he or she has clear authority to do so. The consequence of appearing to authorize use could be liability for any infringement committed on the basis of that implied permission (see 5.2.30). It is primarily the responsibility of the person wishing to publish a copyright work to seek to identify, and to obtain permission from, the current owner or owners of the copyright. The archivist is under no obligation to the intending publisher to identify or contact copyright owners unless specific arrangements have been made with a known copyright owner (in which case the institution is likely to have a duty to the copyright owner but not to the potential publisher). Even if a depositor has given the archivist a licence or assignment, there is likely to be material in the deposit which is the copyright of someone else (see 2.1.2). Where an archivist wishes to publish, the same requirements apply to him or her as to any other publisher.

1988 (CDPA) s16(2)

5.4.21 *Tracing the copyright owner: risk management*

Most archival materials in private copyright are unpublished and many are anonymous, and the copyright is of very long duration; indeed until the passing of the 1995 Regulations it was indefinite in some cases (see 2.2.19 and 2.3.15). It can be very difficult to identify the copyright owner of material created as little as 50 years ago. The prospect of identifying, with any certainty, the person entitled to the copyright in material created in the 19th century and earlier could be daunting, hence the use of the term 'orphan works' to describe this sort of material (see 3.3.20 and see also 2.1.17). While recognizing this, and the similar difficulties facing any person claiming to be the copyright owner and wishing to prove the claim, an archivist should not advise a prospective publisher to go ahead without making abundantly plain that no authorization to publish is given, that the responsibility for any infringement will lie solely with the publisher and that he or she would be well advised to seek legal advice (see 5.2.30).

The question of rights clearance is essentially one of risk management. The publisher must balance the risks of infringement against the benefits of going ahead, and decide how extensive the efforts need to be to identify the copyright owner before proceeding without permission. The Act gives absolute rights to the copyright owner outside the scope of the statutory exceptions; there is nothing about a publisher having to use only reasonable efforts. A court would probably accept that there have to be limits, but the publisher must take the decision, and the risk, as to what he or she thinks those limits might be.

Some assistance is available for the tracing of copyright owners, and the 1956 and 1988 Acts both contain provisions which give a publisher some help in certain circumstances, so it would be reasonable for the archivist to draw the prospective publisher's attention to the following (see 5.4.22–26). Having taken such steps as he or she thinks reasonable, a publisher would be wise to publish, with the works, a disclaimer saying that all efforts have been taken to identify the copyright owners, apologizing for any infringement and inviting copyright owners to make contact.

5.4.22 *Tracing the copyright owner: sources of help*

An Anglo-American university project called WATCH (Writers, Artists and Their

Copyright Holders) has created a voluntary register of copyright owners, primarily of works held in libraries and archives in the UK and North America although in time it hopes to cover the whole of Europe, North and South America and English-speaking countries in other parts of the world. It covers, in descending order of completeness:

- literary authors in the English language;
- other English-language authors in the humanities;
- British and American artists, including photographers, painters, film makers, performers and others in the visual and performing arts, a category much expanded in recent years;
- British and American politicians and public figures;
- literary authors in other European languages; and
- English-language authors outside the humanities.

WATCH is accessible on the internet at www.watch-file.com/.

Other sources of information might be the Library of Congress, and its website at www.copyright.gov/ (searchable for items registered only since 1978); licensing agencies (see 5.4.28ff.); relevant professional, academic or sectoral bodies (such as the British Association of Picture Libraries and Agencies, BAPLA, see 5.4.33); literary agents (try contacting the Association of Authors' Agents or consulting the *Writer's Handbook*); press agencies; and image libraries. If all else fails, the final recourse should be to advertise, by publishing a notice in *The Times* legal notices, the *London Gazette*, and any relevant newspapers, journals and newsletters. The notice should identify the material as precisely as possible, explain what it is intended to do with it, and ask claimants to the copyright to contact the advertiser with evidence to support the claim so that agreement can be reached. It should also apologize for any infringement which might occur if owners do not come forward.

For other issues relating to rights clearance see 6.5.3.

5.4.23 Publication of old works without permission

An unpublished literary, dramatic or musical work, including any illustrations, which is open to public inspection in an archive or similar institution (see 5.3.11) may be published without permission and without infringement of copyright if:

- the work was created before 1 August 1989;
- the author has been dead for more than 50 years;
- the work is more than 100 years old; and
- the publisher did not know the identity of the copyright owner before publication.

It is not clear whether these provisions allow the publication of a work of which the author is unknown; it seems probable that if the work is of a sufficient age that the author must have died at least 50 years earlier, that would be enough (but see 5.4.25). There is no requirement, under these provisions, to make any attempt to identify the copyright owner (as there is in elsewhere in the 1956 and 1988 Acts) or to publicize the plan to publish the work (as there was in the original text of the 1956 Act). However, if it ought to be obvious who the owner is, for instance if the document was written by a member of a prominent and still extant noble family, it might be sensible to be cautious. These provisions do not apply to independent artistic works, though they do cover artistic works that are illustrations to a literary, dramatic or musical work provided they are intrinsic to the understanding of the text, are published as part of the main work and are not reproduced independently (see 5.3.18). The publisher may produce further editions, in the same or altered form, of the publication containing the work, but the same work may not be reproduced in any other publication until copyright in it has expired. However, if only part of the original work is published, the remaining unpublished part is still eligible.

1956 s7(6, 7, 9(d)), cf s7(5)(b); 1988 (CDPA) Sch 1 para 16, cf ss41, 47, exclusion of 1956 s7(7)(a) in Sch 1 para 16(b)

5.4.24 Publication of old works without permission: further use

Once a work has been published using this provision, it may be broadcast, performed in public or recorded (as a sound recording only; video recording did not exist in 1956) without infringement.

1956 ss7(8), 48(1) 'record'; 1988 (CDPA) Sch 1 para 16(c)

5.4.25 Publication of anonymous or pseudonymous works

There is also a dispensation in the 1988 Act for anonymous or pseudonymous works, that is, works whose authors are unknown (see 2.1.17, 5.3.17). This is not the same as works whose first or current copyright owners are unknown, so the dispensation may not be used to avoid the task of tracing the descent of copyright ownership to the present day if the author is known. Copyright will not be infringed by any act done, such as copying (see 5.1.2) or publication (see 5.1.3), to a literary, dramatic, musical or artistic work or a film, whether published or unpublished, where:

- the author (literary, dramatic, musical and artistic works) or any of the persons connected with a film (see 2.4.5) cannot be ascertained by reasonable enquiry; and
- it is reasonable to assume that copyright has expired (but see 5.4.26) or it is reasonable to assume that the author (or all the authors, if it is a work of joint

authorship) or all the persons connected with a film died 70 years or more before the beginning of the calendar year in which the act was done.

The restrictions which formerly hedged this dispensation about for pre-1989 works were lifted by the 2003 Regulations.

1988 (CDPA) s57, 66A, Sch 1 para 15; SI 1995/3297 reg 6(2); SI 2003/2498 Sch 2 repeal of 1988 (CDPA) Sch 1 para 15(3)

5.4.26 Publication of anonymous and pseudonymous works: limitations

For literary, dramatic, musical and artistic works created before 1 August 1989 the reasonable assumption about the expiry of copyright does not apply:

* to any photograph; or
* to any work covered by the Copyright Act 1775 (see 2.2.32).

Also, the assumption about the death of the author does not apply to works or films in Crown copyright or in the copyright of certain international organizations. Despite the exclusions to the first assumption, though, this second assumption may be applied to photographs.

1988 (CDPA) ss57, 66A, Sch 1 para 15; SI 1995/3297 regs 5(2), 6(2)

5.4.27 Acquiescence

If a copyright owner does nothing to prevent someone else from infringing his or her copyright, the result might be that he or she would be found by a court to have acquiesced in the infringement so that no action could be taken against the infringer. A popular tactic for a user to adopt is to write to ask for permission to use a copyright work, stating that it will be assumed that permission is granted unless a reply is received. The result could be that the copyright owner acquiesces in the use if no reply is sent, but it is a risky tactic for the user to adopt. He or she must be sure that the letter has been received, that the recipient of the letter is the copyright owner, and that sufficient time has passed. There is no case law on this type of implied licence (see 3.3.16), but other forms of acquiescence (for instance, not objecting to a pop group performing works but waiting to see how successful the infringing use was, or seeking money for the use of song lyrics while not objecting to the use itself) have involved years, not weeks, of delay. An archivist receiving such a letter should always reply. If he or she has no authority to give permission, the user should be informed. Moreover, it is conceivable that a failure to notify the user that the archivist does not control the copyright could be interpreted as authorizing infringement (see 5.2.30). If the archivist does control the copyright, a reply is still needed to explain what is and is not granted: a written licence (see 5.4.1) is much easier to enforce than an implied one (see 3.3.16).

Redwood Music v Francis Day and Hunter, 1978; *Redwood Music v Chappell*, 1982; *Farmers Build v Carier Bulk Materials Handling*, 1997; *Godfrey v Lees*, 1995; *ZYX Music v King*, 1997, *Ludlow Music v Robbie Williams*, 2001

5.4.28 Collective licensing

The 1988 Act gives statutory backing to collective licensing arrangements for the use of copyright works, which allow users to copy or perform copyright works in return for a fee without having to secure permission from individual copyright owners, and which benefit copyright owners by giving them a better chance of preventing infringement and of receiving an income from royalties. The details of these arrangements vary over time, and are outside the scope of this book, but the following summary may be helpful (see 5.4.29–31).

1988 (CDPA) ss116–144

5.4.29 Collective licensing: licensing bodies

The bodies that grant collective licences are known as licensing and collecting societies. They include:

- Authors' Licensing and Collecting Society (ALCS), representing authors, and a co-owner of the CLA (14–18 Holborn, London EC1N 2LE, or www.alcs.co.uk/);
- Copyright Licensing Agency (CLA), representing the authors and publishers of published literary works (6–10 Kirby Street, London EC1N 8TS, or www.cla.co.uk/);
- Design and Artists Copyright Society (DACS), representing visual artists, including photographers (33 Great Sutton Street, London EC1V 0DX, or www.dacs.org.uk/);
- Directors and Producers Rights Society (DPRS), representing directors and producers in film and television (20–22 Bedford Row, London WC1R 4EB, or www.dprs.org/);
- Educational Recording Agency (ERA) for recordings of broadcasts by educational establishments for non-commercial educational use (150 Southampton Row, London WC1B 5AL, or www.era.org.uk/);
- Newspaper Licensing Agency (NLA), representing the publishers of newspapers and journals (7–9 Church Road, Wellington Gate, Tunbridge Wells, Kent TN1 1NL, or www.nla.co.uk/);
- Music Publishers Association (MPA), representing music publishers in relation to the reproduction of scores (26 Berners Street, London W1T 3LR, or www.mpaonline.org.uk/);

- Performing Right Society (PRS), representing composers and publishers of music for the licensing of performances, and the Mechanical Copyright Protection Society (MCPS), representing owners of copyright in recordings (both at 29–33 Berners Street, London W1T 3AB, or www.mcps-prs-alliance.co.uk/);
- Publishers' Licensing Society (PLS), representing publishers and the other co-owner of the CLA (37–41 Gower Street, London WC1E 6HH, or www.pls.org.uk/).

Information about other licensing and similar bodies may be obtained from the British Copyright Council at the same address as MCPS-PRS or from www.britishcopyright.org/. There is currently very limited provision for pan-European licensing, though there are agreements between some societies. The EU is seeking to encourage movement, but it is likely to be slow.

The societies may have schemes of licensing for particular categories of user (such as schools, universities, industry, government) using materials in its sector whereby any user within the category may take out a licence under standard terms and conditions. Where there is no scheme the licensing body will arrange a tailored licence for the particular use required. The monopoly control of the various societies is subject to the authority of the Copyright Tribunal, which may hear appeals against the terms and costs of licences and refusals to grant licences. A notable case brought to the Tribunal by Universities UK against the CLA resulted in a re-drafting of the licence and a new fee structure.

1988 (CDPA) ss116ff.; *Universities UK v Copyright Licensing Agency*, 2002

5.4.30 Collective licensing: electronic works

Authors and publishers have been reluctant to allow licensing bodies to set up licensing schemes for digital materials, preferring to handle requests for licences themselves on an individual basis, but there is some movement particularly to allow digitization. It is inevitable that licensing schemes for electronic works will become more commonplace. The various CLA schemes currently cover photocopying, faxing, scanning and internal email distribution of copyright material. The ERA licence allows electronic communication of licensed recordings within an educational establishment. The MCPS and PRS jointly have a licence for the podcasting of musical works. The NLA provides an electronic database of newspaper clippings, to which clippings agencies may provide links for their clients but which is not otherwise directly accessible by users.

5.4.31 Collective licensing: significance for archives

Archivists and records managers should be aware that licensing schemes as outlined above are almost exclusively for published works. It may be that DACS would be able to license the use of unpublished photographs and other artistic works, and (although likely to be outside the scope of most archivists professionally) the PRS will no doubt license the performance of unpublished music. However, the CLA, NLA and MCPS deal only with published material.

Also:

- In some cases the existence of a licensing scheme makes invalid exceptions to copyright provided by the Act. This is true for instance of the exception allowing the reprographic copying by educational establishments of published works (see 5.2.15–16). The licensing schemes for educational establishments are well established and generally less restrictive than the statutory exceptions, so archivists and records managers should ensure that any copying of published material that they do for an educational establishment is covered by its licence.
- The existence of licensing arrangements does not invalidate the normal provisions for insubstantial parts of a work or fair dealing. Copying which falls within the generally accepted limits (see 5.2.3–6) does not therefore need a licence, but an archivist or records manager who needs to exceed the limits for official purposes, either routinely or as a one-off, should seek a licence from the appropriate society.
- Societies do not necessarily have authority to license all works by copyright owners they represent nor do they necessarily represent all copyright owners in their sector. Any lists they supply of works or owners excluded from a licence should be studied carefully. Except as notified by the society in such a list, a licensee is entitled to rely on the comprehensiveness of the licence for the whole sector and the society will be liable for any costs arising from an inadvertent infringement.

1988 (CDPA) s136

5.4.32 Licensing of Crown, Parliamentary and public sector material

The Controller of HMSO (see 3.2.28) has made available online a range of 'click-use' licences. These are:

- the PSI licence, which is free, and covers the bulk of 'core' government material in Crown copyright (see 3.2.28), unless the copyright is already waived as with public records (see 5.4.3). The Controller would like also to extend its coverage to material produced by non-Crown public sector bodies, such as local authorities (see below);
- the Parliamentary licence, which covers works in Parliamentary copyright (see 3.2.32), and is also free; and
- the Value-Added licence, which covers Crown copyright works containing material from a variety of sources that has been refined so that it is no longer 'core' information but is available commercially, often in competition with the private sector.

The exceptions to this class licensing regime include:

- material originated by trading funds created under the Government Trading Act 1990, for instance, Ordnance Survey, UK Hydrographic Office, Registers of Scotland, HM Land Registry, Meteorological Office, which do their own licensing, and to which links are given from the website;
- material in which Crown copyright is in any case waived, such as public records (see 5.4.3) and legislation, or which may be reproduced freely subject to conditions, such as some national curriculum material;
- classified material;
- personal material such as birth certificates;
- photograph and film archives;
- material which is not Crown copyright, for which the Controller has no authority to act.

Following a European directive, most public sector bodies including parliaments and assemblies, national and local government bodies and public corporations, must be willing to license the use of their publicly available information by commercial and other users. A public sector body may decline only if no one, including itself, is permitted to use the information for any purpose outside its 'public task' (that is, the task given to it by statute or the equivalent). There are some exclusions:

- information which is the copyright of a third party;
- information held by public service broadcasters;
- information held by educational and research establishments, such as schools, universities, archives, libraries and 'research facilities'; and
- information held by cultural establishments, such as museums, libraries, archives and theatres.

The exclusion of material in an archive covers all the material held, whether among the records or not, but does not apply to an archive that does not exist for educational, research or cultural purposes, such as a company record store. Licensing terms must be clear and fair; guidance on them is available online (see 3.2.28). An archivist or records manager who needs to know about public sector information and its licensing should consult the regulations and the guidance carefully.

Directive 2003; SI 2005/1515 regs 3–5

5.4.33 Fees

An archivist or records manager who has authority to levy copyright fees, for instance for the use of material in the copyright of the employing body or under the terms of a licence or assignment from the copyright owner, should make available to users a scale of fees that will be charged. Indications of the appropriate level of such fees may be obtained from the charges recommended by the British Association of Picture Libraries and Agencies (BAPLA) (18 Vine Hill, London EC1R 5DZ, or www.bapla.org) and from the fees charged for licences by the licensing and collecting societies. For public sector material, guidance would also be available from the Controller (see 3.2.28).

5.4.34 Image library

An archive is entitled to exercise some control over the use of material in its custody irrespective of any copyright in the material, and this may be a useful source of income (see 3.2.6). If reproduction rights are to be exercised, it should be made clear to users:

• which categories of material are subject to control and the payment of fees;
• the scale of fees levied, including a clear statement of the uses which will attract fees, including a definition of those regarded as commercial (such as use on the internet, see 4.1.4) and any provision for remission or waiver of fees, for instance for non-commercial uses;
• the terms and conditions of use that will apply; and
• that they will also need to obtain permission from the copyright owner for the use of copyright material.

Advice on terms, conditions and fees may be obtained from BAPLA (see 5.4.33), and any record office contemplating exploiting its collections is advised to become a member.

5.5   Litigation and legal advice

If an archivist or records manager is unfortunate enough to be involved in litigation over copyright, either as a defendant (for a primary or a secondary infringement, see 5.2.28–33), as claimant (against someone who has infringed a copyright administered by him or her), or as a witness, the first step, to be taken as early as possible, must be to secure good legal advice. This means a lawyer who specializes in intellectual property law, rather than a general practitioner. Names of firms specializing in this area can be obtained from the Law Society's directory of solicitors, either in its published form (see Bibliography) or online at www.lawsociety.org.uk/.

If at all possible it is best to avoid litigation, which is hugely expensive and time-consuming. The courts are keen to encourage the use of Alternative Dispute Resolution and the Patent Office has established a mediation service to assist all parties to a dispute to resolve their differences without going to court. Details and advice on when mediation is and when it is not appropriate are available from the Patent Office website at www.patent.gov.uk/.

6 Copyright in the electronic environment

6.1 Introduction

6.1.1 What is different about the electronic environment?

For many purposes, existing copyright law applies in the same way in the electronic environment as it does to traditional formats. Electronic materials are protected by copyright, and the copyright owners enjoy much the same rights over them as they do over works on paper. Users, too, enjoy much the same exceptions to copyright, allowing them to make use of copyright works for non-commercial research and private study for instance. There are good reasons, though, for discussing copyright in the electronic environment as a distinct issue:

- Although copyright rules still apply, it is very much easier to infringe and the consequences of infringement can be much more damaging, so rights owners are very much more inclined to be energetic in their efforts to prevent or punish infringement than they are with the older media.
- The nature of the internet as a global communications medium makes copyright, an essentially territorial right which differs from country to country, very difficult to apply.
- Some special provisions have been made in the law that apply only, or particularly, to electronic materials.

6.1.2 Use

Since for the most part the law applies to electronic works in the same way as to paper-based ones, the same uses are allowed. Thus, fair dealing (see 5.2.7ff.) and library and archive copying (see 5.3) are permitted, unless there are special provisions restricting them as, for instance, with public record databases (see 8.2). However, it should be borne in mind that fair dealing for the purposes of private study and non-commercial research is limited to those purposes, as is copying under the library and archive regulations, for the use of a single individual only. They do not, for instance, permit communication of the work to the public (see 5.1.6), such as on a website. It should be remembered too that data protection as well as copyright must be taken into account when material contains details of living individuals (see 8.7.2). The simple viewing of a copyright work on a computer screen, for a lawful purpose, is not an infringement because any copying involved is 'transient or incidental', although the saving of the work to disk could be because it involves the permanent copying of the work.

1988 (CDPA) s28A; SI 2003/2498 reg 8

6.1.3 Guidelines

The Joint Information Systems Committee (JISC) for the higher education sector in the UK and the Publishers Association have agreed guidelines for the copying of electronic materials under fair dealing and library privileges. It should be remembered that these guidelines were drafted for the higher education sector and are not intended to be any more than pointers towards good practice even there. For the most part they cover copying for purposes of non-commercial research and private study only; use for teaching might require a licence, and use for any commercial purpose would certainly require permission. The full text of the guidelines may be seen at www.publishers.org.uk/.

As with print materials, only a single copy may be made by or for an individual. A librarian or someone acting for the individual may not make copies of substantially the same extracts for more than one person at substantially the same time and may not make any copy if they know or have reason to believe that the individual intends to make further copies from the copy.

The guidelines apply, as do the normal library privileges, only to literary materials and artistic works that are integral to the text; they do not cover artistic works on their own (see 5.3.18).

6.1.4   Limits to what is allowed

The following would normally be regarded as fair and lawful under the guidelines:

- viewing part or all of an electronic work on screen, so long as any incidental copy made by the computer is deleted afterwards;
- printing out a copy of part (to a maximum of say 5%, see 5.3.12) of an electronic publication;
- copying a part of an electronic publication to disk where the disk is portable or is accessible by only one person at a time;
- transmission across a computer network of part of an electronic publication to enable it to be printed out locally, so long as any incidental copies are then deleted;
- transmission across a network of part of an electronic publication for local storage and use, but not for onward transmission;
- quotation from electronic material for the purposes of criticism, review or current news reporting, so long as the source is properly acknowledged.

6.1.5 What is not allowed

The following would probably be regarded as unfair and unlawful, unless prior permission is obtained:

- the copying of the whole of an electronic work, except an incidental copy for use when viewing on screen;
- transmission across a computer network of the whole of an electronic work, for any purpose;
- the posting of all or part of an electronic publication on a network or a website;
- the making of more than one copy;
- the copying of an artistic work on its own or of one that was not integral to the text.

6.1.6 Moral rights

Moral rights apply to electronic works in the same way as to paper-based ones (see 8.1). The author can assert the right to be identified as the author and an individual can object to having a work falsely attributed to him or her. The ease with which electronic materials can be amended makes the third moral right, the right of integrity, particularly important. Misquotation of a work, or use of extracts in a misleading way, would be infringements.

6.1.7 Other people's works

Since the reproduction of a work (including on CD-ROM or on a website) is in itself a restricted act (see 5.1.2), and if it is in a publicly available electronic form is also publication (see 4.1.1, 5.1.3) or communication to the public (see 5.1.6), it must only be done with the consent of the copyright owner. Out-of-copyright material, and material generated by the owner of a website or by the staff of an organization that owns a website, will be no problem. It is an infringement, though, to copy and reproduce material from someone else's website, or to scan material from a copyright work on paper. Limited licences for scanning some literary works are now available from the Copyright Licensing Agency (see 5.4.29). Without permission, never reproduce someone else's website design, since that is protected by copyrights (see 6.2).

6.1.8 Digital rights management systems

Digital rights management systems (DRMS) have attracted much attention and criticism, some of it justified and some not. It is important to recognize that the term covers a range of technologies with different purposes:

- systems to restrict access to content, for instance by encryption;
- systems to identify owners of rights and to give information on licensing (see 6.5.4); and
- copy protection systems or 'technological protection measures' (TPMs) to prevent unauthorized copying.

The aspects of DRMS which raise most problems in a records context are access controls and copy protection, though Sony found itself in major difficulties with tracking software it put into some CD-ROMs. This modified computer operating systems and in some cases laid systems open to attack by software viruses.

Access controls and copy protection systems are intended to prevent or restrict the use and copying of an electronic work (including a computer program), or to impair the quality of copies made. These present more problems to librarians than to those responsible for archival materials, but archivists and records managers receiving electronic materials should be aware that DRMS may:

- effectively give perpetual control to the rights owner, since the protection does not automatically expire as copyright does;
- be designed to prevent enjoyment by users of the benefits of the statutory limitations and exceptions to rights (see 5.2); and
- prevent the making of preservation copies by 'migration' to new media and new software platforms, copies that are essential to the permanent preservation of works in electronic form.

Whatever the purpose, all forms of DRMS are given statutory protection, making it an infringement, and sometimes a criminal offence, to disable or evade them or to provide equipment to do so. When copies of an electronic work are issued to the public with DRMS the person issuing the copies can take action for infringement against anyone who sells any device or means designed or adapted to circumvent the systems used or who publishes information to help people circumvent it, and can ask the court to order the seizure of infringing materials. The circumvention, for instance, of the systems designed to limit the parts of the world where DVDs may be played is thus an infringement, but on the other hand there is a special exception to allow research into cryptography, unless the research or its publication prejudices the rights of the copyright owner.

Regulations have provided a mechanism, by means of an appeal to the Secretary of State (by individuals or their representatives), to stop rights owners using copy protection devices to prevent people exercising their legitimate freedoms under limitations and exceptions to copyright. If the Secretary of State issues a direction, the rights owner must make it possible for the complainants to use the work as directed or be at risk of being sued for breach of statutory duty. Unsurprisingly, this provision has yet to be used.

1988 (CDPA) ss296, 296ZA–ZG, Sch 5A; SI 2003/2498 regs 24–25, Sch 3; *Sony Computer Entertainment v Owen*, 2002; *Sony Computer Entertainment v Ball*, 2005

6.2 Internet

6.2.1 What is protected

An internet website is not a variety of work in itself, and does not qualify as a form of broadcast (see 2.6.3). A website will normally be a form of database, which might be protected by copyright or database right (see 8.2), or both. The underlying computer programs will be protected as such (see 6.6), and the designs of website screen displays will be protected as artistic works recorded in the program.

The owner of a website needs to ensure that he or she owns or controls all rights in the site. This is especially important if consultants are employed (see 3.2.17). It might not be possible to secure assignments of copyright in all the programs (see 6.6.1) but licences (see 5.4.1), and assignments of copyright in material especially created for the site (see 3.3.8), should be obtained.

There are also quite separate copyrights in the material displayed on websites. These include literary and artistic copyrights in text and images displayed on the pages or included in catalogues accessible from the pages. Protection for these is the same as for other works of the same kinds (see 2.2, 2.3). A catalogue available through the website will also be a database, and the rights in it will be completely separate from the rights in the website itself.

Navitaire v Easyjet Airline, 2005

6.2.2 Publication and communication to the public

It is not explicit in statute that the inclusion of a work on an internet website counts as publication, but it almost certainly does (see 4.1.7, 5.1.3). What it certainly does is communicate the work to the public, which is another restricted act (see 5.1.6) requiring permission. Archivists in particular should note that the library and archive copying provisions (see 5.3) do not allow any communication to the public. A website owner impliedly (see 3.3.16) authorizes the copying of a work on the website by a user who downloads it, but any further use is likely to be subject to the terms and conditions of use of the site.

1988 (CDPA) ss18, 20; SI 2003/2498 reg 6

6.2.3 Protection

There are things that the owner of a website can do to protect the materials made available there, but ultimately the best protection for a work is to keep it off the web. It is helpful to include on the site a reminder to users that copyright and probably moral rights apply (see 3.4). Beyond that:

- Decide how much protection is required: can some material be copied freely or is there a need for some restriction? A statement of the limits of freedoms and restrictions is needed, setting out what users may do, what they may copy, and what they may do with their copies. A Creative Commons licence might be appropriate (see 6.2.4).
- Recognize that free access to and use of material can be beneficial: it can lead to increased demand for other off-line or commercial services. Moreover, free access is what many regard as being the primary benefit of the web.
- If some material must be made available, but it is desired to protect it or limit its use, can it be made available in an area of the website accessible only to certain subscribers, can it be copy-protected or marked in some way to show its origin and to allow the tracing of copies, or can a low-quality copy be used (such as a low-resolution scan of an image)?

The designs of the site itself are copyright (see 6.2.1), and it might include logos, trade marks or other identifying marks of the owner. These need protection as much as the contents of the site.

6.2.4 Creative Commons

Creative Commons is an organization which has prepared free licences for use by anyone, primarily on the web. They are intended to simplify the process of giving permission to others to use material published on the web and to make it simpler for users to find licensed material and to understand what they may do with it. Licences may not be modified if the name 'Creative Commons' or the symbols which identify each option are used. Standard licences have been designed for use in England and Wales and in Scotland, and may include limiting options:

- attribution: users may copy, distribute, play or perform the work or derivative works based on it, so long as they acknowledge the author;
- non-commercial: users may use the work only for non-commercial purposes;
- non-derivative: users may use the work but may not create a derivative work from it; and
- share-alike: allows users to make and distribute derivative works, but requires them to distribute them under an identical licence.

In addition to these licensing options, Creative Commons will assist an author who wishes to relinquish all rights in a work. Note that a Creative Commons licence is not appropriate for the publication of a work in someone else's copyright, so is not suitable for digitization projects.

Further information on licences and how to use them is given on the Creative Commons website at www.creativecommons.org.uk/.

6.2.5 Use

If a website contains links to other websites, those links should be to the home page not an internal page, otherwise the user will probably by-pass advertising and any messages about copyright and related rights that the website owner wishes users to see before they gain access to his or her material. Links should avoid using frames, which conceal the fact that the user has entered another website, since this could amount to passing-off (see 8.6.9). Any employer who provides internet access to staff should have strict rules about its use and particularly about the importance of not infringing the copyright and related rights of website owners. Moreover, those rules should be strictly and publicly enforced, lest the employer become liable for authorizing infringement (see 5.2.30). Internet service providers who make temporary copies of most types of work (but not computer programs or databases) solely in order to transmit them across the web are not liable for infringement by making those copies. A service provider will however become liable if he or she has actual knowledge that an infringement is being committed by a user using the service. Actual knowledge means knowledge received by a notice which identifies the sender and the details of the infringement (see 5.2.33).

1988 (CDPA) s28A, 97A; SI 2003/2498 reg 27; *Shetland Times v Wills*, 1997

6.2.6 Law applicable to the internet

One of the great difficulties with enforcing copyright in works made available on a website is the internet's global nature. There is no international agreement on which laws apply to material made available on websites and which courts have jurisdiction. There has been no copyright judgment on this issue, in the UK or elsewhere, and courts handling website defamation cases in different countries, and even in different states in the USA, have come to varying conclusions, the UK preferring the place of downloading as the place of publication. In a data protection case the European Court of Justice preferred the place of uploading as the place where the offending activity occurred. The Information Society directive seems to take the same approach, saying that the communication to the public right covers all acts of making subject matter available 'to members of the public not present at the place where the act of making available originates'. A copyright judgment is awaited which will decide the issue.

The law differs from country to country, and what may be unlawful in one place may be legitimate in another. For this reason if for no other, do not place material on a website if you do not wish it to be copied, and protect other material (especially logos) with watermark and fingerprinting devices. It may be difficult to take action against someone who infringes a UK copyright by placing material on a website overseas. Legal advice will certainly be necessary as to whether there is an infringement under the UK's or that other country's law, and what can be done about it (see 5.5).

Directive 2001 (Information Society) recital 24; *Young v New Haven Advocate*, 2003; *Wagner v Miskin*, 2003; *Bodil Lindqvist v Kammaraklagaren*, 2004; *King v Lewis and Lion Promotions*, 2004

6.3   Electronic mail

Many of the comments applicable to the internet apply to e-mail, but there are some differences. E-mails may be messages sent to one or many people. In the latter case, it is unlikely that the author would wish, or be able, to control use of the material in the message or any attachment by copyright, although he or she could still seek to insist on the integrity of the message as a moral right. For that reason, messages or attachments should not be forwarded as the work of the original author if they have been changed. A message to a single person, on the other hand, is akin to a letter. It remains the copyright of the author, and there is no implied licence to publish the message or (unless the message says differently) to forward it to someone else. A document should not be sent as an attachment to an e-mail unless the sender owns the copyright in it, or has permission to reproduce it.

6.4   Databases

Databases are discussed below (see 8.2).

6.5   Records in the electronic environment

6.5.1   Electronic media

Electronic media are likely now and in the future to impinge on the work of archivists and records managers in many ways, including:

- use of electronic document and records management systems, which store all files created by an organization as digital media;
- use of standalone or networked PCs for office applications, including word-processing and spreadsheets;
- use of standalone or networked systems for the delivery of public services, such as access to a computerized catalogue and other dedicated databases, access to the internet, and access to commercial packages on CD-ROM;

- delivery of services remotely, such as information about the organization or archive, access to the catalogue, responses to enquiries and freedom of information applications, and scanned images of original documents;
- provision of copies in electronic formats, either from electronic originals or from scanned copies, delivered to the customer on disk or across a network;
- provision of direct access to digitized and digital copies of materials on public access websites; and
- preservation of original electronic material in the archive and public access to it.

6.5.2 Significance of copyright

Copyright and related rights should not be regarded as a major obstacle to the development and use of at least some of these applications, but they must be borne in mind.

Use of most commercial products such as databases will require a licence, particularly if there is to be public access to them or they are to be used for the supply of electronic copies. The library sector is well versed in these issues, and it would be worth consulting the publications of Facet Publishing (the publishing arm of CILIP, see 5.3.12 and Bibliography).

If external assistance is employed for the design of computer systems or websites, for instance, the contract for the commission should specify that copyright in all products is assigned by the contractor to the record office or the parent body (see 3.3.8).

The making available of records to the public by means of an electronic retrieval system, for instance on a PC in a record office or on a website, whether the documents originated electronically or have been scanned, can amount to publication (see 4.1.7). Whereas the supply of copies of copyright works is covered by the library and archive privileges, only the publication of some older copyright works is permitted without permission (see 5.3). Any necessary permission should be obtained from the copyright owner before the service is started.

The making and supply (on disk or as e-mail attachments) of electronic copies of documents is covered by the library and archive and public records provisions (see 5.3). While the declaration form required by the former may carry an electronic signature, the costs of a suitable system to deal with them are not likely to be worthwhile for most libraries and archives, but a signed paper form that is faxed or sent as a digital attachment should be acceptable (see 5.3.15). The making available to the public of electronic copies of copyright works on an internet website is a communication to the public (see 5.1.6), and will normally require permission from the copyright owner.

1988 (CDPA) s175(1)(b); 2000 (Communications) s7

6.5.3   Digitization projects and rights clearance

Most archives, record offices, museums, galleries and libraries are now involved in projects to digitize some or all of their holdings in order to make them available for remote access, usually on the internet. Such projects are vital to the development of modern public services but they must be approached in an orderly fashion which means that copyright issues must be considered at an early stage (see 1.3.5). Issues to bear in mind at the beginning and during the project are:

- Are the materials to be digitized protected by copyright? If only some of them are, can the project be redesigned to exclude all or most of the copyright material? Early artistic works are obvious candidates.
- Are there other issues to take into account besides copyright? Consider moral rights (see 8.1), confidentiality and data protection (see 8.7), and trade marks (see 8.6.8), for instance.
- How much money is available to devote to rights clearance? This is a time-consuming and thus expensive process since it involves trying to identify a current copyright owner then tracing and contacting him or her (see 5.4.20ff.). It must not be left to the last minute.
- What rights do I need? This is a big subject so consult works mentioned in the Bibliography (see 10.2) as well as these notes. There is no point in seeking (and sometimes paying for) more than is needed, but on the other hand it is far better to obtain all the rights that might be needed in the future so that the process of licensing does not have to be repeated. Consider the scope of the project: internet access means you will need world rights whereas a CD-ROM project might not seek to distribute outside the EU. If you are using CD-ROM now, might you wish to use the internet in future? Consider also what you wish to do with the work: is it to be reproduced in facsimile, transcribed, quoted, indexed, shown (films), played (sound recordings), performed? Is the website freely accessible or is it restricted to approved users? Do you wish to be able to supply copies, to allow users to take copies, to license further use by users? Be careful to ensure that everything you might wish to do is covered by the licence you obtain, and ensure that you retain and keep up-to-date contact details for the rights owner if you might need to be in touch in the future, for instance if their consent is needed for commercial use by a user of the site.
- For how long do I need the rights? Rights owners will not necessarily be willing to grant rights for lengthy terms, so be realistic. Consider seeking a clause allowing for automatic renewal at set intervals if the licence is not terminated.
- In what form do I need the rights to be? Do I need an assignment (see 3.3.8) or will a licence be sufficient (see 5.4.1)?
- What do I do if I cannot trace the copyright owner? This is an issue of risk management (see 5.4.20ff.). What are the chances of a copyright owner realizing that his or her work has been used and objecting? Is the risk associated with digitizing

and making available works whose rights have not been cleared sufficiently small to be worth taking? In general terms, it is probably fair to say that older works are lower risk than more recent ones; works evidently intended for public consumption are lower risk than ones dealing with confidential matters; and anonymous works are lower risk than ones whose author is known. There will inevitably be exceptions to these generalizations, though, so the decision must rest with the project manager.

• It is possible that rights owners will refuse permission. Be prepared for this and do not think you can ignore it.

6.5.4 Rights information

Rights owners are entitled to require that information about their rights is attached to digital copies of their works. This can be included in the metadata for the document and should preferably be written in a digital rights expression language which can be interpreted by computers and search engines. The information given should, among other things, identify the work by some unique identifier, the rights owner(s) (including the author), the uses permitted and the conditions of use. The Open Digital Rights Language Initiative is seeking to secure international ageement for an open source language for this purpose.

6.5.5 Electronic document and records management

It is government policy that government departments and other bodies should cease to rely on paper records and should instead create electronic records and store them electronically, and other bodies are moving in the same direction. The maintenance of paper files poses no or few copyright problems, since none of the restricted acts is routinely infringed, although the use of files whether active or closed can lead to infringement notably by copying for some other purpose.

There is a range of activities involved in creating and managing electronic files which could lead to infringement:

• Paper materials must be digitized, which involves copying (see 5.1.2, 6.5.6).
• Multiple copies must be made, for instance for back-up storage on different servers or for users to read (see 6.5.6).
• Files must be migrated to new media and new formats in order to ensure their preservation and accessibility, all of which involves copying (see 6.5.7).
• Records must ultimately be selected for permanent preservation and be made available to the public, which might involve a communication to the public (see 5.1.6, 6.5.8).

A few tentative solutions are offered below to these problems of infringement, but it is clear that legislative change at a national level (within the constraints of EU law) is needed before a records manager can lawfully deal with the large quantities of material for which he or she is responsible. Solutions which apply to just some individual files are of little value.

Directive 2001 (Information Society) art 5(3)(e)

6.5.6   Records management: copying

There is no exception in UK law which clearly covers copying for the routine purposes of records management: although back-up copies of computer programs may be made (see 6.6.2), the same does not apply to data. However, the impact of such copying on a rights owner is likely to be minimal. The courts occasionally recognize that 'technical infringements' are too trivial to be worth worrying about, and it is to be hoped that this would fall into that category. For Crown and NHS bodies there may be some help from the public proceedings exception (see 5.2.17).

1988 (CDPA) s50A; *Blair v Osborne and Tomkins*, 1971; *ZYX Music v King*, 1997

6.5.7   Records management: migration

The process of migration of electronic files is a much more significant issue for records managers. Migration can take two forms: conversion of the files to a new medium (for instance from tape to disk) and conversion of the data to a new format as computer programs are updated and replaced.

When records management is handled within the context of an archive, and the files are part of the permanent collection, the archive preservation exception (see 5.3.8) will apply to media migration at least on one occasion though whether it would allow repeated migrations is uncertain. There is no equivalent provision for files still held by the creating body, so records managers must hope that this too would be considered only a technical infringement.

Format migration raises more fundamental issues because the change to new operating systems and functional programs can have the effect of altering the actual data. If the result is that only a substantial part, rather than the whole, of a file has been copied the infringement could be said to be less but there is then raised the possibility that the author's moral right of integrity is infringed by a mutilation of the original work (see 8.1.7).

6.5.8   Records management: communication to the public

The communication to the public of works preserved in records management systems is likely to remain beyond the scope of any exception in national or European law. It is the electronic equivalent of publishing and goes far beyond what parliaments or governments are likely to force rights owners to accept. The same issues apply as to any other project to allow remote access (see 1.3.5, 6.5.2).

6.6   Computers and computer programs

6.6.1   Copyright protection

Computer programs and preparatory design material for them are literary works in copyright terms, and the normal rules apply. However, regulations have made some special provisions, which apply to computer programs of any date. An adaptation of a computer program means an arrangement or altered version or a translation (a conversion into a different computer language or code), and is an infringement if done without permission. It is not fair dealing to convert a program from a low-level to a high-level language (except as part of decompilation, see 6.6.2).

The circuit diagram for a computer or similar device is both a literary and an artistic work, as a compilation of notations for components and as a graphic work (see 2.1.2). There is no copyright in a computer programming language, which is regarded as being an idea or principle (see 2.1.4), nor in a command structure, which is seen as being a small language. When a computer program generates a graphic display which is static on the screen that display is an artistic work fixed (see 1.1.5) in the code. Icons used on on-screen buttons are also artistic works (see 2.3). However, a variable character-based display is not fixed and not artistic and so is not of itself a copyright work.

Commissioned programs will normally be the copyright of the programmer or his or her employer (see 3.2.12, 3.2.17–18). The programmer is unlikely to agree to a full assignment of copyright to the person commissioning it because so much programming is generic and must be available to the programmer for use on other projects, but a partial assignment or exclusive licence covering just the tailored parts, together with a licence for the rest, should be secured if possible (see 3.2.17, 3.3.8, 5.4.1).

1988 (CDPA) ss3(1), 21(3)(ab) and (4); SI 1992/3233 regs 3, 5, 7, 12; *Anacon v Environmental Research Technologies*, 1994; *Aubrey Max Sandman v Panasonic UK*, 1998; *Mackie Designs v Behringer*, 1999; *Navitaire v Easyjet Airline*, 2005; *Clearsprings Management v Businesslinx*, 2006

6.6.2   Lawful users

There are special provisions covering the activities of lawful users of a computer program. A lawful user is a person who has a right to use the program, by licence or otherwise. No licence or other agreement may restrict the freedom of a lawful user:

• to make any back-up copy necessary for his or her lawful use;

- to decompile the program, by converting it from a low-level to a higher-level language, and in the process to copy it.

A back-up copy is not 'necessary' in all circumstances. If, for example, the manufacturer of a CD-ROM has a policy of supplying replacement copies of disks that are damaged or have become unusable, there is no need to make back-up copies.

Decompilation is permitted only in order to obtain information to enable the user to create a new program which can operate with the original program or another one. It would be an infringement to decompile a program if the user already had the necessary information; did more than was necessary to obtain the information needed; supplied the information to someone else unless that was necessary to create the new program; or used the information to create a new program substantially similar to the original.

1988 (CDPA) ss50A and 50B, 296A; SI 1992/3233 reg 8; *Sony Computer Entertainment v Ball*, 2005

6.6.3 Lawful use

Lawful use permits a lawful user to observe, study or test the functioning of a program in order the discover the ideas and principles underlying it, so long as this is during the course of normal use of the program, and no licence may restrict this freedom.

A lawful user may also copy or adapt a program if that is necessary for his or her lawful use, but only provided such copying or adaptation is not prohibited by any licence or agreement. Any program or package that is bought for use on computers will come with a licence, and it is important to study the licence carefully to ensure that all required uses of the material are authorized. If variations are needed (for instance to allow more people to use the program or package at the same time) the licensor should be contacted and a revised licence purchased. It is normal for software to be supplied 'shrink-wrapped' on a CD-ROM, with a label saying that opening the wrapping indicates acceptance of the terms of a licence to use the software. This is legitimate so long as the user has the opportunity to read the licence before opening. If the licence cannot be read before the packaging is opened, the user cannot be contractually bound by it (see 5.4.1). If the user decides not to open the pack, for any reason, it may be returned. Online 'click-use' licences are similar.

1988 (CDPA) ss50BA, 50C; SI 1992/3233 reg 8; SI 2003/2498 reg 15; *Beta Computers (Europe) v Adobe Systems (Europe)*, 1996

6.6.4 Technological protection

Computer programs may be protected by anti-copying measures, which are themselves protected from circumvention (see 6.1.8).

7   Special cases

7.1   Records of local authorities

7.1.1   *Ownership of copyright*

In normal circumstances, a local authority will be the first owner of copyright in works created by its employees (see 3.2.12), including, for instance, employed officers of civil parishes. Where officers were not actually employed but were effectively volunteers, there might be complications (see 7.4). Moreover, many local authority files will contain material in the copyright of others (including the Crown). This might include letters received, invoices from suppliers, government circulars, advertising literature and so on. Material created by individuals and bodies working on commission for the authority will normally be the copyright of the authors (see 3.2.17), unless the contract contained an assignment of copyright to the authority (see 3.3.8). Archivists and records managers must be aware of the distinction between material which is and is not the copyright of their parent authority, and ensure that they do not commit an infringement by authorizing the publication (see 4.1.2, 5.1.3) or communication to the public (see 5.1.6) of works which are not in the authority's copyright (see 5.2.30).

7.1.2   *Pre-20th-century records*

Given that there was no provision for automatic ownership by employers of copyright in unpublished works until the passing of the 1911 Act (see 3.2.12), the strict ownership of copyright in records of 19th-century and earlier local administration could be very difficult to determine. However, in many cases the principles of equitable ownership might be useful (see 3.3.17–18): the author as legal owner of the copyright would be deemed to have been acting for the equitable owner (such as the parish or the union). This could apply, for instance, to records created by overseers of the poor, surveyors of highways, boards of guardians and other officers of local administration, and the equitable rights would since have descended to the present local authority.

On the other hand, a modern local authority is unlikely to have any claim to the copyright in records of a body such as a turnpike trust, a private institution that owed no duty to the parish. In such a case, copyright might have been owned jointly by the members of the board or might have belonged to the clerk (probably a local attorney) who did all the work. Local authority copyright ownership would apply only to records created after responsibility for a road had passed to a local highways board.

1911 s24

7.1.3   Local authority archivists

Local authorities in England and Wales are empowered by the Local Government (Records) Act 1962 to provide archive facilities, take records into their care, make them available to the public, provide finding aids to them, and exhibit them. However, the Act explicitly reminds local authorities, and their archivists, that it does not give authority to do anything that infringes copyright in the material held. The library and archive copying provisions (see 5.3.5ff.) thus apply, except in the case of material no longer in copyright, material in the copyright of the authority itself (see 7.6) or public records on deposit (see 5.3.1–2).

1962 s1(2)

7.1.4   Local government reorganization

In the many reorganizations of local government over the years, it has usually been possible to determine the identity of the successor to an authority that has been abolished; the copyright in works created by that abolished body would have passed to the successor along with the files. More recently, reorganizations have not been so clear cut and special provisions have had to be made. These are outlined below.

In any doubtful case, a local authority archivist or records manager should try to get hold of the relevant agreements and consult the authority's legal advisers. It is not possible to give general guidance which will cover every case. The duration of the copyright is as for any other works (see Chapter 2); the notional 'death' of an abolished authority has no effect on duration.

7.1.5   1974 reorganization in England and Wales

Under the Local Government Act 1972, the local government of England and Wales was radically reorganized with effect from 1974, creating new metropolitan counties and a new structure of county and district councils. In many cases, the transition from abolished to successor authority was sufficiently clear for there to be little doubt about the successor in title to the copyrights. Where necessary, local agreements were reached, and these should be on the files of the legal department of the successor authority. To give certainty in England, however, the Local Authorities (England) (Property etc.) Order 1973 provided for property (which would include copyright) of abolished authorities to be transferred to and to vest in successor authorities and for deeds and agreements (which would include assignments of copyright) in favour of abolished authorities to have full force in favour of successor authorities.

1972 s254; SI 1973/1861

7.1.6 1986 reorganization of metropolitan counties and London

The Local Government Act 1985 abolished, as from 1986, the Greater London Council and the metropolitan counties created in 1974, transferring their functions to the City of London and the district and borough councils which had previously formed the second tier or to residuary bodies which were required to distribute functions before they themselves were abolished. The Act also created joint authorities for such things as the fire and passenger transport services. For the most part property and rights (including copyright) passed to the successor authorities or residuary bodies, but the Local Government Reorganization (Property etc.) Order 1986 made further provision for property and rights, including the transfer of ownership of records. Detailed advice on any particular problem should be sought from the successor authority's legal advisers.

1985 (Local) ss62, 100; SI 1986/148

7.1.7 1995 reorganization in England

The Local Government Act 1992 provided for the review by a Local Government Commission of local government in England outside the metropolitan counties. The Commission could recommend the replacement of existing county and district authorities by single-tier authorities, and the Secretary of State could by order implement the change, with or without amendments. The Local Government Changes for England (Property Transfer and Transitional Payments) Regulations 1995 required successor authorities, where there was more than one, to reach agreement on the identification and future ownership of property and rights; if they could not reach agreement, the matter went to arbitration. Such agreements determine the ownership by the successor authorities of copyrights owned by the abolished authorities, and should be available for consultation in the successor authorities' legal departments.

The same regulations provided for agreements on the transfer of ownership in property contained in archival and local history collections, and related rights and liabilities. In this case, no agreement could specify more than one successor authority for any item in such a collection. Where the abolished authority owned rights, including copyright, in archival materials, therefore, those rights transferred with the documents.

1992 ss17, 19; SI 1995/402 regs 5, 6, 19

7.1.8 1996 reorganization in Wales

The structure of two tiers of counties and districts created for Wales in 1974 was amended in 1996 by the creation of single-tier counties and county boroughs. Property and rights (including copyright) of the abolished authorities passed to their successor authorities. Where public bodies were affected by the reorganization, they could make agreements with the successor authorities for the transfer or retention of property and rights (including copyright), copies of which should be available with the successor authorities' legal advisers.

1994 (Wales) ss17, 56

7.1.9   1975 and 1996 reorganizations in Scotland

Scottish local government was reorganized in 1975 by the Local Government (Scotland) Act 1973 into regions, islands areas and districts. The Act vested the records of abolished authorities in their successors, and the Local Authorities (Property etc.) (Scotland) Order 1975 provided for the transfer of property (including rights such as copyright) to the successor authority responsible for each function, unless successor authorities agreed a different distribution between themselves. Copies of such agreements should be available among the records of the legal advisers of those successor authorities. The regions and districts were abolished in 1996 by the Local Government etc. (Scotland) Act 1994, which created new single-tier local government areas. The Local Authorities (Property Transfer) (Scotland) Order 1995 required successor authorities to reach agreement on the distribution of property (including records) and rights (including copyright), and again such agreements should be available from the legal advisers.

1973 ss200, 222; 1994 (Scotland) s15; SI 1975/659; SI 1995/2499

7.1.10 Regional bodies in England

The unelected regional assemblies in England, outside London, are associations of relevant local authorities and other bodies. They employ their own staff and are capable of owning copyright in works they and their staff create (but see 7.4.2). The Greater London Authority is of a different nature but also owns its own copyrights, whether works were created by staff of the Mayor or the Assembly.

Regional development agencies are public records-creating bodies, but works created by them are not Crown copyright but copyright of the relevant agency.

1998 (Regional Development) s3; 1999 ss1, 67

7.2   Records of ecclesiastical and religious bodies

7.2.1   Ownership

The records of any ecclesiastical or religious body may have been created, collected and deposited (if they are in the diocesan or some other record office) by diocesan, parochial or other authorities. These authorities are the owners, and in some cases also the custodians, of the records themselves and thus have rights to exercise some control over such things as copying, publication and exhibition, irrespective of the copyright position. They may also be the owners of the copyright, but in many cases they will not be.

7.2.2 Church of England

The clergy of the Church of England and the Scottish Episcopal Church at all levels when occupying ecclesiastical offices (such as benefices and vicarages in team ministries) are regarded by the Church, and the courts, as ecclesiastical office-holders not as employees, serving God and the people. There is no employer, and there is no contract of employment, actual or implied, with the parish, the bishop, the archbishop or other Church authorities; a clergyman owes nothing but a duty of 'due' or 'canonical' obedience to an ecclesiastical superior. This means that the incumbent, not the Church, is the first legal owner of copyright in works of which, say, the vicar or curate is the author on behalf of a parish, such as correspondence. However, the copyright position is not necessarily quite that simple. It may be that the current rector, vicar or curate as the current office-holder, or the parochial church council as an undying corporation, might have a claim in equity to works created on behalf of the parish by an earlier incumbent (see 3.3.17, and see also 7.4). Whatever the precise legal position, for practical purposes archivists would be well advised to continue to regard the current incumbent as the first port of call in such cases.

Ordained clergy are capable of being employees, for instance as chaplains to schools. The position of individuals who are not ordained will depend on their particular circumstances. Many, such as secretaries, will have the status of employees (see 3.2.12), while a volunteer secretary or other officer will not (see 7.4). People such as lay readers might be employed; it depends on whether the church and the individual intended to create a legal relationship (see 3.3.8).

Canons Ecclesiastical C14(3); *In re Employment of Church of England Curates*, 1912; *Barthorpe v Exeter Diocesan Board*, 1979; *Diocese of Southwark v Coker*, 1997

7.2.3 Records of religious bodies other than the Church of England

The employment status of clergy in the Roman Catholic Church and the Church of Scotland, ministers of non-conformist churches, rabbis of synagogues, Sikh priests, Salvation Army officers and similar individuals is comparable to that of Church of England clergy (see 7.2.2). In each case, the intention when taking up office is to be under a spiritual rather than a legal obligation, so copyright is again likely to lie with individual authors rather than the religious body. However, for practical purposes the first enquiry should be addressed to any modern parent body or current senior figure (for example, the office of a bishop or archbishop or the headquarters of a church or religious organization), or to the current priest, minister, rabbi or other individual as appropriate.

Records of such bodies as synods, meetings of elders, boards of deputies and monthly meetings are created by volunteers in some cases (see 7.4), but in others by employees (see 3.2.12).

Scottish Insurance Commissioners v Church of Scotland, 1914; *Rogers v Booth*, 1937; *President of the Methodist Conference v Parfitt*, 1984; *Davies v Presbyterian Church of Wales*, 1986; *Santokh Singh v Guru Nanak Gurdwara*, 1990; *Birmingham Mosque Trust v Alavi*, 1992

7.2.4   Parish and non-parochial registers

The Church of England has recognized that there is no copyright at all in the contents of its registers of baptisms, marriages and burials for lack of originality (see 2.1.9). This applies both to an individual entry and to an entire register. There is thus no need to ask readers to complete a declaration form (see 5.3.15) when requesting copies. The registers of parochial baptisms and burials themselves are, however, the property of the incumbent of the parish, the churchwardens or the parochial church council, and they have the right to control access to and copying of them and especially commercial or extensive use, whether still in the parish or in a diocesan record office. Roman Catholic and Church of Scotland parochial registers and non-parochial registers are equally unoriginal, but similar permission should be sought from the priest, minister, clerk, rabbi or equivalent as owners of them. Any registers created since 1 January 1998 will presumably qualify as databases; as such there could perhaps be a copyright but probably not a database right in them (see 8.2). For local marriage registers see 7.3.13.

1812 s5; *Legal opinions concerning the Church of England*, p. 208e (Legal Advisory Commission of the General Synod).

7.2.5   Records of ministry

Works produced as part of his or her ministry by a clergyman, priest, minister, rabbi or other individual, such as the texts of sermons or prayers, should normally be regarded as the copyright of their author, in the same way as other literary works.

7.3   Legal records

7.3.1   Court-holding authority and judgments

The court-holding authority is the first owner of copyright in documents (such as indictments and enrolments) drafted by officials of any court of law who are employees of the authority (see 3.2.12). The court-holding authority is owner of the copyright in judgments delivered by the court. However, many judgments are published in court reports (see 7.3.5). If lengthy extracts are to be used from judgments, it would be as well to secure the permission of the individual judge (if he or she is still alive) as well as from the court-holding authority and (where appropriate) the publisher of the court report.

7.3.2 The Crown as court-holding authority

The Crown is (or was) the court-holding authority for the following categories of court in England and Wales:

- the Privy Council (for appeals from Commonwealth countries which still retain that link);
- the Court of Appeal (Civil and Criminal Divisions);
- the High Court (Chancery Division, Queen's Bench Division and Family Division and their predecessors);
- the Crown Court;
- assizes and quarter sessions;
- county courts;
- magistrates' courts (since 2005) (but see 7.3.3);
- tribunals.

Once the new Supreme Court is created to replace the Appellate Committee of the House of Lords (see 7.3.3) the Crown will be the court-holding authority since the Court's members will be office-holders of the Crown.

In Scotland, the Crown is the court-holding authority for the higher courts: the Court of Session, the High Court of Judiciary and the sheriff courts, and was the court-holding authority for the post-Reformation commissary courts. The Crown is the court-holding authority for all courts in Northern Ireland: the Court of Appeal, the High Court, the Crown Court, the county courts, and the magistrates' and coroners' courts.

2005 (Constitutional Reform) s23; *Crown Copyright in the Information Age*, Cm 3819 (1998)

7.3.3 Other court-holding authorities

Parliament is the court-holding authority for the Appellate Committee of the House of Lords (but see also 7.3.2), so works created by its members are in Parliamentary copyright (see 3.2.32). The court-holding authority for coroners' courts is the local authority. The court-holding authority for manorial courts was the lord of the manor (see 7.10). For ecclesiastical courts (including those of the pre-Reformation Church, the Church of England and the Church of Scotland), the court-holding authority was normally the appropriate bishop or archbishop, but see 7.3.4 for their probate jurisdiction.

Justices of the peace (magistrates) in England and Wales are officers of the Crown and any works created by them personally in that capacity are Crown copyright. However their clerks have not always been employees of any court-holding authority. Thus it appears that copyright in most magistrates' court (petty sessions, police court) records lies as follows:

- Until 1851 justices' clerks were all fee-paid in private practice, and themselves owned the copyright.
- Between 1851 and 1878 justices' clerks were increasingly employed by the local authority, so the copyright position varied from place to place.
- Between 1878 and 1951 all clerks were employed by the local authority, which was the court-holding authority.
- Between 1951 and 2005 clerks were employed by magistrates' courts committees as court-holding authority.
- Since 1 April 2005 the Crown is court-holding authority as the courts are now part of HM Court Service.

In Scotland the local authority was the court-holding authority for burgh, police and justices' courts, and is the authority for district courts.

1877; 1949 (Justices); 2003 (Courts)

7.3.4   Probate and inheritance

Until 1858 in England and Wales, jurisdiction over probate matters (the proving of wills and the granting of letters of administration) was handled by ecclesiastical courts scattered around the country. The most important of these were the prerogative courts of York and Canterbury. The ecclesiastical jurisdiction, together with the jurisdiction of some temporal peculiars, was abolished by the Court of Probate Act 1857, and replaced by a new civil court with one central and 40 district registries, whose records are Crown copyright. The records of the pre-1858 courts were transferred to the new registries and have since been deposited in record offices, but the Act made no mention of the ownership of those records or of any rights in them. That being so, the copyright in the records, including in letters of administration issued by the courts but not in wills proved by them (see 7.3.9), should be presumed to have transferred to the successor at law of the old courts, which is the Crown, although the copyright did not as a result become 'Crown copyright' (see 3.3.10). All such records are public records.

In Scotland, inheritance of movable property was dealt with by church courts until the Reformation, as in England and Wales. Jurisdiction over the inheritance of movable property passed to the commissary courts in 1563 and on their abolition in 1824 to the sheriff courts (see 7.3.2). Thus, the post-Reformation testaments confirming the execution of an estate are Crown copyright (but see 7.3.9 for wills). The feudal nature of land owning in Scotland means that the records relating to heritable property (primarily the register of Sasines and various Chancery records) are also Crown copyright.

In Ireland, as in England and Wales, ecclesiastical jurisdiction over probate was abolished in 1858, and a new Court of Probate established in Dublin, and after 1922 in Belfast. The pre-1858 records were deposited in the new probate registries 'so as to be easy of reference, under the control and direction of the Court', but almost all the original wills were lost in 1922. The copyright position in Northern Ireland is as for England and Wales; for the Republic see 7.7.1–5.

1823 s6; 1857 (Probate) ss3, 89; 1857 (Ireland) ss5, 6, 96; 1958 Sch 1 para 4(1)(n)

7.3.5 Court reports

There are two kinds of account recording what happened during a trial, and they have different copyrights.

- Published court reports, which appear in many published series and in some newspapers (see 11.4), are prepared by qualified barristers employed by the publishers. They record the significant elements of the cases made by counsel, and the reasoning and judgments of the judges. Those that appear after some delay are approved before publication by the judges, and so are regarded as authoritative statements of judgments for the purposes of precedent in later trials. For the most part they have no other official status and as reports they are the copyright of the publishers (who may be the Crown), but see 7.3.1 for the judgments themselves.
- Shorthand transcripts of the proceedings of the trial are taken by shorthand writers either employed directly by the court or employed by companies operating under contract with the court. The contracts reserve the copyright in the transcripts to the Crown.

7.3.6 Writs

Writs issued by a court in connection with civil proceedings are likely to involve two distinct copyrights. The form of the writ is Crown copyright; the Crown permits the copying of blank forms and their publication without formality. The details with which the form is completed (such as the reasons for suing someone) are the copyright of the author, usually the person issuing the writ or a solicitor. The reproduction of a completed writ thus requires the permission both of the author of the details and, in theory though not in practice, of the Crown. Writs issued by a court in criminal proceedings are Crown copyright, and permission will be required in most cases for the copying or publication of them.

7.3.7 Affidavits and witness statements

The first owner of the copyright in affidavits and witness statements will not always be easy or even possible to determine, but under the Act the position will be as follows:

- If a document was recorded in the deponent's own words, the deponent will have been the first owner of the copyright (see 2.2.8).
- If a document was drafted by, for instance, a solicitor or police officer (see 3.2.18, 7.3.10–11) using the ideas of the deponent but not reproducing his or her precise words, the writer (or the writer's employer) will have been the first owner of the copyright (see 2.2.9, 3.2.12).
- If a document was drafted before 1 August 1989 'under the direction or control of Her Majesty' it is Crown copyright. Thus an affidavit or witness statement made before that date on the direction of a court of which the Crown was the court-holding authority (see 7.3.2) will be Crown copyright, regardless of who actually did the recording.

In practice, it will often be impossible to determine the precise circumstances in which such a document was created. Unless internal or other evidence suggests a different author or first owner, therefore, it would normally be appropriate to treat the deponent or the deponent's employer as the author and first owner.

7.3.8 Exhibits

The copyright status of exhibits filed for or produced during court proceedings will normally be unchanged by their use for that purpose, and the court will normally have no more right to the copyright in them than does the depositor in a record office of letters he or she has received. However, if before 1 August 1989 the Crown was the first publisher of unpublished exhibits or other works, they became Crown copyright (see 3.2.28).

7.3.9 Wills

It is normally assumed that the testator is the author of a will for copyright purposes and that the testator's legal heirs will be the owners of the copyright in the text, whether the original or a registered copy. This may or may not strictly be the case. In fact, authorship and first ownership of copyright in a will, and of any codicils, will depend on the circumstances in which they were drafted (see 2.2.14).

If the testator drafts or dictates the precise terms of the will or codicil, he or she is the author and ownership of the copyright will lie with him or her and subsequently with the legal heirs. If, however, the will or codicil expresses the intentions of the testator but is drafted in the words of a solicitor or some other person, that person will be the author and first owner of the copyright unless he or she is the employee of the testator at the time of drafting, and that person's legal heirs will be the present owners of the copyright unless it was assigned elsewhere.

In practice, it is likely to be impossible to determine the circumstances in which a particular will or codicil was drafted. Any successors of a solicitor would be hard pressed to prove their right to the copyright, and the testator's legal descendants are likely at least to have a claim in equity (see 3.3.17). Unless there are clear indications to the contrary, therefore, it will normally be reasonable to regard the testator's direct descendants (if they can prove their descent) as the current owners of the copyright.

For the effect of a will on the copyright in any items bequeathed see 3.3.

7.3.10 Metropolitan Police

The records of the Metropolitan Police Service up to the establishment of the Greater London Authority are public records. Where works were created by the Service they are all now the copyright of the Metropolitan Police Authority. The Authority has no objection to the use of copyright material for the purposes of research or private study. The use of copyright material for academic, educational, charitable or other non-profit-making purposes (including use on non-commercial radio) is permitted, so long as the following acknowledgement is used (with appropriate amendment as necessary):

> Material in the [name of the Record Office] in the copyright of the Metropolitan Police Service is reproduced by permission of the Metropolitan Police Authority.

The use of copyright material for any commercial or profit-making purpose (including commercial radio) and for television requires the permission of the Departmental Record Officer, Metropolitan Police Service, 20th Floor, Empress State Building, Lillie Road, London SW6 1TR.

7.3.11 Other police forces

Copyright in material created by police authorities other than the Metropolitan Police is the property of the relevant authority.

7.3.12 Records of civil registration

The civil registration of births, deaths and marriages has been compulsory in England

and Wales since 1837, in Scotland since 1855 and in Ireland since 1864 (with the exception of non-Roman Catholic marriages, which were registered from 1845), and in civil partnerships in the UK since 2005. The registers are not public records, so there is no right of access to or copying of them on those grounds (see 5.3.1). The Crown claims the copyright in the design of the register volumes and certificates (extracts in Scotland) as artistic works (see 2.3.2), not in the information, so no restriction is placed on the transcription and publication of the information obtained from them. The registers are unpublished; artistic copyright in those created before 1989 will not expire until 2039 at the earliest if they are engravings (see 2.3.21) but expires 50 years after creation if they are not engravings (see 2.3.20). The certificates are published, so copyright expires 50 years after issue (see 2.2.23, 2.3.20). However, reproduction of certificates could qualify as fraud, a criminal offence, so great care needs to be taken. Guidance on the Crown copyright in certificates and registers has been issued as Guidance Note 7 and is available online (see 3.2.28 and also 7.3.13).

1836 (Births) ss18, 30, 43; 1844 ss3, 64; 1854 ss26, 46; 1863 (Births) s30; 1953 ss25, 37; 1958 Sch 1 para 2(2)(b); 1965 (Scotland) ss13, 22, 53; 2004 (Civil Partnership) ss30, 98, 155–156; SI 1976/1041 regs 34, 38–39, 45; SI 2005/3176 regs 13–17

7.3.13 Records of registration of marriage

Whereas the registration of births and deaths is a purely civil matter, the registration of some marriages is handled by people other than the registrars. The copyright position remains the same (see 7.3.12), but in some cases the position over the supply of copies does not.

In England and Wales since 1837, marriages have been solemnized in register offices, parish churches, Friends meeting houses and Jewish synagogues, and in certain categories of licensed premises, notably churches of other denominations and more recently in places such as hotels and stately homes. For marriages in licensed premises the local registrar attends and the registers remain in his or her custody. However, registers are supplied in duplicate to Church of England parish clergy, clerks of meetings and secretaries of synagogues by the Registrar General. Only one is returned when complete to him, the other being retained locally or in the custody of the diocesan record office. The person having custody of a local register may issue a marriage certificate, and a Church of England parish clergyman and the chief officer of a diocesan record office may make copies from registers in their custody. See the Guidance Note referred to in 7.3.12.

In Scotland, marriages have also been solemnized in churches, Friends meeting houses and synagogues, and more recently in other places, but the marriage is authorized by the issue of a schedule by the registrar which is signed at the ceremony and returned to the registrar who then completes the register. The records thus all remain in the hands of the registrar.

In Ireland, the registration of all but Roman Catholic marriages began in 1845. As in England, duplicate registers were supplied to and kept by clergy of the United Church of England and Ireland, Presbyterian ministers, clerks of meetings and secretaries of synagogues, and they were authorized to supply certified copies. The arrangements for the registration of Roman Catholic marriages from 1864 were similar to those in Scotland. The marriage registers of most religious denominations in Northern Ireland are now held by the Public Record Office of Northern Ireland but there is no special provision allowing copying of them.

1836 (Marriage) s23; 1836 (Births) ss30, 35; 1844 ss63, 65, 68; 1854 s46; 1863 (Marriages) ss11–12; 1949 (Marriage) ss63–65; 1977 (Marriage) ss8, 15; 1978 (Parochial) ss6, 10, 14, 16–18, 20

7.4 Office-holders and members

7.4.1 Ownership of copyright

There can be no doubt that, in accordance with the statute, the author is the first owner of the copyright in a work created by a person acting in a voluntary or honorary capacity (for instance, as an office-holder or member) for an organization or individual, or working under an express or implied contract for services (that is, as a contractor not an employee) (see 3.2.17–18). In practical terms, though, this can at times be nonsense, and equity rather than strict law may provide the answer (see 3.3.17 and 7.4.3).

7.4.2 Members of representative bodies

Members of representative bodies including Parliament, the Scottish Parliament, the National Assemblies of Wales and Northern Ireland, and local and regional authorities and assemblies, when acting in their capacity as members, are first owners of the copyright in their works. If they take on a post under a contract of service they are employees and the employing body is the first owner, but the mere holding of an office, such as chairman or leader of the council, would not normally be under such a contract. If an MP, peer, member of the Scottish Parliament or of the National Assemblies of Wales or Northern Ireland becomes a government minister, minister of the Scottish Administration or Assembly secretary, all the works they create in that capacity (including, for instance, ministerial speeches) are Crown copyright. Copyright in works created by the same individuals in their constituency capacities (including, for instance, constituency and election speeches) would be owned by the author. See also 3.2.32–36.

7.4.3 Honorary and voluntary office-holders

Honorary and voluntary, and in some cases stipendiary, office-holders are not normally employees; it depends on whether they intended to have a legal relationship with the body concerned. If not employees they are, strictly, the first owners of the copyright in the works they produce in that capacity. This would include, for example, honorary secretaries and treasurers of charities and learned societies, secretaries to parochial church councils and perhaps unpaid clerks to poor law unions. In practice, few are likely to have assigned their copyright to the body for which they act but most would probably regard the body as having some rights over the material or even as being the copyright owner. In such cases, the bodies might be able to exercise rights in equity (see 3.3.17 and 7.4.1), and for practical purposes they should be regarded as the point of contact for archivists.

Barthorpe v Exeter Diocesan Board of Finance, 1979

7.5   Public records

7.5.1   Special provisions

Special copyright provisions for the copying of public records are described in 5.3.1–2. Special dispensations for Crown copyright material in public records are described in 5.4.2–5.

7.5.2   Census returns

Returns of decennial censuses of population for all parts of the UK are public records and Crown copyright literary works. Many local record offices and libraries hold microfilm copies of some of the returns, which are made available for public inspection. The original returns for England and Wales, 1841–1901, are held by and made available in The National Archives and online. Those for Scotland, 1841–1901, are held by, and available on microfilm at, the General Register Office (Scotland) in Edinburgh. The few surviving 19th-century returns and the returns for 1901 for Northern Ireland are held by and available on microfilm at the Public Record Office of Northern Ireland in Belfast. All these records, except for those in Scotland which are not preserved in a 'public record repository', are covered by the waiver of Crown copyright in public records (see 5.4.3).

7.5.3   Census returns: Ireland

The few surviving 19th-century returns of decennial censuses of population, and the returns for the 1901 and 1911 censuses, for areas now in the Republic of Ireland, are now in the National Archives of Ireland in Dublin. Under the terms of the Copyright Act 1911 they are, and continue to be (at least in theory), Crown copyright. Later censuses are covered by legislation of the Irish Free State and the Republic of Ireland, and the copyright belongs to the Irish Government (see 7.7.1–5).

1911 s18; 1927 ss168, 174(1)

7.6   Records of a repository's parent institution or authority

7.6.1   Ownership of copyright

Except in the case of public records, there are no special copyright provisions for the records of a repository's parent institution or authority. This means that the repository is not entitled to copy or license the reproduction of any material among the records of the parent institution or authority which is the copyright of an individual or another institution (for instance letters received), except as this is permitted under the general provisions for copying and publication or the special provisions for libraries and archives (see 5.2 and 5.3).

7.6.2   Guidance from management

An archivist who is responsible for the care of the records of a parent institution or authority should secure guidance from senior management on the use of material among the records that is in the parent institution or authority's own copyright. This guidance should certainly include authority to supply copies to users, so as to reduce the burden of compliance with the special regulations for copying by libraries and archives (see 5.3), and might extend to explicit authority to grant licences for the use of copyright material.

7.7   British Isles outside the UK

7.7.1   Republic of Ireland: copyright history

The Copyright Act 1911, when it was passed, applied to southern Ireland as part of the UK. When the two Parliaments for the south and north were established by the Government of Ireland Act 1920, copyright was a subject reserved by Westminster. That Act was repealed by the Irish Free State (Consequential Provisions) Act 1922 (session 2), and under the Irish Free State (Agreement) Act 1922 and the Irish Free State Constitution Act 1922 (session 2), the south became a self-governing dominion within the British Empire. The 1911 Act applied to self-governing dominions only if their local legislatures decided that it should, and local legislatures could amend or repeal that or any other Westminster copyright legislation so long as no existing rights were prejudiced. The Irish Free State duly provided its own copyright law by the Industrial and Commercial Property (Protection) Act 1927 which applied retrospectively as from 6 December 1921, but material created before that date continued to be protected under the 1911 Act. The Republic of Ireland ceased to be a dominion in 1949 by the Ireland Act 1949, and since then the Republic has twice passed new copyright legislation: the Copyright Act 1963 (see 7.7.4) and the Copyright Act 2000 (see 7.7.5). Strong similarities to the law in the UK remain, however, because the law of the Irish Republic is rooted in the common law tradition (see 1.1.1, 1.2.2), and both countries are now required to implement the harmonized aspects of European law, such as those for the duration of copyright (see 1.2.8).

1911 ss25, 26; 1920 s4(1); 1927 s174

7.7.2   Republic of Ireland: 1911 Act

The provisions of the Copyright Act 1911 continued to apply in the Republic, in particular to the subsistence of copyright and the ownership of it in works created in Ireland before 6 December 1921 (but see 7.7.5). This means that, for works to which the Act continues to apply:

- the first owner of a commissioned engraving, photograph or portrait is normally the person who commissioned it (see 3.2.20);
- where a testator who was the author bequeathed to a particular person or institution a manuscript of a work, the ownership of the manuscript is taken to be prima facie proof of ownership of the copyright, unless the copyright was explicitly bequeathed elsewhere (see 3.3.3); and
- there is no protection for films as such, but those that can be shown to be original dramatic works are protected as dramatic works, and each frame is protected as a photograph (see 2.4.1).

1911 ss5(1)(a), 17(2), 35(1) 'dramatic work'; 1927 s174(1)

7.7.3   Republic of Ireland: 1927 Act

The 1927 Act was very similar to the 1911 Act. It covered works created by citizens of the Irish Free State, works published in the State and works created or published elsewhere if there was reciprocal protection, if they were created after 6 December 1921. Some of the provisions that were continued from the 1911 Act, and that may still be significant (but see 7.7.5), are those applying to the following:

- commissioned engravings, photographs and portraits (see 3.2.20);
- the employer as the first owner of the copyright of a work produced in the course of employment (see 3.2.12);
- reversionary interests in assigned copyrights (see 3.3.12);
- presumptions about the ownership of copyright in a bequeathed manuscript (see 3.3.3);
- authorship of photographs (see 2.3.7); and
- films as original dramatic works (see 2.4.1).

Significant differences are:

- The right of the copyright owner to control the translation of his or her work into the Irish language expired ten years after first publication, unless the owner had arranged for such a translation to be published within that period.
- The ownership of all infringing copies of a work that infringed the whole or a substantial part of another person's copyright belonged to that person.
- Crown copyright was replaced by a Government copyright, owned by the Government of the Irish Free State. This applied to any work prepared or published by or under the direction or control of the Provisional Government or any minister or department (from 6 December 1921 onwards); and to any work prepared, printed or published by or under the direction of the Government of the Irish Free State, any minister or department, or by or under the authority of the Stationery Office. The reference to the Stationery Office meant that any work (including the original manuscript) by a private author became the copyright of the Government if it was officially published.

1927 ss154(2)(a), 158, 160, 167(2), 168, 171, 177 'dramatic work'

7.7.4 Republic of Ireland: 1963 Act

The 1963 Act in the Republic of Ireland was closely modelled on the UK's 1956 Act, much of the text having been copied word for word. As a result, most of what this book says about parts of the 1956 Act that are still in force may also apply to the Republic, for works created during the period from 1 October 1964 (when the 1963 Act came into force) to 1 January 2001 when the 2000 Act came into force (but see 7.7.5). It should, though, be borne in mind that as the jurisdictions are separate, court judgments in Ireland may have differed from those in the UK. Some significant differences between the statutes are:

- 1956 Crown copyright provisions (see 3.2.28) are replicated for the benefit of 'the Government' of the Republic.
- The 1956 provisions for the copying by institutions such as libraries, museums and archives of works over 100 years old (see 5.3.11) and for their publication (see 5.4.23) are not included, so archivists and publishers in the Republic may not rely on them.
- A literary, dramatic, musical or artistic work was published even if reproductions of an insubstantial part were issued to the public.

1963 ss3(1, 2), 51; SI 1964/177 (Ireland)

7.7.5 Republic of Ireland: 2000 Act

Copyright in the Republic of Ireland has since 1 January 2001 been governed by the Copyright and Related Rights Act 2000 as amended. The Act updates the law to take account in a single statute of technological developments, changes arising from European Union directives and changes in international law, but there are still very close family similarities to the UK statute, and some provisions are identical. For one significant amendment of the Act in relation to exhibitions, see 4.2.2.

There are special provisions in the Irish Act, with prescribed conditions including the use of declaration forms as in the UK, for the copying of works in the permanent collections of prescribed archives and libraries for non-commercial curatorial purposes. These cover copying for insurance, security, cataloguing, exhibition, for the supplying of copies of certain works to other similar institutions and for preservation purposes. Works in archives and libraries which in the UK are called unpublished works are described as works which have 'not been lawfully made available to the public' (as they have not been made available to the public with the rights owner's explicit permission, and so cannot have been published), a very different use of the expression 'made available to the public' from that used in the UK (see 4.1.10). There is no exclusion preventing the copying of artistic works by archives and libraries, nor is there any limitation of research in these institutions to non-commercial research. Instead, the archives and libraries supplying the copies must be 'not conducted for profit', a quite different interpretation of the directive from that adopted in the UK. For the comparable UK provisions see 5.3.

Fair dealing is very similar to the UK provision, except that fair dealing for the purposes of commercial research is not explicitly excluded, and the work must have been made available to the public if fair dealing for research and private study (but oddly not criticism and review, see 5.2.10) is to apply. Instead the Act adopts part of the Berne Convention's three-step test (see 5.2.1), specifying that use must be 'for a purpose and to an extent which will not unreasonably prejudice the interests of the owner of the copyright'. This test appears to be even more subjective for users to apply than the UK's non-commercial one (see 5.2.8). The reprographic copying of sheet music is not permitted under fair dealing for research or private study.

Duration of copyright in unpublished works is either the same as was provided for in the 1963 Act or 50 years after commencement of the 2000 Act (that is, to 31 December 2051), whichever is earlier. This could in some cases lead to an even longer term than for similar works in the UK (for which see especially 2.2.17).

Government and Oireachtas copyrights are much the same as Crown and Parliamentary copyrights in the UK.

There is no copyright in a film as such made before 1 October 1964, but there is copyright in the individual frames as photographs and, where appropriate, in the film as a dramatic work.

Directive 2001 (Information Society) art 5(2)(c); 2000 (Ireland) ss40, 50, 59–70, 191–193, Sch. 1 paras 3(5), 30(2); SI 404/2000 (Ireland); SI 427/2000 (Ireland) regs 3(1), 6, Sch 2 form B; SI 16/2004 (Ireland) reg 6

7.7.6 Channel Islands

The Channel Islands are a group of dependent territories of the British Crown, outside the UK, the EU and the EEA (see 1.2.8), and outside the terms of the TRIPS Agreement (see 1.2.5), though to some extent bound by treaties made by the UK. Each of the Islands has its own form of government. Jersey continues, so far, to apply a version of the Copyright Act 1911 but is expected to acquire new legislation in 2007; the Bailiwick of Guernsey (including Alderney, Sark and other smaller islands) has however passed a new Copyright Ordinance. Both bailiwicks are planning to come within TRIPS when they have amended all their relevant legislation.

7.7.7 Jersey

For Jersey, the 1911 Act has some significant differences from the 1988 Act in force in the UK, so the advice in this book should be used only with caution there. Some significant variations in the 1911 Act are:

- Although there is a defence of fair dealing for private study, research, criticism, review or newspaper summary, there are no specific provisions for archival copying.
- The standard term of protection is life of the author plus 50 years. Protection in the UK for a work originating in Jersey will be for this shorter period (see 1.2.10).
- The first owner of a commissioned engraving, photograph or portrait is normally the person who commissioned it (see 3.2.20).
- Where a testator who was the author bequeathed to a particular person or institution a manuscript of a work, the ownership of the manuscript is taken to be prima facie proof of ownership of the copyright, unless the copyright was explicitly bequeathed elsewhere (see 3.3.2).
- Copyright in photographs is for 50 years from the date of taking, and the first owner of the copyright is the owner of the negative (see 2.3.7).
- There is no protection for films as such, but those that can be shown to be original dramatic works are protected as dramatic works (see 2.4.1).
- A map, chart or plan is a literary work, not an artistic one.
- Even though computer programs did not exist in 1911, they have been found to fall within the definition of a literary work in Jersey.

1911 ss2(1)(i), 3, 5(1)(a), 17(2), 21, 35(1) 'dramatic work', 'literary work'; *Oliver v ABN-Ambro Bank*, 1995; *Comprop v Moran*, 2002

7.7.8 Bailiwick of Guernsey

For the Bailiwick of Guernsey, the new Ordinance (which came into force on 1 January 2006) is very similar, and is for the most part identical, to the latest version of the UK's

1988 Act, so much of this book is directly applicable. Important points to note, though, are:

- Duration of copyright in literary, dramatic, musical and artistic works, of any date, is for the 70-year term with no special provisions for older unpublished works, so archivists have many fewer copyright problems.
- Authorship of works created before 2006 is determined for everything but moral rights by the 1911 Act provisions, which means that for photographs the author was the owner of the negative, even for purposes of duration (compare 2.3.7).
- There is no copyright in a film as such (but see 2.4.1), a broadcast or a typographical arrangement created or published before 2006.
- Crown copyright applies as in the UK, with the standard term of duration, and it vests in the Receiver General of the Bailiwick, but copyright in works created under the direction or control (see 3.2.28) of the States and other official bodies (but not in commissioned works) belongs to the States as States copyright for 50 years after creation.
- Reversionary interests (see 3.3.12) may be assigned since 1 January 2006.
- Provisions covering copyright in documents bequeathed are the same (see 3.3.2–5) except that the 1911 Act (see 3.3.3) applies for works created up to 31 December 2005 and the new Act applies thereafter (see 3.3.4).
- The normal fair dealing provisions apply, with one significant addition. It may be fair dealing to use a work for any purpose so long as the two tests for the effect on the rights owner contained in the Berne Convention's three-step test (see 5.2.1) are passed. The Ordinance gives guidance on the issues to be taken into account: whether the use is commercial; the nature of the work used; the quantity and substantiality of what is taken; the effect of the use on the market for the source work and on its value; and the availability of a commercial copy.
- Provisions for library and archive copying are very similar to those in the UK, but the implementing regulations (which will, for instance, define a prescribed archive) have yet to be passed.

Ordinances to cover other rights have also been passed, based where appropriate on relevant EU directives, covering databases, performance rights, registered and unregistered designs and trade marks.

2005 ss34–36, 50–57, 115, 189, 191, Sch 1 paras 6–9, 11, 17–18, 23–24

7.7.9   Isle of Man

The Isle of Man is a self-governing possession of the Crown with its own legislature, outside the UK, the EU and the EEA (see 1.2.8). The Isle of Man is however a party to the World Trade Organization and thus to the TRIPS Agreement (see 1.2.5), which requires compliance with most of the Berne Convention, and it has special agreements which ensure reciprocal treatment for its nationals and nationals of EU and EEA countries. It has its own Copyright Act of 1991, largely identical to the UK Act of 1988, which came into force on 1 July 1992. The Isle of Man and the EU have given mutual recognition to protection of databases made by their citizens, in accordance with the EU's database directive.

Significant differences from the current UK legislation include:

- The standard term of copyright is life of the author plus 50 years. Protection in the UK for a work originating in the Isle of Man will be for this shorter period.
- Copyright in unpublished literary, dramatic and musical works expires on 31 December 2042 at the earliest.
- There is no limitation of 'research' under either fair dealing or library and archive copying.
- Cable programmes are separately protected from broadcasts and there is no infringement by 'communication to the public' so use of a work on the internet will probably infringe by inclusion in a cable programme.
- The public records copying exception applies to records in the Public Record Office, General or Diocesan Registry or the Manx Museum.
- Crown copyright vests in the Treasury or (for maps) the Department of Local Government.
- Unpublished literary, dramatic, musical and artistic works of any date, and published works since 1 July 1992 made under the direction or control of the Tynwald are Tynwald copyright for 50 years from creation.

1991 ss12, 20, 29, 37–43, 49, 156–158, Sch 1 paras 12, 38–42; EC Council decision 2003/239/EC; SI GC 316/92; SI 2003/2501 regs 3–5

7.8 Electoral registers

7.8.1 Copyright status

There are no special copyright provisions for electoral registers, so they are covered as published literary works (see 4.1.6, 7.8.5) by the relevant general provisions of the various Copyright Acts. Their preparation and use are governed by the electoral legislation in force at the time they were compiled. The restrictions imposed by the latest legislation apply only to registers compiled after 16 October 2002 in England and Wales and after 18 November 2002 in Scotland and Northern Ireland, but data protection requires restrictions on earlier ones nevertheless.

SI 2002/1871 reg 2(2); SI 2002/1872 reg 2(2); SI 2002/1873 reg 2(4)

7.8.2 Author and first owner

Electoral registers were first compiled under the Representation of the People Act 1832, and the arrangements were improved by the Parliamentary Voters Registration Act 1843. Under both, lists were prepared by overseers of the poor in the shires and the boroughs, posted in public places for inspection, and passed to the clerks of the peace (for the shires) and town clerks (for the boroughs). The lists were then amalgamated into registers and printed for sale. All registers created before 1 July 1912 are likely to be published works of unknown authorship, in which copyright has expired (see 2.2.19). If the author is known, the continuation of the copyright would depend on his date of death (see 2.2.10).

A legal opinion of the Treasury Solicitor in 1924 decided firmly that under the Copyright Act 1911 (and thus also under the 1956 Act) electoral registers were Crown copyright (see 3.2.28). In consequence, all registers created between 1 July 1912 and 31 July 1989 as published works are out of copyright once they are over 50 years old. Registers made after 1 August 1989 will be copyright of the local authority, with duration based on the life of the registration officer who is 'an officer of the council', an employee.

1983 s8; TNA: T 161/241, file S25383

7.8.3 Current registers

Registers are prepared each year in accordance with the provisions of the Representation of the People Act 1983 as amended by the Representation of the People Act 2000 and implementing regulations. As soon as a new register comes into use, the previous one lapses (see 7.8.4). The 2002 Regulations have created a two-tier structure with full and edited versions of the register; electoral registration officers may not make the full registers available to the public generally except under suitable supervision. Amending regulations in 2006 have clarified that copies of full registers in England, Wales and Scotland may be supplied to a public library (statutory library authority in Scotland) or local authority archive service for public use under supervision. Users may only make handwritten notes and are not permitted to make copies, and may not search electronic versions of the register by names of individuals. Supervision must be to a standard to ensure that these requirements are met and the Electoral Commission has urged electoral registration officers to offer help with defining the appropriate level of supervision. The full edition of all the registers will be available in the British Library in paper and digital forms, and in digital form also in the National Library of Scotland and the National Library of Wales. They may be consulted under the same conditions as in other libraries.

Regulations specify the fees for the sale of copies of the edited register but also provide that any person may make a copy (whether handwritten or by other means) of the whole or part of it.

SI 2001/341 regs 7, 93, 97, 97A–B, 107, 109A; SI 2001/400 regs 7, 43, 91; SI 2001/497 regs 7, 43, 96 108; SI 2002/1871 regs 6, 10, 15; SI 2002/1872 regs 6, 9, 14; SI 2002/1873 regs 6, 13, 21; SI 2006/752 regs 16, 21; SI 2006/834 reg 19

7.8.4 Past registers

The latest regulations have said nothing about access to electoral registers made before autumn 2002. However, they have specified that full registers made since then may be consulted and copied once they are ten years old for research (including historical research) purposes only, under the conditions specified in the Data Protection Act 1998 (see 8.7.2). It seems that it is intended that earlier registers should be subject to the same rules in order to comply with data protection law. Edited registers that have lapsed have no special status, and it is difficult to see why copying that is permitted when they are current should cease to be permissible thereafter.

SI 2002/1871 reg 2(2, 3); SI 2002/1872 reg 2(2, 3); SI 2002/1873 reg 2 (4, 5); SI 2006/752 reg 21(9, 10); SI 2006/834 reg 19(9, 10)

7.8.5 Publication and duration

All electoral registers that are in force are published, in the sense both of the Representation of the People legislation and of the copyright legislation, with consequential implications for the duration of copyright (see 7.8.2).

1988 (CDPA) s175; SI 1986/1081 regs 51, 53–54; SI 2001/341 reg 43(1, 1A), 97A–B; SI 2001/400 reg 43; SI 2001/497 reg 43; SI 2002/1871 reg 10; SI 2002/1872 reg 9; SI 2002/1873 reg 13; SI 2006/752 reg 16

7.9 Business records

7.9.1 Complexity

Copyright in the records of companies and other business enterprises, especially if they are defunct, is likely to be complex. Material which was created by employees of the company, including copies of out-letters, design drawings, reports to shareholders, some publicity material and some accounts, will be the copyright of the company if created on or after 1 July 1912, but may be owned by descendants of the author if created before then (see 3.2.16). However, letters and orders for goods received by the company, accounts prepared by external accountants, publicity material prepared by external consultants, and most commissioned reports are all likely to be the copyright of their respective authors, unless the business has been far-sighted enough to secure assignments. The ownership of the physical items (see 3.2.3), and even the right to use them for the purposes for which they were prepared (such as an advertising campaign) (see 3.2.18, 3.3.17), do not affect the copyright position. Archivists should thus ensure that they secure authority for the copying, publication and exhibition of material that is the copyright of the depositor, and preferably obtain an assignment of the copyright, but must remember that the permission of other individuals or bodies will often still be required.

7.9.2   Directors

Copyright material produced by the directors of companies can present special problems. Until the 1980s the courts seem to have treated all directors alike, as managers not employees. Since then the position has been less clear-cut. A few directors are employees, acting under a contract of service (see 3.2.12). In such a case, any material they produce in accordance with that contract will be the copyright of the company. Most directors, though, have no formal contract and the copyright status of any works they produce will not be easy to determine. There are three broad categories into which work by such a director might fall:

- General management. A director as manager is unlikely to be an employee, and will probably be owner of copyright in works of which he or she is the author.
- Regular non-management tasks performed for the company. The products of such work are likely to count as being produced in the course of employment, unless any contract explicitly provides otherwise.
- Occasional non-management tasks performed for the company. The ownership of copyright in the products of this sort of work will depend on the particular circumstances. If the director was paid a fee to undertake a certain project or has personally received royalties for its exploitation, the copyright would be treated as belonging to the individual. In the absence of such indicators, a director might be regarded by a court as being merely the trustee for the company as the equitable owner of the copyright (see 3.3.17), or might be treated for this purpose as an employee.

It is quite possible for even the sole owner of a company to be an employee as well as a director. The law regards the company and the individual as distinct entities, so an owner, as representing the company, can give instructions to himself as employee.

Unless the copyright ownership is clear, an archivist would probably be best advised to treat the company (or its current successor) as the first point of contact.

Normandy v Ind Coope, 1908; *Antocks Lairn v I Bloohn*, 1972; *Roban Jig and Tool Co v Taylor*, 1979; *Gardex v Sorata*, 1986; *Ultraframe UK v Fielding*, 2003

7.9.3   Defunct companies

Most companies become defunct by being taken over or going bankrupt. In the former case, the copyrights owned by a company will simply be among the property purchased by the new owner, while in the latter case the receiver will sell the copyrights along with the other property so as to realize as much as possible in order to pay off the company's debts. If the assets have been sold off piecemeal, it may not be easy to trace the new copyright owners; the receivers are likely to be the best source of information. If a company is dissolved with no outstanding debts there may be no successor company. In that case, the remaining assets including the copyrights become *bona vacantia* (see 3.3.19).

7.10   Estate and manorial records

7.10.1   Ownership of the records

Under the Law of Property Act 1922 and the Manorial Documents Rules 1959, as amended, manorial documents created before 1923 are protected so that so far as possible they are preserved in good condition and in facilities which allow access to them for legal purposes. Ownership of them may lie with the present lord of the manor (if any), with an earlier lord of the manor, or with some other person to whom they have been sold, and control of them remains with the owner even if they are deposited in an approved place of deposit under the Rules. Those who need to consult the records for legal purposes are entitled to do so, but inspection and copying for historical research purposes of deposited records is possible only with the consent of the lord of the manor. Thus there are hurdles to be surmounted over the ownership, care and control of the records themselves before the question of ownership of the copyright in them is considered. However, neither the 1922 Act nor the Rules apply to deeds and other evidences of title or to non-manorial estate records.

SI 1959/1399; SI 1963/976; SI 1967/963

7.10.2   Copyright

The normal rules for the ownership of copyright in documents apply to estate and manorial records: it should not be assumed that the owner of the records or the present owner of the estates to which they refer necessarily owns the copyrights (see 3.2.3). The present and previous owners of the estates will presumably own the copyright in materials that they created themselves or that were created by employees such as secretaries, bailiffs or stewards, though only the larger estates are likely to employ such people nowadays and the rules for employer ownership may apply only to works created after 1 July 1912 (see 3.2.16). The present owner of the estates will probably own no copyright in the records of his or her predecessors, and the owner of the records will probably own no copyrights at all, unless they have been assigned to him or her by the previous copyright owner or they have passed by inheritance or bequest (and such transfers will in any case not cover all the different copyrights likely to subsist in the records) (see 3.3). Where titular lordships of the manor have been sold but with no title to the relevant estate, no copyrights are likely to have been transferred.

7.10.3 Contracts for services

Many, and perhaps in recent times even most, estate documents were drafted for the landlord by lawyers, surveyors, architects, accountants and others. Such people were, for the most part, self-employed professionals not employees of the landlord, and as such were working under contracts for services (see 3.2.17–18). They will normally have retained their copyright in any works of which they were the authors, including, for example, title deeds and accounts.

7.11 Hospital and medical records

7.11.1 National Health Service to 1990

Most records created within the National Health Service until 1990, with some exceptions as noted below, are Crown copyright. Where hospitals and other bodies which were absorbed into the National Health Service in 1948 owned the copyright in their records and those records passed to the NHS, that copyright passed to the Crown. It did not, as a result, become 'Crown copyright', however (see 3.3.10), and the duration will be determined as if the copyright were still privately owned. All these records, whether created before or after 1948, are likely to contain material that was not created by the NHS or the body that originally owned them; items such as letters received, for instance, will be the copyright of the authors.

1946 ss6, 69; SI 1948/567; SI 1948/1292

7.11.2 National Health Service since 1990

Since 24 July 1990 in Scotland and 1 April 1991 in England and Wales, copyright in works created within National Health Service bodies (regional health authorities, district health authorities, special health authorities and NHS trusts) or by their employees has belonged to the individual bodies, not the Crown.

1990 (NHS) ss32, 60, Sch 6 para 21; SI 1990/1329; SI 1990/1520

7.11.3 National Health Service medical staff

Most staff working within the NHS, including consultants and other specialist staff within hospitals, are employed by the relevant authority or trust under standard terms and conditions of service appropriate to their positions. Copyright in works produced by them in accordance with those terms is owned by the Crown (see 3.2.28) or the authority or trust as appropriate (see 3.2.12–17). Many such staff, however, are also permitted to carry out private work so long as it does not conflict with their NHS duties; material produced as a result of such private work will normally be the copyright of the individual.

Doctors, dentists and opticians providing NHS primary care services are normally working in private practice under a contract for services with the NHS. Copyright in works produced by them will normally be owned by the individual. In some cases they are employed by a company or other body which has the contract with the NHS, in which case the copyright will be owned by the employing body.

7.11.4 Private health care services

Copyright in records created in private practices and private institutions (such as hospitals and clinics) will be owned by the institutions or individuals concerned, depending on the circumstances in each case. Property, including copyrights, owned by hospitals not absorbed within the NHS in 1948 remained with the governing bodies of the institutions or the local authority, as appropriate.

1946 s6

7.12 Maps, charts and plans, together with engravings and prints

7.12.1 Copyright status

The copyright positions of maps and related material (including charts, plans, architectural drawings and elevations, and at least some engineering drawings) and of engravings and other forms of print (see also 2.3.2), was decidedly tangled until the passing of the 1988 Act. They are all now classified as artistic works, and this has significant implications for an archivist's freedom to make copies from them (see 5.3.18). Ordnance Survey maps are Crown copyright (see 3.2.28); until 1923 they were printed from engravings, and this would be important for any unpublished maps printed before that date because it means that they remain in copyright (see 7.12.7). Under some circumstances a map might also be classified as a compilation of data (places, names, heights and so on), which is a form of literary work (see 2.2.3).

It should be borne in mind that an 'engraving' may be both the printing plate or equivalent and the print or other work taken from it. The type of work which can be covered is surprisingly wide: a frisbee is an engraved 'print'.

James Arnold and Co v Miafern, 1980; *Geographia v Penguin Books*, 1985; *Wham-O Manufacturing v Lincoln Industries*, 1985

7.12.2 Protection before 1912: engravings and prints

Prior to 1912, published maps, charts, plans, engravings, lithographs and prints were protected by the Engraving Copyright Acts 1734 and 1766 and the Prints Copyright Act 1777. These Acts together provided copyright protection for any published 'historical print, or any print or prints of any portrait, conversation, landscape or architecture, map, chart or plan, or any other print or prints whatsoever'. To qualify for protection the plate and each print had to carry the date of publication and the name of the proprietor.

From 1842, works that did not qualify might have gained protection under the Literary Copyright Act if they were described and treated appropriately (see 7.12.3). Works that did qualify and that were described and treated by their publishers as engravings continued to enjoy protection under the 1734, 1766 and 1777 Acts. Protection under these Acts was for 28 years after the year of publication. Works that were not published were potentially protected by the common law (see 1.2.2). Works still in copyright on 1 July 1912 (whether published or unpublished) were protected thereafter by the provisions of the 1911 and subsequent Acts (see 7.12.5–6).

1734 s1; 1766 s1; 1777 s1; 1852 s14; *Stannard v Harrison*, 1871

7.12.3 Protection before 1912: maps as 'books'

Maps, charts and plans that were separately published and that were described as such by their publishers were included in the definition of 'books' in the Literary Copyright Act 1842, 'for maps are intended to give information in the same way as a book does'. They therefore had to be registered at Stationers' Hall (see 1.2.1). This provision was alongside that still provided by the Engravings Acts (see 7.12.2), so works that were illustrations to books and thus not separately published could have been protected by those Acts instead, if they met the qualification requirements. Under the 1842 Act, protection for works published during the life of the author was for seven years after the death of the author or 42 years after publication, whichever was later, and for works first published after the author's death, 42 years after publication. Works still in copyright on 1 July 1912 were protected thereafter by the provisions of the 1911 and subsequent Acts (see 7.12.5–6).

1842 ss2, 3; James LJ in *Stannard v Lee*, 1871, at 349

7.12.4 Drawings for engravings from 1862

The unpublished drawings on which published maps, charts, plans and engravings were based were first given statutory protection by the Fine Arts Copyright Act 1862. Protection was for seven years after the death of the author so long as they were registered. Those that were unregistered had limited but perpetual protection under the common law (see 1.2.2). Those that were still in copyright or that were covered by the common law on 1 July 1912 were protected thereafter as artistic works under the 1911 and subsequent Acts (see 7.12.5–6).

1862 s1

7.12.5 Protection since 1912: engravings and prints

Under the Copyright Act 1911, all published and unpublished engravings (including etchings, lithographs, woodcuts, prints and other similar works that were not photographs, but excluding any that were maps, charts or plans, see 7.12.6), were classified as artistic works. This included relevant works created before 1 July 1912 that were in copyright on that date under earlier Acts (see 7.12.2–4). Those that were still in copyright on 1 June 1957, and all engravings made between that date and 31 July 1989, were given special provision by the 1956 Act for the duration of copyright. All engravings made since 1 August 1989 have been treated in the same way as all other artistic works. If the copyright under the 1956 provision would expire later than it would under the amended 1988 Act, then it still applies. For guidance on the duration of copyright in these works see 2.3.12–16, and for Crown copyright works 7.12.7.

1911 ss3, 35(1) 'literary work', 'artistic work', 'engraving'; 1956 s3(4)(a)

7.12.6 Protection since 1912: maps, charts and plans

Under the Copyright Act 1911, all maps, charts and plans (whether printed from engravings or not, and whether published or unpublished) were defined as literary works. This included relevant works created before 1 July 1912 that were in copyright on that date under earlier Acts (see 7.12.2–4). Those that were still in copyright on 1 June 1957 were reclassified as artistic works by the Copyright Act 1956. All maps, charts and plans created since that date are also artistic works. All were treated in the same way as other artistic works except that those which were engravings were given special provision by the 1956 Act for the duration of copyright. For guidance on the duration of copyright in these works see 2.3.12–16, and for Crown copyright works 7.12.7.

1911 ss3, 35(1) 'literary work'; 1956 ss3(1), 48(1) 'artistic work', 'drawing'

7.12.7 Crown copyright

All Crown copyright (see 3.2.28) maps (including Ordnance Survey maps) and engravings are now artistic works. For the duration of copyright in these works see as follows:

- engravings created before but unpublished on 1 August 1989: 2.3.21;
- engravings created and published before 1 August 1989: 2.3.22;

- other maps, charts and plans, and drawings for engravings (whether published or unpublished), created before 1 August 1989: 2.3.20;
- unpublished works created on or after 1 August 1989: 2.3.26;
- published works created on or after 1 August 1989: 2.3.27–28.

Artistic works may not generally be copied by libraries and archives (see 5.3.18). However, the Ordnance Survey has made an agreement with the Libraries and Archives Copyright Alliance (LACA) to permit limited copying in libraries and archives of its copyright printed mapping for purposes of private study, non-commercial research, criticism, review, current news reporting and parliamentary and judicial proceedings. A poster is available from the Ordnance Survey which should be displayed by any copier which is used by members of the public who are permitted to copy maps. In addition, the Ordnance Survey has agreed that librarians and archivists may make copies for users on terms similar to those for library copying of published works (see 5.3.12). Copies may be made for the purposes of private study or non-commercial research and users must pay a reasonable fee to cover at least the cost of production of the copy. A declaration form may be used if desired. For the most part only a single copy of 'a reasonable proportion' of a map is permitted but 'in appropriate circumstances' (such as for inclusion in a thesis) the Ordnance Survey will not object to up to four copies being made of an area up to 625 cm^2 (the area of an A4 sheet). Whether the copying is by the user or the librarian, each copy must be accompanied by an acknowledgement (unless such an acknowledgement is impossible for reasons of practicality or otherwise) (see 5.2.7): '© Crown copyright. Reproduced by permission of Ordnance Survey.' Further information about the agreement can be obtained from CILIP (see 5.3.12) or the Map Department at the British Library (96 Euston Road, London NW1 2DB, or www.bl.uk/ then links to Maps).

The Ordnance Survey will issue licences for copying for commercial purposes (including planning purposes), and has prepared tailored ones for different sectors including local authorities and universities. Information about such licences may be obtained from Ordnance Survey at Romsey Road, Southampton SO16 4GU, on its customer helpline (08456 050505) or www.ordnancesurvey.co.uk/.

1988 (CDPA) s39(2)

7.12.8 Relationship to design right

Some works described collectively as maps, charts and plans, notably but not exclusively engineering and architectural drawings, will also qualify for protection as designs, which could have implications for the copyright in them (see 8.6 and especially 8.6.5).

7.12.9 Enclosure awards and maps

Enclosure awards and maps made by assistant commissioners, their valuers and surveyors under the 1845 and later general Enclosure Acts are Crown copyright. Copyright in most such maps will have expired, but that in the awards is likely still to subsist (see 2.2.21, 2.3.20–21). Copyright in other awards and maps may be less easy to determine. Where commissioners were appointed they would have shared the copyright as joint authors of the award, even if it was actually written by a clerk (see 2.2.6, 2.2.21, 3.2.7). However, the map is likely to have been prepared by a surveyor, who would have been the author and first owner of the copyright in it (see 2.3.6, 2.3.12–13). Crown copyright in the Enclosure Acts themselves expires 50 years after the year in which each Act received Royal Assent (see 2.2.23, 3.2.28). Those awards and maps that are in The National Archives are public records; where local record offices have copies of them The National Archives, Kew, would have no objection to further single copies being made for research or private study purposes (see 5.3.24). Locally deposited contemporary copies of the maps, including copies to be found, for instance, among court records, are subject to the control of the relevant archive once any remaining copyrights have expired.

7.12.10 Tithe apportionments and maps

The Tithe Commissioners and their assistant commissioners were all public servants, and the apportionments and maps prepared by them are (or were) all Crown copyright (see 2.2.21, 2.3.20–21). In those cases where a map originally prepared for another purpose was used as the tithe map, the copyright would have been owned by the surveyor (see 2.3.6, 2.3.7, 2.3.12–13). Those apportionments and maps that are in The National Archives are public records; where local record offices have copies of them The National Archives, Kew, would have no objection to further single copies being made for research or private study purposes (see 5.3.24). Locally deposited diocesan and other contemporary copies of the maps are subject to the control of the relevant archive once any remaining copyrights have expired.

7.12.11 Valuation Office maps

Maps and related field books created under the Finance Act 1910 by the Valuation Office are (or were) all Crown copyright (see 2.2.21, 2.3.20–21). They are also all public records.

7.13 Transport records

7.13.1 Copyright ownership

Most transport records were created by private companies, and copyright will lie with the creators or their successors (see 7.9). Copyrights owned by companies nationalized under the Transport Act 1947 passed to the British Transport Commission. These companies included almost all railway companies, together with the canal and docks companies that they had established or taken over, and companies involved in long-distance road haulage. Most of the haulage companies were sold off again, with their copyrights, from 1953 onwards.

7.13.2 Railways and canals

The copyrights in most railway and canal companies passed to the British Railways Board, which assigned some of them elsewhere:

- Copyright in records of canal companies is now administered by the Head of Archives and Records, The Waterways Archive, The Boat Museum, South Pier Road, Ellesmere Port, Cheshire CH65 4FW.
- Copyright in railway company and British Railways works of art, posters and photographs is now administered by the Picture Librarian, Science and Society Picture Library, Science Museum, Exhibition Road, London SW7 2DD.
- Copyright in railway company pseudo-heraldic devices, monograms and similar works is now administered by the National Railway Museum, Leeman Road, York YO26 4XJ.
- Copyright in most other records of railway and canal companies and in other records of the British Transport Commission or the British Railways Board is administered by the Secretary, British Railways Board (Residuary) Ltd, Whittles House, 14 Pentonville Road, London N1 9HF.
- Copyright in the records of London Transport is administered by London's Transport Museum, Covent Garden Piazza, London WC2E 7BB.

8   Other intellectual property rights

8.1 Moral rights

8.1.1 Definition

Moral rights are the rights, even more intangible than copyright, which attach to the author's personality as expressed in his or her work. They recognize that the products of the human mind and spirit are so closely tied to the personality of the author that protection is needed, since the corruption of the one inevitably damages the other. They are of great importance in some parts of Europe, notably France and Germany, but are of much less significance in the UK where emphasis has traditionally been given to economic rights rather than the personality of the author (see 1.1.1). As a result, they were not for the most part recognized in the UK until the passing of the 1988 Act. Some of the elements of moral rights were covered by such things as the law of defamation, but copyright law was silent on the subject except through the creation by the 1956 Act of a civil offence of false attribution of a copyright literary, dramatic, musical or artistic work. Action had to be taken in 1988 in order to bring the UK into line with the provisions of the Paris Act (1971) of the Berne Convention (see 1.2.5). The result is a group of rights strictly limited in application and scope, which apply to the author as an individual. They are the right of attribution (to be identified as the author); the right of integrity (to object to changes to the work); the right to object to false attribution; and (not really a moral right at all) the right of privacy of a person who commissions certain photographs or films.

For moral rights in performances see 8.5.3.

1956 s43

8.1.2 Importance for archives

For the most part moral rights will not have a direct bearing on the work of archivists but they could affect anyone wishing to publish or exhibit a copyright work, and since archivists may at times wish to do both things, and will be called upon to advise others who wish to do them, they must be aware of them. Moral rights in the UK are hedged about with many limitations and exceptions, not all of which can be described in this book. Those that seem likely to be of concern to archivists are mentioned, but careful study of the statute, or a good guide to it, is advisable for anyone who needs more detailed knowledge.

8.1.3 Authors and types of work

Moral rights apply only to literary, dramatic, musical and artistic works and to films. They do not apply to sound recordings, except where a work covered by a moral right is reproduced in a sound recording. Two of the rights (attribution and integrity) apply to authors, while the other two (false attribution and privacy) apply to any person. An author is determined solely under the terms of the 1988 Act, and not under those of the Act in force at the time the work was made. This is of particular significance for photographs where for moral rights purposes the photographer is always the author (see 2.3.7). For films, the author's rights apply to the principal director, not (say) the author of the screenplay and not the producer. Note that authors and directors have the rights of attribution, integrity and false attribution even if they are acting in the course of employment, though the rights are quite likely to be restricted (see 8.1.6, 8.1.8).

1988 (CDPA) ss77(1), 80(1), Sch 1 para 10

8.1.4 Duration and waiver

All moral rights, except the right relating to false attribution, subsist for the same period as the copyright. The right relating to false attribution ends 20 years after the person's death. Moral rights may not be assigned to anyone else but they may be waived, temporarily or permanently. They are inherited by the person's personal representatives or as directed in a person's will, except that the right relating to false attribution may only be inherited by the person's personal representatives.

1988 (CDPA) ss86, 87, 95

8.1.5 Right of attribution

The author of a copyright literary, dramatic, musical or artistic work and the principal director of a copyright film has the right in certain circumstances to be identified as the author or director if the work (or a substantial part of it) is published commercially (see 4.1.4), performed in public or broadcast, issued to the public as part of a film or sound recording, or, in the case of an artistic work, exhibited in public. Before it can be enforced the author or director must previously have asserted the right (unless the work is in Crown or Parliamentary copyright, see 8.1.6, and see also 3.4):

- by including a statement of authorship in an assignment of copyright, in which case the assignee (and any successors) is bound by the assertion;
- by signing an instrument in writing, in which case anyone to whose attention the assertion is brought (for example, anyone reading a book, through a statement at the front) is bound by it;

- for an artistic work that is publicly exhibited, by attaching the author's name to the original or a copy made under the author's direction, or to a frame or mount, in which case anyone into whose hands the work comes is bound by the assertion, regardless of whether it is still visible;
- for an artistic work of which copies are publicly exhibited, by including an assertion in a licence authorizing the copying, in which case the licensee and anyone in possession of such a copy is bound by the assertion, whether or not they have been told about it.

Archivists would be well advised to acknowledge the author of a work without worrying about whether the right has been asserted. In this context it will normally be better to do something than nothing. The most likely time this will be needed is during the exhibition of artistic works; all that is required is a reasonably prominent caption giving the name of the artist.

1988 (CDPA) ss77–78, 89(1)

8.1.6 Right of attribution: exceptions

The right does not apply in the following cases:

- to the author of a literary, dramatic, musical or artistic work who died or the director of a film that was made before 1 August 1989;
- to anything permitted under an assignment or licence from the copyright owner of a literary, dramatic, musical or artistic work created before 1 August 1989;
- to the author of a piece of music or of the words of a song when the work is performed in public, or broadcast;
- to a computer program, the design for a typeface or a computer-generated work;
- where the employer of the author or director was the first owner of the copyright and approved its publication or use;
- to a work in Crown or Parliamentary copyright, unless the author or director is identified in or on published copies of the work; no other assertion by the author is then required;
- to any work made for the reporting of current events;
- to publication in a newspaper, magazine or collective work of reference (for instance an encyclopedia or collection of essays) of a literary, dramatic, musical or artistic work created for that purpose or made available with the consent of the author for that purpose.

1988 (CDPA) ss77–79, Sch 1 para 23; SI 2003/2498 Sch 1 para 18

8.1.7 Right of integrity

The author of a copyright literary, dramatic, musical or artistic work and the director of a copyright film have the right in certain circumstances to object to derogatory treatment of the whole or part of the work. Derogatory treatment means additions and alterations to, deletions from or adaptations of the work (except translation of a literary or dramatic work or transcription of a musical work) which distort or mutilate it or are otherwise prejudicial to the honour or reputation of the author or director. The work may apparently, however, be destroyed in its entirety without infringement of the right, since nothing then remains to prejudice the author. It is possible for an author to object to a treatment which is prejudicial but which is not a distortion or mutilation, but not to a mutilation or distortion if it is not prejudicial. The author must persuade the court that his or her view of the effect of the treatment is reasonable, which appears to be a high hurdle. The right may be exercised if the altered work is published commercially (see 4.1.4), performed in public or broadcast, issued to the public as part of a film or sound recording or, in the case of an artistic work, exhibited in public.

There have so far been few cases considering the right of integrity in the UK, and in none has prejudice been found. In one, minor amendments and colour changes to a promotional leaflet did not amount to derogatory treatment, and the judge explicitly made a comparison to a judgment in France where the colourization of an entire black and white film was derogatory. Other cases have considered a reduction in the size of cartoons reproduced in a book and meaningless words added to a recording of a piece of music.

1988 (CDPA) ss80, 89(2); *Huston v Turner Entertainment*, 1992; *Tidy v Trustees of the Natural History Museum*, 1998; *Pasterfield v Denham*, 1999; *Confetti Records v Warner Music UK*, 2003

8.1.8 Right of integrity: exceptions

The right does not apply in the following cases:

- to the author of a literary, dramatic, musical or artistic work who died or the director of a film that was made before 1 August 1989;
- to anything permitted under an assignment or licence from the copyright owner of a literary, dramatic, musical or artistic work created before 1 August 1989;
- to a computer program or a computer-generated work;
- where the employer of the author or director was the first owner of the copyright and approved the treatment, so long as the author or director has not been identified as such (see 8.1.5); however, even if the author or director has been identified, the right does not apply if a 'sufficient disclaimer' is also published;

- to a work in Crown or Parliamentary copyright, unless the author or director is identified in or on published copies of the work (see 8.1.5), and even then it does not apply if the altered work contains a 'sufficient disclaimer';
- to any work made for the reporting of current events;
- to publication in a newspaper, magazine or collective work of reference (for example an encyclopedia or collection of essays) of a literary, dramatic, musical or artistic work created for that purpose or made available with the consent of the author for that purpose.

A 'sufficient disclaimer' means a clear and reasonably prominent indication in the publication or film, alongside the name of the author or director, that the work has been subjected to treatment to which the author or director has not consented.

1988 (CDPA) ss81, 82, 178 'sufficient disclaimer', Sch 1 para 23; SI 2003/2498 Sch 1 para 18

8.1.9 False attribution

Any person has the right not to have the whole or part of a literary, dramatic, musical or artistic work or a film falsely attributed to him or her as author or director. The right is infringed if a person issues to the public copies of a work bearing the false attribution; exhibits in public an artistic work bearing a false attribution; performs in public or broadcasts a literary, dramatic or musical work as being the work of someone when the infringer knows it is not; and shows in public or broadcasts a film as having been directed by someone when the infringer knows it was not. The right applies to literary, dramatic, musical and artistic works of any date, and to films made on or after 1 August 1989. The right has had a longer life than other moral rights in UK law, having appeared in the 1956 Act, and is related to the long-standing concept of passing-off (see 8.6.9). As the Master of the Rolls said as long ago as 1842: 'A man is not to sell his own goods under the pretence that they are the goods of another man; he cannot be permitted to practise such a deception.'

1956 s43; 1988 (CDPA) ss84, 89(2), Sch 1 para 22(2); Lord Lauderdale MR in *Perry v Truefitt*, 1842, at 752; *Noah v Shuba*, 1991

8.1.10 Right to privacy of certain photographs and films

Any person who, on or after 1 August 1989, commissions the taking of a photograph or the making of a film for private and domestic purposes has the right not to have copies of the whole or any substantial part of the work issued to the public, or the work exhibited, shown in public or broadcast. The intention is to protect, for instance, wedding photographs, but note that the right belongs to the person commissioning the images who is not necessarily the subject. A similar right existed under the common law for a work created before 1 August 1989.

It may be that data protection could be used to stop a photographer publishing or exhibiting his or her pictures of people if they were not taken on commission (see 8.7.2), but there is also little to stop a photographer publishing or exhibiting non-intrusive pictures of people and other pictures, such as pictures of a record office, whether commissioned or not, unless an obligation of confidence can be established (see 8.7.3–4).

1988 (CDPA) ss85, 89(1), Sch 1 para 24; *Pollard v Photographic Co*, 1889; *Stedall v Houghton*, 1901

8.2   Databases and database right

8.2.1   *Origin*

As a result of an EU directive (see 1.2.8), the Copyright and Rights in Databases Regulations 1997 created a right called database right. This gave particular rights to the creators of databases and changed the nature of copyright protection for them. Databases may now attract database right, or be protected by copyright as literary works, or both. The database right (see 8.2.7) applies to the investment involved in obtaining, verifying and presenting the contents of the database, while copyright in a database (see 8.2.4) applies to intellectual creation in the database's design and the selection of its contents. Neither affects the continuance where appropriate of the quite distinct rights in the individual items making up the contents of the database which will in many (but not all) cases be copyright works themselves, with a variety of copyright owners. Clearance to use material in a database may thus not be simple to obtain. Also, many databases are used to store information (including photographs) about individuals. If those individuals are still living, the Data Protection Act will apply (see 8.7.2). Unless otherwise stated, the comments below relate to a database itself and not to the items making up its contents.

SI 1997/3032

8.2.2   *Definition*

A database, whether protected by copyright or database right or both, is a collection of independent works, data or other materials which are arranged in a systematic or methodical way and are individually accessible by electronic or other means. The Regulations offer no other definition, but the directive on which they are based provides that a recording, or an audiovisual, cinematographic, literary or musical work as such (for instance a CD of songs, a single film, a novel or a symphony) is not a database. A database need not be on or for use on a computer: it could be a card index, a filing system or perhaps even a microfilm. Many works previously regarded as compilations (see 2.2.3) are now databases, including (it would seem) catalogues, encyclopedias, most CD-ROMs and (perhaps) internet websites. If it attracts copyright, the database as a whole is a literary work even if it consists of non-literary works, such as pictures, numbers or passages of music. A computer database program is not, in itself, a database; it becomes one only when it is structured by the user (the maker) as required, and data are added. The program is separately protected (see 6.6.1).

Directive 1996 recitals 17, 19; 1988 (CDPA) s3A(1); SI 1997/3032 reg 6

8.2.3 Copyright: databases created before March 1996

Any database that was entitled to copyright protection before 1 January 1998 and that was completed on or before 27 March 1996 continues to enjoy copyright protection for the full term as a literary work. To qualify, it would merely have to be an original compilation (see 2.1.9).

SI 1997/3032 reg 29

8.2.4 Copyright: databases created after March 1996

A database that was created on or after 27 March 1996 qualifies for copyright protection as a literary work only if it satisfies a special definition of originality that applies in the UK solely to databases. It is original only if by reason of the selection or arrangement of the contents it constitutes the author's own intellectual creation. This means that there must be an individual who was the author of the database, so an anonymous database (as for example one created by a group of unnamed individuals working for a company) is unable to attract copyright. Moreover, the database cannot be copyright if it is in a standard form and there was no intellectual creativity in the selection of the contents; the author must have created it him or herself using his or her own skill and ingenuity. Thus a database would probably not qualify for copyright if it were a simple card index of basic data, a microfilm of a single class or series of documents, a telephone directory in alphabetical order, or if it were constructed on a commercially available program using straightforward data. On the other hand, an encyclopedia, a classified directory or a carefully designed CD-ROM containing a selection of hitherto unrelated documents or images which together form a genuinely creative work could qualify for copyright protection as databases. There is little case law on this as yet, but it is thought to be likely that relatively few databases will pass the test in future.

1988 (CDPA) s3A(2); SI 1997/3032 regs 6, 29

8.2.5   Copyright: duration and author

Any copyright in a database has the same duration and authorship as for any other literary work, whether in private, Crown or Parliamentary copyright (see 2.2.16ff.). In many cases, a database will be a work of joint authorship (see 3.2.7), but, where individual parts can be securely attributed to particular authors, those parts will be protected as works of those authors alone. If an older database is anonymous, as will happen in many cases, copyright in it will last for the same time as for any other anonymous literary work.

8.2.6   Copyright: rights and exceptions

If a database qualifies for copyright protection, for the most part the owner of the copyright enjoys the same rights and the user of the database enjoys the same exceptions as for any other literary copyright work (see 5.1, 5.2). However:

- the use of data from a database does not infringe copyright in the database itself unless the form or arrangement of the database or a substantial part of the selection of the contents is also taken; and
- any user who is entitled to use the database may do anything which is required for the purpose of gaining access and using the contents of the database without infringement of the copyright in the database, and no agreement or contract can prohibit or restrict this freedom.

Directive 1996 recital 38; 1988 (CDPA) s29, 50D; SI 1997/3032 regs 8, 9

8.2.7   Database right

Database right is a property right that subsists in a database if there has been a substantial investment in obtaining, verifying or presenting the contents of the database. It may apply to any database that was completed on or after 1 January 1983 and that qualifies for protection. A database qualifies for protection if its maker, or one or more of its makers, was an individual resident in the EEA (see 1.2.8) or a body operating in an EEA state. The investment in a database may be substantial in qualitative or quantitative terms, or both, and it may consist of the investment of financial, human or technical resources. It seems that what is 'substantial' in this context would vary: a substantial investment by a big company would have to be bigger than one by a small company (see 8.2.9).

- Investment in obtaining data means gathering data together from external sources but not creating it in the first place: no matter how much has been invested in creating data, that investment will not help in establishing database right. The

European Court of Justice has decided that a database will be protected only if its creation was an end in itself, not a means to some other end. The right, it seems, is intended to encourage innovation in developing databases, not to assist other activities which happen to depend on databases. As a result the scope of the right is quite narrow: only databases of collected items, such as photographs, seem likely to be protected.

- Verification involves checking data obtained or already in the database for accuracy even if few changes have to be made as a result.
- Presentation means making the data more accessible to the user but must be distinguished from the separate rights, if any, of the owner of a computer database program.

1988 (CDPA) s172A; SI 1997/3032 regs 18, 30; *British Horseracing Board v William Hill*, 2005

8.2.8 Database right: maker

The maker of a database is the first owner of the database right in it. The maker is the person who takes the initiative in obtaining, verifying or presenting the contents, and takes the risk of investing in the database, and may thus be a company or other body as well as an individual. An employer is the maker of a database that was made by an employee in the course of employment, and the Crown is the maker of a database made by an officer or servant of the Crown in the course of his or her duties. The two Houses of Parliament, separately or together, are makers of databases made under their direction or control. A database is made jointly if two or more people shared the work and the risk. Database right may be assigned or bequeathed by the maker in the same way as copyright (see 3.3).

SI 1997/3032 regs 14, 15, 23

8.2.9 Database right: restricted acts

Database right restricts the unauthorized extraction or re-utilization (directly or indirectly) of all or a substantial part of the contents of a database. In this context:

- extraction means the permanent or temporary transfer of contents to another medium by any means or in any form, such as the making of individual copies of extracts;
- re-utilization means making contents available to the public by any means (see 4.1.10);
- substantial may be assessed in terms of quality, quantity or both (compare 5.2.3–6); in quantitative terms, substantial must be assessed in relation to the rest of the

database: a substantial part of a very large database would have to be much bigger than a substantial part of a small one; in qualititative terms, substantial must be assessed in relation to the investment in obtaining, verifying or presenting what has been taken: if that investment was not substantial (see 8.2.7) the material taken is not a substantial part; and

- the repeated and systematic extraction or re-utilization of insubstantial parts of the contents may amount to a substantial part (as defined above), so the extraction of a little each day may not be allowed without permission.

Directive 1996 art 7(2); SI 1997/3032 regs 12, 16; *British Horseracing Board v William Hill*, 2005

8.2.10 Database right: duration

Database right expires at the end of the year 15 years after the database was completed. However:

- database right in a database completed between 1 January 1983 and 31 December 1997 lasts for 15 years commencing on 1 January 1998;
- when a database is made available to the public (see 4.1.10) while database right in it still subsists, a new period of 15 years commences from the year in which it was first made available; and
- any substantial change to the contents of the database, including accumulated additions, deletions or alterations, that amount to a substantial new investment qualify the resulting database for a new period of protection for 15 years. The new period of protection will probably not apply, though, to unamended data if they can be distinguished.

The effect of this is that database right in a database subject to repeated substantial new investment (see 8.2.7) could be perpetual.

SI 1997/3032 regs 17, 30

8.2.11 Database right: assumption as to expiry

If the database has no label or other mark identifying the maker and it is not possible to discover the identity of the maker by reasonable enquiry, and it is reasonable to assume that database right has expired (that is, that it was completed more than 15 years ago), it is not an infringement of the right to extract or re-utilize substantial parts of the contents.

SI 1997/3032 reg 21

8.2.12 Database right: lawful users

A lawful user is a person who, by licence or otherwise, has a right to use the database. It seems reasonable to assume that the lawful purchaser of a database (such as a CD-ROM) is a lawful user, but it is far from clear how many of that purchaser's friends would qualify. Certainly, if an organization buys a database it needs to ensure that it has any appropriate licences to cover use by its staff. For the most part, anyone allowed access to an archive or library will be a lawful user of a database that is legitimately made available there. However, with some electronic databases, whether or not a person is a lawful user might depend on the terms of any licence obtained by the library or archive to cover its use. Lawful use of a database available across the internet will depend on the terms and conditions of access (if any) to the relevant website. If a person is a lawful user of a database that is available to the public (see 4.1.10) in any manner under a licence or other agreement, no condition may be placed on that user by the licence or agreement to restrict his or her freedom to extract or re-utilize insubstantial parts of the contents.

SI 1997/3032 regs 12, 19(2)

8.2.13 Database right: permitted uses: insubstantial parts

A lawful user of a database which has been made available to the public in any manner (including to only a limited segment of 'the public', see 4.1.10) shall be entitled to extract or re-utilize insubstantial parts of the contents for any purpose. As usual, insubstantial must be considered in qualitative or quantitative terms, or both (see 5.2.3–6), but could be quite a lot if the database is large (see 8.2.9).

SI 1997/3032 reg 19(1)

8.2.14 Database right: permitted uses: fair dealing

Database right in a database that has been made available to the public in any manner (including to only a limited segment of 'the public', see 4.1.10) is not infringed by fair dealing with a substantial part of the contents by a lawful user for the purpose of illustration for teaching or research, so long as it is not for any commercial purpose and the source is indicated. It is as yet unclear what 'illustration' in this context means. The supply of extracts (in whatever form) from a database to illustrate a class or lecture in a school or university would presumably qualify, and it may be that use of such extracts for examination purposes would too. Use of extracts for commercial training courses, on the other hand, is not fair dealing. There is no certainty as to whether 'illustration' also qualifies research; if it does, it is far from clear what would be permitted. Commercial research cannot be fair dealing (see 5.2.8).

SI 1997/3032 reg 20(1)

8.2.15 Database right: permitted uses: public lending

The public lending of a database (for example, on a CD-ROM) is not an infringement of database right, provided it is not lent for direct or indirect commercial advantage and it is lent by an establishment that is accessible to the public. The charging of a fee for the service is permitted, so long as it covers only the costs of the establishment. The use that the borrower makes of the database, of course, is a different matter. This exception does not apply to on-the-spot reference use of a database, so a library or archive needs the maker's permission or a licence to make available a database for reference use.

SI 1997/3032 reg 12(2–4)

8.2.16 Database right: permitted uses: public administration

Database right is not infringed by anything done for the purposes of parliamentary or judicial proceedings or the reporting of those proceedings, nor by anything done for the purposes of a royal commission or statutory inquiry or the reporting of their proceedings that were held in public.

All or a substantial part of the contents of a database that are open to public inspection under statute or are on a statutory register may be extracted so long as the contents consist of factual information and the purpose of extraction does not include re-utilization of more than an insubstantial part (see 8.2.9) by making the material available to the public. However, if the information is about matters of general scientific, technical, commercial or economic interest, both extraction and re-utilization are permitted in order to disseminate the information. Extraction and re-utilization of a database that is open to public inspection under statute is permitted in order to facilitate the exercise of the statutory rights.

SI 1997/3032 Sch 1 paras 1–3

8.2.17 Use in various circumstances: libraries and archives

The following notes discuss the likely range of circumstances in connection with databases in libraries and archives. In all cases, it is very important to remember that the contents are likely to be protected by a multitude of different copyrights, quite independently of the database right, and that these last for much longer than database right unless the database is repeatedly updated or changed.

8.2.18 Use in various circumstances: manual databases

Most manual databases are likely to pose few problems with database right. Those created by an archive or its parent institution will be accessible to staff and the public on terms set by the archivist or his or her superiors. Access to manual databases that have been deposited as records in the archive will be governed by the terms of the deposit, and after 15 years at most database right in the database deposited will expire.

8.2.19 Use in various circumstances: administrative databases

Many institutions, including libraries and archives, will make use of a range of databases for their own purposes: the various catalogues, the administration of collections, the recording of information about users, the running of the finances, and so on. In part these might be manual, but they are much more likely to be dependent on computers. Any of them that contain details of living individuals will fall under the Data Protection Act, and must be treated accordingly (see 8.7.2). The software for the databases will in almost all cases have been supplied by an external contractor, who will provide a licence for the use of his or her copyright material (see 6.6). That licence has nothing to do with database right, since the database was created by the archive and its maker is the archive or its parent institution. When such a database is not available to the public, it is up to the archivist to define the lawful users and control access and use as appropriate. Any approved user of the record office (however defined by the archivist) will be a lawful user of a database that is provided for public access.

8.2.20 Use in various circumstances: public record databases

The normal exception for the copying of public records applies to databases and their contents, so public record databases and their contents may be copied without infringement of any copyright either in the database or its contents (see 5.3.1–2). There is a new exception covering database right in public records, but it is not all-embracing. It gives the repository the right to make available to the public (re-utilize) any public record database, but the making of copies (extraction) of the contents may be an infringement of database right, so the database right must belong to the record office or its parent body, or any extraction must fall within the terms of a licence or of the other exceptions (see 8.2.13–16, 8.2.21).

SI 1997/3032 Sch 1 para 5

8.2.21 Use in various circumstances: deposited electronic databases

An electronic database that is deposited with an archive as an addition to its collections is unlikely to be of continuing commercial value, and if it has not been substantially changed within the previous 15 years the database right in it will already have expired. At the latest, database right will expire 15 years after deposit. Once database right has expired it cannot be revived, but if it still subsists at the time of deposit, and is assigned by the maker to the archivist, it is possible (though unlikely) that substantial investment in the periodic re-formatting (presentation) of such an electronic database would qualify the database for a new term of database right protection each time. If the right is assigned to the archivist (see 3.3.8), there should be no problem with the public use of the database. Failing that, use will be limited to what is permitted by the exceptions (see 8.2.13–16) or by the terms of a licence (see 8.2.22).

SI 1997/3032 reg 23

8.2.22 Use in various circumstances: licences

Licences for the use of databases may be issued by collecting societies (see 5.4.28–31) as part of licensing schemes, or individually by licensing societies or the individual owners of database rights.

There are licensing schemes available for some sectors, such as those for institutions in higher education run by CHEST (the Combined Higher Education Software Team) which has purchased from certain makers the right to issue licences in its sector. More common are individual licences, one for each database. The archivist must ensure, when securing rights to re-utilize (make available to the public or to a limited public such as the members of staff of the institution) and for staff and users to extract substantial parts of the material in a database, that the licence covers all the people who need or may need to be lawful users (see 8.2.12). No licence may prevent a lawful user from extracting an insubstantial part for any purpose, so it is particularly important to get the definition in the licence of a lawful user right: the staff of the archive together with all approved users of the archive are likely to be the main categories. The licence must also provide clear rules as to how much may be extracted and for what purposes.

SI 1997/3032 reg 19(2), Sch 2

8.3 Publication right

8.3.1 Definition

Publication right is a right equivalent to copyright which is acquired by the first person after 1 December 1996 to publish a previously unpublished literary, dramatic, musical or artistic work or a film after copyright has expired. It expires 25 years after the end of the year of first publication. It is important to note that no one can ever acquire publication right in a work that has been published while still in copyright; and no one can acquire publication right in a previously unpublished work until copyright has expired.

SI 1996/2967 regs 1(2), 16, 17

8.3.2   Publication

Publication in this context has a different meaning from publication as it applies to copyright (see 4.1.1–8). This can cause some confusion, since it means that a work may be an unpublished work in copyright terms (which can affect the duration of copyright) but a published work in publication right terms. For publication right purposes, publication includes making the work available to the public in any way, perhaps including in a record office (see 8.3.5). It also means:

- the issue of copies to the public (that is, normal publication);
- making the work available by means of an electronic retrieval system (for instance, on the internet);
- the rental or lending of copies of the work to the public (see 5.1.4);
- the performance, exhibition or showing of the work in public; and
- communicating the work to the public (for example, by broadcasting or on a website, see 5.1.6).

If any of these acts is done to the work before copyright expires it is already published for the purposes of publication right, which as a result can never subsist in it. Any of these acts after copyright expires qualifies a previously unpublished work for publication right.

SI 1996/2967 regs 16, 17; SI 2003/2498 Sch 1 para 27

8.3.3   Qualification

A work qualifies for publication right if it is first published in the EEA (see 1.2.8) and the first publisher, or at least one if there is more than one, is a national of an EEA state. No work qualifies for publication right if Crown or Parliamentary copyright subsisted in it. Moreover, for publication right to subsist, publication must be with the explicit consent of the owner of the physical medium on which the work is recorded. Thus, if the work is actually owned by the library or archive (rather than merely being deposited there) the librarian or archivist may withhold consent, or give it only in return for royalties.

SI 1996/2967 regs 16, 17

8.3.4   Rights and exceptions

The owner of publication right has all the same rights in relation to the work as the copyright owner previously had except moral rights, and these will apply equally to the original item and to the published version (see 5.1.1–10). Fair dealing and most of the other exceptions to copyright also apply, including all of those covering archives and libraries, so copies of the original item may continue to be provided and copies of extracts from the published version may be made (see 5.2, 5.3). However, the provisions covering assumptions as to the expiry of copyright do not apply (see 5.4.23–26).

SI 1996/2967 regs 16, 17

8.3.5   Application to traditional archives: literary, dramatic and musical works

The list of ways by which a work can be communicated to the public (published) for the purposes of publication right (see 8.3.2) is not exhaustive, and the intention (of the UK government at least, but see 7.7.5) was to allow publication right only to works which had genuinely never previously been 'made available to the public' (see 4.1.10) in any way. The consequence of this is that the making available to the public of a work in a record office apparently counts as publication for publication right purposes. All literary, dramatic and musical works that are unpublished and have never been made available to the public will remain in copyright until at least the year 2039 (see 2.2.17, 2.2.20), so publication right cannot apply to them until then. If they are made available to the public in a record office while still in copyright it may be that there can never be any publication right in them; this is likely to affect all or most such works in archives.

Directive 1993 (Term) art 4; SI 1996/2967 regs 16, 17

8.3.6   Application to traditional archives: artistic works of known authorship

Copyright in most unpublished artistic works of known authorship expires 70 years after the death of the author (see 2.3.12–13). This means that publication right can subsist on first publication of such previously unpublished works by an author who died more than 70 years ago. In practice, most archivists might already own any such publication right because by making the work available to the public (see 4.1.10) they are perhaps making it available to the public (and thus publishing it) in publication right terms (see 8.3.2). So the archivist will own the publication right in most unpublished artistic works if they were first made available to the public at least 70 years after their author died. On the other hand, if someone were to publish the work after that time, and only then were it to be made available to the public in the record office, the publisher would own the publication right. Where the work was first made available to the public less than 70 years after the author died there can be no publication right.

SI 1996/2967 regs 16, 17

8.3.7   Application to traditional archives: artistic works of unknown authorship

Copyright in most unpublished artistic works of unknown authorship will expire in 2039 at the earliest. However, copyright in photographs of unknown authorship created before 1 June 1957 expires 70 years after creation if they are not made available to the public during that time (see 2.3.17, 4.1.10). Thus the archivist might be the owner of the publication right if they are first made available to the public in the record office more than 70 years after creation, and the publisher will own it if they are first published in some other way. If the photographs are made available to the public less than 70 years after creation, the duration of the copyright will be extended and there will never be any publication right in them.

SI 1996/2967 regs 16, 17

8.3.8   Application to film archives

Most commercial films are made to be shown in public, which counts as publication for publication right purposes (see 8.3.2). Publication right can thus apply only when copies of the film have never been issued to the public and the film has never been shown in public. This would cover, for instance, family and other private films, in-house films made by businesses, and films that were never released by the film companies that made them. Films made before 1 June 1957 qualify for copyright as dramatic works or photographs (or both), so copyright in them expires as for those works (see 2.4.1, 2.4.10, 8.3.6). Copyright in later unpublished films is likely to persist until the year 2039 at the earliest (see 2.4.9ff.). Publication right can thus only apply before 2039 to unpublished non-fiction films made before 1957 whose director died more than 70 years ago (see 2.4.10). As with traditional archival materials (see 8.3.5–6), it is possible that the archivist will own the publication right in any film that was first made available to the public after copyright in it expired. If it was made available to the public while still in copyright, there can never be any publication right in it.

SI 1996/2967 regs 16, 17

8.4   Public Lending Right

Public Lending Right was created by the Public Lending Right Act 1979; the current scheme was established in 1982 and has been subject to successive variations. It exists to provide some return for 'eligible' authors, translators, editors and compilers for the lending of their copyright works by public libraries. It is not strictly a right under copyright law, but lasts for the same period as copyright. Only books that have been registered with the Registrar of the scheme qualify for payments, which are made from a central (government) fund. Authors may register their books for the Right online at www.plr.uk.com/. Public libraries may lend only books, as defined by the scheme, and are restricted in the lending that they may do outside the scheme, hence the qualification to the definition of a prescribed library for lending purposes (see 5.2.14). Since Public Lending Right does not cover rental, public libraries may only supply such things as videos and CDs for rent under licence from the copyright owner or a collecting society. This is only a very brief summary; for further details see the Regulations and guidance available in works on copyright in libraries (see 10.2).

For the quite distinct rental and lending right, see 5.1.4 and 5.2.14.

1988 (CDPA) s40A; SI 1982/719; SI 1990/2360; SI 1996/2967 regs 11, 34

8.5 Performers' rights

8.5.1 Relevance to archives

Rights in performances are set out in the 1988 Act as amended by the 1996 Regulations. They are summarized here because, although they are not relevant to most traditional archival materials, there are some provisions of which archivists, particularly those with responsibility for collections of film and sound recordings, should be aware. If an archivist or records manager works for a company or body that commissions films and sound recordings, it would be worth ensuring that the commissioning department makes the necessary arrangements with the performers at the time the works are made, to allow use as required.

It is important to distinguish between performers' rights, which are the rights of the performers themselves, and performing rights. The latter are the rights of copyright owners in works (such as pieces of music) that may be performed; performing rights in music are normally administered by the Performing Right Society (see 5.4.29).

1988 (CDPA) ss180ff.; SI 1996/2967 regs 20ff.

8.5.2 Performances

A performance for the purpose of performers' rights is:

- a dramatic performance (including dance and mime);
- a musical performance;
- a reading or recitation of a literary work (whether or not that work qualifies for copyright because it has previously been written or recorded, so an ad lib speech or lecture qualifies);
- a performance of a variety act or similar presentation.

A performance qualifies for protection if it was made in or by a subject of the UK, a citizen of a member state of the EU or a signatory state of the 1961 Rome Convention (see 1.2.6). A performance also qualifies for some of the rights if it was made in or the performer was a subject of a signatory state of the TRIPS Agreement (see 1.2.5, 3.1.5).

1988 (CDPA) ss 3(1), 180, 206, 211(1); SI 1995/2990

8.5.3 The rights

A performer's rights are of three kinds: non-property rights and property rights, which relate respectively to live and recorded performances, and moral rights. Some similar rights are given to companies with exclusive recording contracts with the performer. The performer may be amateur or professional. The following is merely a summary; anyone who needs to understand performers' rights in detail should consult the 1988 Act and the 1996 Regulations.

- Non-property rights are infringed if, without the performer's consent, someone makes a film or sound recording of a live performance; makes a live broadcast of a performance; makes a recording of such a broadcast; or gives a public performance of or broadcasts an infringing recording.
- Property rights are infringed if, without the performer's or rights owner's consent, someone copies a recording of a performance (whether or not the first recording was legitimate); issues copies of a recording of a performance to the public; lends or rents copies of a recording to the public; or makes the recording available by electronic transmission for access when and where a member of the public chooses (see 4.1.10).
- Moral rights are similar to the moral rights of authors (see 8.1). They give the right to the performer or group (if collectively named) to be identified if they have asserted the right; and the right to object to derogatory treatment of the performance by distortion, mutilation or other modification that is prejudicial to the reputation of the performer or group.

Property and non-property rights relate to performances made at any time, but moral rights apply only to performances made on or after 1 February 2006.

1988 (CDPA) ss 180(3), 182, 182A–CA, 183–188, 191A, 192A, 205C–H; SI 1996/2967 regs 20ff.; SI 2006/18 regs 6, 8

8.5.4 Consent and waiver

Each performer taking part in a performance owns rights in the performance, so consent for the making and use of recordings is required from each of them. The consent does not have to be in writing, but it is easier to prove that it has been given if it is. Consent may be given for any of the acts restricted by non-property rights for a specific performance, for performances generally and for future performances. Consent for acts restricted by property rights is normally by licence, and is binding in most cases on successors and assignees.

Moral rights may be waived by an instrument in writing signed by or on behalf of the rights owner(s), and the waiver may be whole or partial, temporary or permanent.

1988 (CDPA) ss191B, 193, 205J; SI 1996/2967 reg 21; SI 2006/18 reg 6

8.5.5   Duration and transmission

All performers' rights expire 50 years from the end of the year in which the performance took place, or, if during that time a recording was released with the consent of the rights owner, 50 years from the date of release of the recording. This means that property and non-property rights apply retrospectively only to performances given or recordings released up to 50 years ago.

Performers' rights of all kinds belong initially to the performers themselves, even if they are performing in the course of employment. Non-property rights may not be assigned or passed to any other person or body, except by inheritance or bequest (see 3.3.1ff.), while property rights may be assigned in the same way as copyright (see 3.3.8). Moral rights are also not assignable, but may be explicitly bequeathed. If they are not bequeathed but the property rights are, the moral rights pass with the property rights, otherwise moral rights pass to the residuary legatee (see 3.3.1, 3.3.6). Individuals or bodies that own recording rights under exclusive recording contracts with performers may assign the benefits of the rights by assigning the contract.

1988 (CDPA) ss185, 191, 191B, 192A, 205L–M; SI 1995/3297 reg 10; SI 2006/18 reg 6

8.5.6   Exceptions

There is no longer any exception which allows the recording of a performance or the copying of a recording of a performance for private or domestic purposes, though a temporary copy may be made to enable a lawful use of the recording (such as into the memory of a computer to enable a recording to be played). For the most part, other exceptions that apply to copyright (see 5.2.1–25 and 5.3) also apply to performing rights. Thus, the following are among the permitted acts:

- fair dealing for criticism, review and news reporting (but not for research or private study);
- the copying and the supply of a copy of any recording that is a public record (see 5.3.1), but, as with copyright, subsequent use of the copy could be an infringement unless another exception applies;
- the lending of copies of recordings of a performance by a prescribed library or archive (except a public library or an archive in a public library) (see 5.2.14 and 5.3.6), and

any other lending of copies of recordings so long as reasonable royalties are paid or the lending is under licence;

- the recording of broadcasts for deposit in designated archives (see 5.3.25); and
- copying for instruction or examination and recording of broadcasts by or on behalf of educational establishments (such as by an archive, see 5.2.15–16).

1988 (CDPA) ss182A, Sch 2; SI 2003/2498, Sch 2

8.5.7 Consequences

An archivist or records manager with responsibility for recordings of performances, including films, sound recordings and video recordings made up to 50 years ago, or who works for a body that commissions such recordings, should be careful to ensure that consents or licences have been obtained from all performers involved in the recordings before allowing the recordings to be used for public performances, broadcasts or the making of copies, and that performers are properly acknowledged (for instance in a printed programme). In many cases, it may be possible to secure licences from the relevant collecting societies, such as the British Equity Collecting Society (BECS) for such people as actors and other stage performers, circus artists, and theatrical and film producers (66 Great Russell Street, London WC1B 3BN, or www.equitycollecting.org.uk/) and Phonographic Performance Ltd (PPL) for musical performers and record companies (1 Upper James Street, London W1F 9DE, or www.ppluk.com/).

Archivists and records managers should remember that copyright restrictions could also apply, and so need information about whether the rights of the various contributors of different copyright works (the music, the script, the artwork, and so on) have been cleared. Rights probably will have been cleared in the case of the product of a production company, but a work commissioned by a company could be different; it may be that the company secured only limited rights of exploitation for its own purposes, which might not cover archival and historical uses.

8.6 Designs, patents and trade marks

8.6.1 Monopoly rights

Unlike copyright, designs, patents and trade marks are all monopoly rights which are likely to have limited application to most archives and archive materials. The significance of the monopoly is that it is possible to infringe innocently, by independently designing, making or using something which has already been designed or registered. Action can be taken against an innocent infringer, but the penalties will be different from those for a deliberate infringer.

The following notes are intended only as brief introductions to the relevant rights, in order to assist archivists and records managers to decide whether the rights affect them.

If they are affected, more detailed guidance should be sought from suitable reference works (see 10.2), from lawyers (see 5.5) or from patent or trade mark agents. For patent agents contact the Chartered Institute of Patent Attorneys (CIPA) at 95 Chancery Lane, London WC2A 1DT, or www.cipa.org.uk/; for trade mark attorneys contact the Institute of Trade Mark Attorneys (ITMA) at 2–6 Sydenham Road, Croydon, Surrey CR10 9XE, or www.itma.org.uk/.

Corelli v Gray, 1911–16

8.6.2 Registered designs

Any protection for designs created before 1 August 1989 is provided by the Registered Designs Act 1949 as originally passed, so long as an application for registration was made before that date. Registration could be obtained for a design that was new or original. A design was features of shape, configuration, pattern or ornament applied to an article by an industrial process which were appreciated by the eye but which were not dictated solely by the function of the article. The right lasted for five years but could be renewed twice giving a maximum term of 15 years, but this has now been extended by two further renewals to a maximum of 25 years (see below). The owner of the right was the author of the design unless it was created 'for good or valuable consideration', in which case the owner was the person who paid.

A design for which an application for registration was made on or after 1 August 1989 and before 9 December 2001 could be registered if it was new and consisted of features applied to an article by an industrial process that appealed to the eye, and that were neither a method nor principle of construction nor features dictated solely by the function of the article. A design could not be registered if, among other things, it consisted of printed matter primarily of a literary or artistic character, such as book jackets, maps and plans, but note that manuscript literary or artistic material was not so excluded. The author was owner of the right unless the design was commissioned 'for money or money's worth' or was made in the course of employment. A registration could be renewed every five years, up to a maximum of 25 years.

A directive of the EU has required further changes, which were implemented by regulations in 2001 and 2003. A design may now be registered if it is new and has individual character, that is, it does not look to an informed person like an earlier design. A design consists of the appearance of the whole or part of a product resulting from the features of, in particular, the lines, contours, colours, shape, texture or materials of the product or its ornamentation. The specific exclusion of 'matter of a literary or artistic character' has disappeared, but the definition of a design appears to exclude most of them anyway, since a product is defined as 'any industrial or handicraft item other than a computer program'. However, some care might be needed since a work of artistic craftsmanship (see 2.3.5) could be a handicraft item, and typefaces (see 2.3.2) are identified as products. Duration of protection remains at a maximum of 25 years from the application, but this term now also applies to pre-1989 applications.

The European Union has also now introduced its own design registry, based in the trade mark registry, the Office for Harmonization in the Internal Market (OHIM) (see 8.6.8). Applicants may choose to register there, for protection throughout the EU, and may also have protection for three years prior to registration under a new European design right.

Protection for a design of any date covers the design when applied to the product or products for which registration was made, and now also a design 'which does not produce on the informed user a different overall impression'. Thus, if a design has been registered for use on wallpaper alone there is unlikely to be any infringement if it is applied to wrapping paper, and there is never likely to be an infringement if a design is reproduced as an illustration in a book, though there might be an infringement of copyright in the design as an artistic work (see 5.2). There is strict liability, so a person who is unaware that a design has been registered can still infringe, though such a person will not be liable for damages.

1949 (Designs) ss1, 2, 4, 7–9; 1988 (CDPA) ss265, 267–269; SI 1989/1105 rule 26(3); SI 1995/2912 rule 26(3); SI 2001/3949 regs 2, 5, 13; SI 2001/3950 rule 12; SI 2003/550 reg 2

8.6.3 Design right

Design right requires no registration, and it is possible for design right to subsist in a registered design, so long as the design was first recorded on or after 1 August 1989. Any aspect of the shape or configuration (whether internal or external) of the whole or part of an article qualifies as a design for design right. However, a design must be original (in the same sense as a copyright work, see 2.1.5ff., except that a design is not original if it is commonplace in the relevant field) and it may not be a principle or method of construction, a feature which enables the article to function with another article (for instance a spare part), or mere surface decoration (that is, enhancing the appearance but having no influence on the shape or construction of the article). Before design right can subsist, the design must have been recorded either as a design document or as an article made to the design; it then lasts for a maximum of 15 years. A design document is defined as any record of a design, including a record in the form of a drawing, written description, photograph or computer file. Infringement of the design right is only by the reproduction of the design (either by making an article to the design or by copying a design document) for commercial purposes.

1988 (CDPA) ss213, 216, 226, 263 'design document'; *Jo-y-Jo v Matalan Retail*, 2000

8.6.4 Design right and copyright

It is possible for both copyright and design right to subsist in a single design, but this can have particular consequences:

- Where the design is for the making of a typeface or an artistic work (such as a work of architecture or a sculpture) it is an infringement of copyright in the design document (see 8.6.3) or in a model recording the design to make an article from it (for example, to make a scale model from an engineering drawing for the sculpture *The Angel of the North*).
- Where the design is not for the making of a typeface or an artistic work (for example, an engineering drawing for a special form of nut and bolt), it is not an infringement of the copyright in the design document or in a model recording the design, or of the author's moral right of attribution (see 8.1.5), to make an article to the design or to copy an article made to a design (for example, by making a Teletubby costume, which is itself not an 'artistic work'), though it might be an infringement of design right.

The copyright in typefaces is subject to its own limitations (see 2.3.32). The intention is to stop copyright being used to prevent commercial exploitation of functional items which do not themselves attract copyright.

1988 (CDPA) ss51, 79(4)(f), Sch 1 para 19; *BBC Worldwide v Pally Screen Printing*, 1998; *Lambretta Clothing v Teddy Smith (UK)*, 2005

8.6.5 Design right and copyright: manufacture

If an artistic work is exploited by the making and marketing of at least 50 articles made by an industrial process (that is, made for commercial purposes, even if individually made by hand), copyright and moral rights in the artistic work are affected. The exclusion of artistic works from the provisions mentioned above (see 8.6.4, first bulleted paragraph) ceases to apply 25 years from the first marketing of the articles (or 15 years from first marketing if that took place before 1 August 1989), unless the articles made using the work are:

- films;
- works of sculpture other than those intended to be used for commercial reproduction;
- wall plaques, medals and medallions; or
- printed matter primarily of a literary or artistic character, including book jackets, calendars, greetings cards, maps, plans and advertisements.

Thus artistic works such as a drawing of a teapot, a hand-drawn map, an architectural drawing of a house, or an engineering drawing of a toy car would continue to attract full copyright and moral rights protection for the full term if reproduced commercially for a calendar, as printed maps, by the construction of a single house or in an animated film. However, it would cease to be an infringement of copyright to copy those artistic works by making articles such as teapots, topographical models, houses or toy cars 25 years after the copyright owner has approved the use of those works to make more than 50 similar articles for commercial purposes. It would still of course be an infringement of copyright in the artistic work to copy it in some other way (for instance, by photocopying the drawing).

1956 s10(3); 1988 (CDPA) ss52, 79(4)(g), Sch 1 para 20; SI 1989/1070

8.6.6   Design right and copyright: infringement of both rights

Where both design right and copyright subsist in the same work and there has apparently been infringement of both design right and copyright, the design right is taken not to have been infringed. The effect of this is that the infringement of both rights (for instance by the photocopying of a design document, see 8.6.3) may only be pursued as an infringement of the copyright.

1988 (CDPA) s236

8.6.7   Patents for invention

Patents for invention are registered in the UK under the Patents Act 1977 as amended by the 1988 Act and later regulations, or may be registered for the whole of the EU at the European Patent Office. To qualify, the subject of an application must be new (that is, it must not have been previously revealed to the public), involve an inventive step (that is, not be obvious to a person skilled in the relevant art) and be capable of industrial application. A patent may be for a product (such as a new form of pen) or a process (such as a new way to make a pen), but it may not protect a literary, dramatic, musical or artistic work or any other aesthetic creation, nor a computer program. Patents last for 20 years from the filing of the application.

Archivists and records managers are unlikely to have much need of knowledge of how to apply for a patent, or of whether a patent registration is valid. If they do, they should consult a qualified patent agent (see 8.6.1). However, they might need to know about how they might infringe.

Infringement is by the making of a patented product or the using of a patented process, so the reproduction in a book of an image of a patented product is not an infringement of the patent, though there is likely to be a design drawing and such reproduction might well infringe the copyright, and conceivably any design right, in that. A patentee may not sue for infringement until the patent is granted, but once it has been granted may sue for infringements that have occurred since the application was made. However, if someone was legitimately doing something before a patent was applied for, he or she will not infringe the patent by continuing to do it, by allowing business partners or assignees to do it, or by selling products.

1977 (Patents) ss1–5, 25, 60; *Merrell Dow Pharmaceuticals v H N Norton*, 1996

8.6.8 Trade marks

Trade marks are registered and protected in the UK under the Trade Marks Act 1994 or may be registered in the EU Registry, Office for Harmonization in the Internal Market (OHIM). Protection is effectively endless, so long as the registration is renewed at the necessary intervals (every ten years) and the mark is actually used. A trade mark is a sign that is capable of being represented graphically, a requirement that can be interpreted quite widely provided the description is sufficiently precise that an ordinary person would understand from it what the trade mark was. A trade mark must also be capable of distinguishing goods and services of one undertaking from those of another and be distinctive in itself. its purpose is to guarantee to a consumer that all goods or services bearing the mark have been made or supplied under the control of the trade mark owner. Once registered a trade mark may be further protected by the use of the symbol ® or the letters RTM beside it to warn off infringers; it is a criminal offence to use the symbol or letters by an unregistered mark. The ™ symbol may be used to indicate that an unregistered mark is being used as a trade mark; infringement by use of such a mark would be treated as passing-off (see 8.6.9).

It is an infringement in connection with goods, packaging or services (regardless of whether there is any intention to mislead) to use an identical or similar mark especially if there is a likelihood of confusion or the use takes unfair advantage of the mark.

Like patents, rights in trade marks are monopolies, so it is possible to infringe innocently (see 8.6.7). Use of a trade mark will not infringe if it is merely descriptive, to describe one of the characteristics of the goods or services rather than to indicate origin. It would be unlikely (depending on the circumstances) to be an infringement of the trademark to reproduce in a book a picture of a chocolate wrapper bearing the manufacturer's trade mark, although there could be an infringement of copyright in the artwork for the wrapper and in the mark as a (probably anonymous) artistic work unless its inclusion could be shown to be incidental (see 5.2.13). A trade mark that consists of words alone and in no special form is unlikely to qualify for copyright protection.

1994 (Trade Marks) ss 1, 10, 42, 43, 95; *Trebor Bassett v The Football Association*, 1997; *Arsenal Football Club v Reed*, 2003; *Davidoff v Gofkid*, 2003

8.6.9 Passing-off

It is possible for a trade mark, a style of packaging, a company name, an internet domain name or even (in limited circumstances) the name of an individual to have legal protection even if it does not qualify for copyright or registered trade mark protection, by means of a civil action for passing-off under the common law. Passing-off law protects goodwill in goods or services that has been acquired in the course of trade. Goodwill is 'the attractive force that brings in custom', while trade is defined quite widely and can cover not only a commercial company but also a profession, a charity or an individual who is a well known author, though it will not otherwise protect an individual's name. Passing-off occurs when someone misrepresents him or herself in order to misappropriate the goodwill, so that there is, or is likely to be, confusion on the part of the public. The misrepresentation does not have to be deliberate fraud and can be entirely innocent, so that for instance a person could honestly use his or her name without knowledge of another's use of the same name, but might still be held to be passing-off goods or services using that name if the result was that the public was, or was reasonably likely to be, confused. Parody is permitted so long as the true authorship is as prominent as the spoof attribution (see also 8.1.9).

An unregistered trade mark may be protected by the use of the symbol ™ next to it. It is a criminal offence to use the ® symbol (see 8.6.8) with an unregistered mark.

An action for passing off is expensive because of the quantity of evidence that is required, for instance to prove possession of goodwill and confusion of the public. The company Mothercare, for instance, failed to prevent Penguin publishing a book called *Mother Care/Other Care* about the benefits of mothers caring for their own children, since it was descriptive use and there was no likelihood of confusion.

Lord MacNaghten in *Commissioners of Inland Revenue v Muller & Co's Margarine*, 1901, at 224; *Marengo v Daily Sketch*, 1948; *Wright, Layman & Umney v Wright*, 1949; *Mothercare UK v Penguin Books*, 1988; *British Diabetic Association v Diabetic Society*, 1996; *Alan Clark v Associated Newspapers*, 1998

8.7 Confidentiality

8.7.1 Confidential records

Copyright is far from being the only restriction on the use of records held by archives. Few collections will not have some material that falls under the terms of the Data Protection Act, and many are likely also to have material that is or has been confidential. The following notes do not attempt to give detailed advice, and archivists and records managers would be well advised to consult the relevant statutes and published guidance (see 10.2).

8.7.2 Data protection

The data protection principles in the Data Protection Act are drafted to be consistent with the Human Rights Act, so that compliance with the one will ensure compliance with the privacy requirements of the other. Archivists and records managers should be aware that data protection applies to manual as well as computer records that contain personal data (even down to the level of name and address) about living individuals, so long as the records are arranged in a way that makes specific information on an individual as readily accessible as it would be if stored on a computer. The mere mention of an individual's name does not necessarily amount to personal data, especially if the focus is on something else. Data protection can also apply to photographs, though probably not to a non-intrusive photograph of a person in a public place. There are special provisions for 'sensitive' data about individuals, including information about racial origin, physical or mental condition, or sexual life. All personal data must be kept securely, unless the exception covering access to data kept for historical research applies. Personal data may be kept indefinitely for purposes of historical research and may be made available to the public, so long as:

- they are not used to take decisions about living individuals;
- they are not used in a way that could cause substantial damage or distress to living individuals; and
- the results of research into living individuals are anonymized.

If data of historical value do not meet these requirements, they may be kept for subsequent release but must be kept securely.

Personal data may not be transferred to a country outside the EU which does not have comparable protection. However, putting data onto a website does not contravene this, even though a website is potentially accessible from anywhere in the world, so long as the internet service provider is based in a member state.

The National Archives, the National Archives of Scotland and the Public Record Office of Northern Ireland have jointly issued *Data Protection Act 1998: A Guide for Records Managers and Archivists*, which is available online from the website of The National Archives, at www.nationalarchives.gov.uk/.

Campbell v MGN, 2004; *Bodil Lindqvist v Kammaraklagaren*, 2004; *Durant v Financial Services Authority*, 2004

8.7.3 Law of confidence

The law of confidence is part of the common law, so there is no statute defining its nature or extent. Instead, there are certain basic principles that apply, whose interpretation will depend on the circumstances in which the information was communicated between the parties:

- The information must be confidential, that is, it must not already be public knowledge. It is possible, though, for some parts to be public knowledge while others remain confidential, or for publicly available information to have been used in a confidential way.

- There must be an obligation of confidence, which is dependent on some level of understanding, agreement or knowledge on the part of the recipient. The test of this is based on whether a 'reasonable man' would recognize that the information received was confidential. A person who does not know that information is confidential is under no obligation, but if the recipient knows or ought to know that it is, he or she would normally be bound. If for instance an obviously confidential document is blown from an open window into the street or a private diary is accidentally dropped, the person who finds them should know that they are confidential. However, even where there is an obligation it is not absolute: it may for example be lawful under some circumstances to break a confidence to prevent a crime, to defend one's reputation or if the breach is otherwise in the public interest (see 5.2.25).
- For breach of confidence to be actionable, the revealing of the confidential information must normally have resulted in damage, usually to the confider but perhaps also to a third party such as the confider's family.

Coco v A N Clark (Engineers), 1969; *Lion Laboratories v Evans*, 1985; *Attorney General v Guardian Newspapers*, 1988; *Stephens v Avery*, 1988; *Shelley Films v Rex Features*, 1994

8.7.4 Obligation of confidence

It is not normally too difficult to decide whether information is confidential, or to decide that damage might be caused by disclosure. The difficulty tends to be in deciding whether there is an obligation of confidence.

An obligation of confidence can arise without any explicit agreement (either oral or in writing) if it is implicit in the circumstances. Two companies working together on a project are likely to owe a duty of confidence to one another even if they have no contract saying so, and so do a married couple (or in modern circumstances a couple in a long-term relationship).

There is an implied obligation on every servant or employee not to disclose information or documents received in the course of employment, and a similar obligation arising from confidential relationships such as between doctor and patient or solicitor and client.

An obligation of confidence might arise even if the information is unsolicited, for instance because a letter says 'In Confidence' at the top. An archivist who does not wish to be bound by an unsolicited obligation should return the information at once with a note to say that no obligation of confidence is accepted. If the organization receiving the information is an authority within the meaning of the Freedom of Information Act 2000 (see 5.3.3–4) it will have to consider carefully which obligation takes precedence.

The confidentiality owed to people responding to a survey (such as of readers in a record office) will depend largely on the terms under which the information was sought.

The presumption is likely to be that there is no relationship of confidence, but it would be sensible to clarify the position by a statement on the form such as that replies would be treated as confidential only if appropriately marked.

An obligation of confidence diminishes over time, and the duty owed must be increasingly weighed against the public interest in openness (see 5.2.25).

Any obligation of confidence expires on the death of the party (or the death of the last of the parties) to whom the confidence is owed.

Prince Albert v Strange, 1848–9; *Philip v Pennell*, 1907; *Saltman Engineering v Campbell Engineering*, 1948; *Argyll, Duchess of, v Argyll, Duke of*, 1967; *Seager v Copydex*, 1967; *Initial Services v Putterill*, 1968; *Coco v A N Clark (Engineers)*, 1969; *Lion Laboratories v Evans*, 1985; *Stephens v Avery*, 1988; *A v B and C*, 2002

8.7.5 Privacy

A right to privacy in the UK has been gradually developed by the courts. The statutory law in this area derives from the Human Rights Act 1998 (incorporating the European Convention on Human Rights into UK law) and the Data Protection Act 1998 (see 8.7.2). The Convention says that 'everyone has the right to respect for his private and family life, his home and his correspondence'.

Privacy has developed as a child of the law of confidence (see 8.7.3–4), but it has its own tests:

- Does the claimant have a reasonable expectation of privacy? A person in a clearly public place will normally have no expectation of privacy, but some activities (such as dining in a secluded area of a public restaurant) might nevertheless be private. The sending of private papers, marked confidential, to a few friends is unlikely to remove the expectation of privacy, and the authorized publication of images of a private event do not make the rest of that event public. The invasion of privacy by photography is regarded as especially offensive.
- Which of the human rights of privacy and freedom of expression has precedence in the particular circumstances, bearing in mind that each is equally important? What is the justification for interfering with one or the other right, and is the damage caused by the interference proportional to the benefit gained? The public interest will be of importance here (see 5.2.25), so that freedom of expression might win if a newspaper could show that it was in the public interest to reveal information about which the person had lied. In the view of the European Court of Human Rights, the right to freedom of expression relates to the expression of ideas. Photographs which convey information but not ideas may well not be covered so that the right to privacy of the subject of the pictures would be superior.

1998 (Rights) Sch 1, art 8, 10; *Campbell v MGN*, 2004; *Von Hannover v Germany*, 2004; *Douglas v Hello!*, 2005; *HRH the Prince of Wales v Associated Newspapers*, 2006

8.7.6 Moral rights

There is a moral right of privacy in photographs and films commissioned for private and domestic purposes (see 8.1.10).

8.8 Artist's resale right (*droit de suite*)

Following pressure from France, which has had the right for some time, an EU directive has introduced a right for artists to receive a share of the money raised by the resale of their works. Regulations have introduced the right to the UK. The author or authors of an artistic work (including some which might be defined for copyright purposes as works of artistic craftsmanship, such as glassware and tapestries) is entitled to a percentage of the price paid for the work each time it is sold, after it first leaves the artist's possession, so long as the sale is through a professional art dealer and is above a minimum value. The right cannot be assigned but may be bequeathed, and it may not be waived. It lasts for the same period as copyright in the work.

The collection of the royalty must be handled by a collecting society. There are two non-profit societies seeking to be appointed by artists as their agent: DACS (see 5.4.29) and the Artists Collecting Society, set up for this purpose by the Bridgeman Art Library for the Society of London Art Dealers. It may be contacted at 17–19 Garway Road, London W2 4PH, or www.bridgeman.co.uk/. There is also a commercial body, Artists' Rights Administration Ltd (447 Kenton Road, Middlesex HA3 0XY, or www.aradmin.com/).

Directive 2001 (Artists); SI 2006/346

9 Appendix

9.1 Charts for the duration of copyright

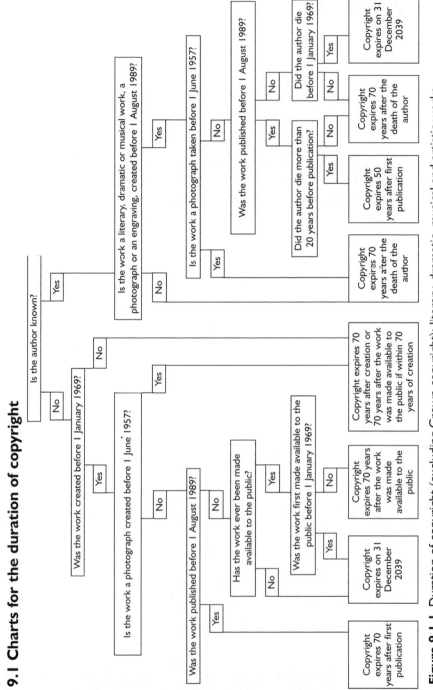

Figure 9.1.1 Duration of copyright (excluding Crown copyright): literary, dramatic, musical and artistic works

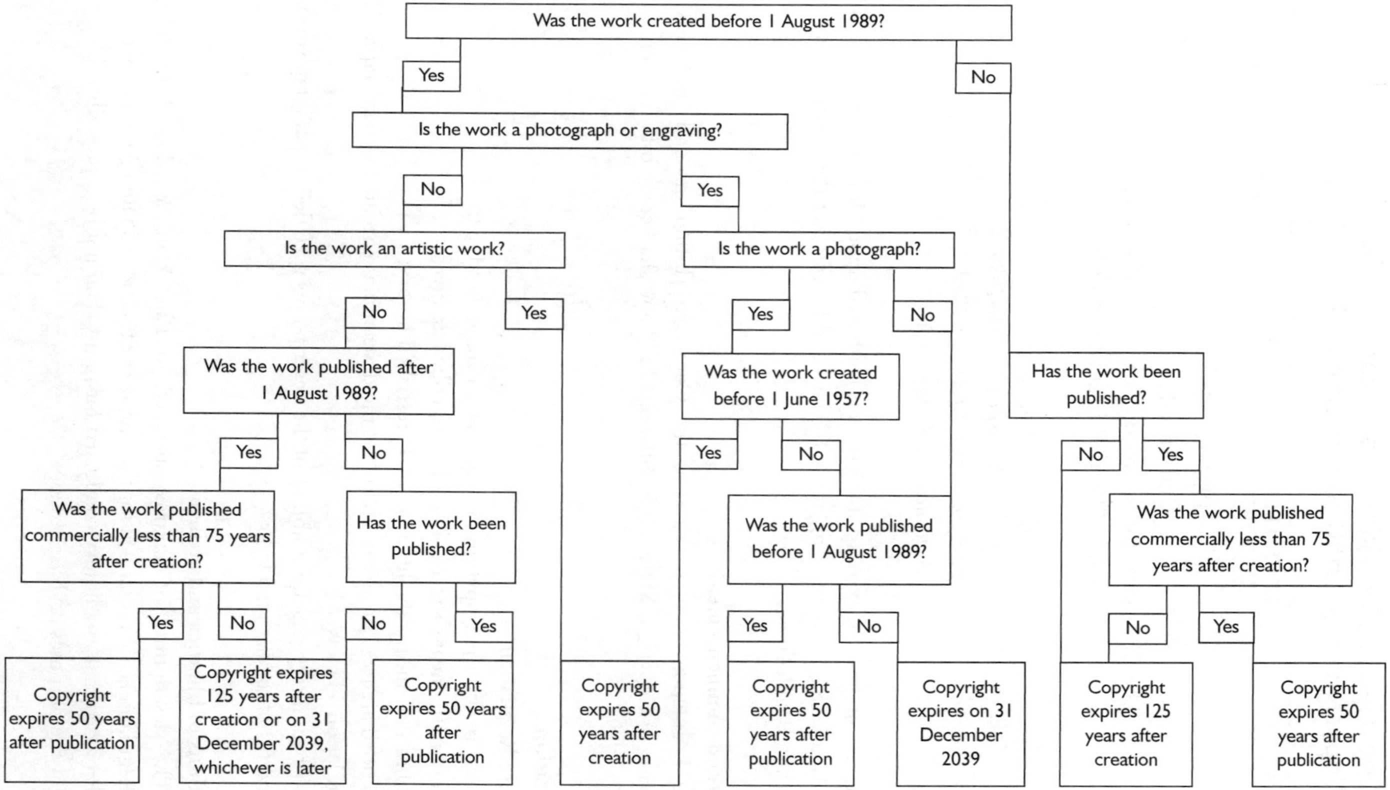

Figure 9.1.2 Duration of Crown copyright: literary, dramatic, musical and artistic works

9.2   Copyright (Librarians and Archivists) (Copying of Copyright Material) Regulations 1989

STATUTORY INSTRUMENTS

1989 No. 1212
COPYRIGHT
The Copyright (Librarians and Archivists) (Copying of
Copyright Material) Regulations 1989

Made 14th July 1989
Laid before Parliament 18th July 1989
Coming into force 1st August 1989
Amended 31st October 2003

The Secretary of State, in exercise of the powers conferred upon him by sections 37(1), (2) and (4) and 38 to 43 of the Copyright, Designs and Patents Act 1988, hereby makes the following Regulations:

Citation and commencement
1   These Regulations may be cited as the Copyright (Librarians and Archivists) (Copying of Copyright Material) Regulations 1989 and shall come into force on 1st August 1989.

Interpretation
2   In these Regulations –
"the Act" means the Copyright, Designs and Patents Act 1988;
"the archivist" means the archivist of a prescribed archive;
"the librarian" means the librarian of a prescribed library;
"prescribed archive" means an archive of the descriptions specified in paragraph (4) of regulation 3 below;
"prescribed library" means a library of the descriptions specified in paragraphs (1), (2) and (3) of regulation 3 below.

Descriptions of libraries and archives
3   (1)   The descriptions of libraries specified in Part A of Schedule 1 to these Regulations are prescribed for the purposes of sections 38 and 39 of the Act: Provided that any library conducted for profit shall not be a prescribed library for the purposes of those sections.

(2) All libraries in the United Kingdom are prescribed for the purposes of sections 41, 42 and 43 of the Act as libraries the librarians of which may make and supply copies of any material to which those sections relate.

(3) Any library of a description specified in Part A of Schedule 1 to these Regulations which is not conducted for profit and any library of the description specified in Part B of that Schedule which is not conducted for profit are prescribed for the purposes of sections 41 and 42 of the Act as libraries for which copies of any material to which those sections relate may be made and supplied by the librarian of a prescribed library.

(4) All archives in the United Kingdom are prescribed for the purposes of sections 42 and 43 of the Act as archives which may make and supply copies of any material to which those sections relate and any archive within the United Kingdom which is not conducted for profit is prescribed for the purposes of section 42 of the Act as an archive for which copies of any material to which that section relates may be made and supplied by the archivist of a prescribed archive.

(5) In this regulation "conducted for profit", in relation to a library or archive, means a library or archive which is established or conducted for profit or which forms part of, or is administered by, a body established or conducted for profit.

Copying by librarian of article or part of published work

4 (1) For the purposes of sections 38 and 39 of the Act the conditions specified in paragraph (2) of this regulation are prescribed as the conditions which must be complied with when the librarian of a prescribed library makes and supplies a copy of any article in a periodical or, as the case may be, of a part of a literary, dramatic or musical work from a published edition to a person requiring the copy.

(2) The prescribed conditions are –

    (a) that no copy of any article or any part of a work shall be supplied to the person requiring the same unless –

        (i) he satisfies the librarian that he requires the copy for purposes of research for a non-commercial purpose or private study and will not use it for any other purpose; and

        (ii) he has delivered to the librarian a declaration in writing, in relation to that article or part of a work, substantially in accordance with Form A in Schedule 2 to these Regulations and signed in the manner therein indicated;

    (b) that the librarian is satisfied that the requirement of such person and that of any other person –

        (i) are not similar, that is to say, the requirements are not for copies of substantially the same article or part of a work at substantially the same time and for substantially the same purpose; and

(ii) are not related, that is to say, he and that person do not receive instruction to which the article or part of the work is relevant at the same time and place;

(c) that such person is not furnished –

(i) in the case of an article, with more than one copy of the article or more than one article contained in the same issue of a periodical; or

(ii) in the case of a part of a published work, with more than one copy of the same material or with a copy of more than a reasonable proportion of any work; and

(d) that such person is required to pay for the copy a sum not less than the cost (including a contribution to the general expenses of the library) attributable to its production.

(3) Unless the librarian is aware that the signed declaration delivered to him pursuant to paragraph (2)(a)(ii) above is false in a material particular, he may rely on it as to the matter he is required to be satisfied on under paragraph (2)(a)(i) above before making or supplying the copy.

Copying by librarian to supply other libraries

5 (1) For the purposes of section 41 of the Act the conditions specified in paragraph (2) of this regulation are prescribed as the conditions which must be complied with when the librarian of a prescribed library makes and supplies to another prescribed library a copy of any article in a periodical or, as the case may be, of the whole or part of a published edition of a literary, dramatic or musical work required by that other prescribed library.

(2) The prescribed conditions are –

(a) that the other prescribed library is not furnished with more than one copy of the article or of the whole or part of the published edition; or

(b) that, where the requirement is for a copy of more than one article in the same issue of a periodical, or for a copy of the whole or part of a published edition, the other prescribed library furnishes a written statement to the effect that it is a prescribed library and that it does not know, and could not by reasonable inquiry ascertain, the name and address of a person entitled to authorize the making of the copy; and

(c) that the other prescribed library shall be required to pay for the copy a sum equivalent to but not exceeding the cost (including a contribution to the general expenses of the library) attributable to its production.

Copying by librarian or archivist for the purposes of replacing items in a permanent collection

6 (1) For the purposes of section 42 of the Act the conditions specified in paragraph (2) of this regulation are prescribed as the conditions which must be complied

with before the librarian or, as the case may be, the archivist makes a copy from any item in the permanent collection of the library or archive in order to preserve or replace that item in the permanent collection of that library or archive or in the permanent collection of another prescribed library or archive.

(2) The prescribed conditions are –

(a) that the item in question is an item in the part of the permanent collection maintained by the library or archive wholly or mainly for the purposes of reference on the premises of the library or archive, or is an item in the permanent collection of the library or archive which is available on loan only to other libraries or archives;

(b) that it is not reasonably practicable for the librarian or archivist to purchase a copy of that item to fulfil the purpose under section 42(1)(a) or (b) of the Act;

(c) that the other prescribed library or archive furnishes a written statement to the effect that the item has been lost, destroyed or damaged and that it is not reasonably practicable for it to purchase a copy of that item, and that if a copy is supplied it will only be used to fulfil the purpose under section 42(1)(b) of the Act; and

(d) that the other prescribed library or archive shall be required to pay for the copy a sum equivalent to but not exceeding the cost (including a contribution to the general expenses of the library or archive) attributable to its production.

Copying by librarian or archivist of certain unpublished works

7 (1) For the purposes of section 43 of the Act the conditions specified in paragraph (2) of this regulation are prescribed as the conditions which must be complied with in the circumstances in which that section applies when the librarian or, as the case may be, the archivist makes and supplies a copy of the whole or part of a literary, dramatic or musical work from a document in the library or archive to a person requiring the copy.

(2) The prescribed conditions are –

(a) that no copy of the whole or part of the work shall be supplied to the person requiring the same unless –

(i) he satisfies the librarian or archivist that he requires the copy for purposes of research for a non-commercial purpose or private study and will not use it for any other purpose; and

(ii) he has delivered to the librarian or, as the case may be, the archivist a declaration in writing, in relation to that work, substantially in accordance with Form B in Schedule 2 to these Regulations and signed in the manner therein indicated;

(b) that such person is not furnished with more than one copy of the same material; and

(c) that such person is required to pay for the copy a sum not less than the cost (including a contribution to the general expenses of the library or archive) attributable to its production.

(3) Unless the librarian or archivist is aware that the signed declaration delivered to him pursuant to paragraph (2)(a)(ii) above is false in a material particular, he may rely on it as to the matter he is required to be satisfied on under paragraph (2)(a)(i) above before making or supplying the copy.

Revocations

8   The Regulations mentioned in Schedule 3 to these Regulations are hereby revoked.

Eric Forth
Parliamentary Under Secretary of State,
Department of Trade and Industry
14th July 1989

N.B. These regulations were amended by SI 2003/2498, Sch.1 para 26.

SCHEDULE 1   Regulation 3

PART A   Regulation 3(1) and (3)

1 Any library administered by –
   (a) a library authority within the meaning of the Public Libraries and Museums Act
       1964 in relation to England and Wales;
   (b) a statutory library authority within the meaning of the Public Libraries
       (Scotland) Act 1955, in relation to Scotland;
   (c) an Education and Library Board within the meaning of the Education and
       Libraries (Northern Ireland) Order 1986, in relation to Northern Ireland.

2 The British Library, the National Library of Wales, the National Library of Scotland,
   the Bodleian Library, Oxford and the University Library, Cambridge.

3 Any library of a school within the meaning of section 174 of the Act and any library
   of a description of educational establishment specified under that section in the
   Copyright (Educational Establishments) (No.2) Order 1989.

4 Any parliamentary library or library administered as part of a government
   department, including a Northern Ireland department, or any library conducted for
   or administered by an agency which is administered by a Minister of the Crown.

5 Any library administered by –
   (a) in England and Wales, a local authority within the meaning of the Local
       Government Act 1972, the Common Council of the City of London or the
       Council of the Isles of Scilly;
   (b) in Scotland, a local authority within the meaning of the Local Government
       (Scotland) Act 1973;
   (c) in Northern Ireland, a district council established under the Local Government
       Act (Northern Ireland) 1972.

6 Any other library conducted for the purpose of facilitating or encouraging the study
   of bibliography, education, fine arts, history, languages, law, literature, medicine,
   music, philosophy, religion, science (including natural and social science) or
   technology, or administered by any establishment or organization which is
   conducted wholly or mainly for such a purpose.

PART B   Regulation 3(3)

Any library outside the United Kingdom which is conducted wholly or mainly for the
purpose of facilitating or encouraging the study of bibliography, education, fine arts,
history, languages, law, literature, medicine, music, philosophy, religion, science
(including natural and social science) or technology.

SCHEDULE 2   Regulations 4 and 7
FORM A

DECLARATION: COPY OF ARTICLE OR PART OF PUBLISHED WORK

To:

The Librarian of   Library
[Address of Library]

Please supply me with a copy of:
    *the article in the periodical, the particulars of which are [   ]
    *the part of the published work, the particulars of which are [   ]
required by me for the purposes of research or private study.

2   I declare that –
    (a) I have not previously been supplied with a copy of the same material by you or
         any other librarian;
    (b) I will not use the copy except for research for a non-commercial purpose or
         private study and will not supply a copy of it to any other person; and
    (c) to the best of my knowledge no other person with whom I work or study has
         made or intends to make, at or about the same time as this request, a request for
         substantially the same material for substantially the same purpose.

3   I understand that if the declaration is false in a material particular the copy supplied
    to me by you will be an infringing copy and that I shall be liable for infringement of
    copyright as if I had made the copy myself.

                                                              †Signature

                                                              Date

Name
Address

*Delete whichever is inappropriate.
†This must be the personal signature of the person making the request. A stamped or
typewritten signature, or the signature of an agent, is NOT acceptable.

FORM B

DECLARATION: COPY OF WHOLE OR PART OF UNPUBLISHED WORK

To:

The *Librarian/Archivist of   *Library/Archive
[Address of Library/Archive]

Please supply me with a copy of:
the *whole/following part [particulars of part] of the [particulars of the unpublished work] required by me for the purposes of research or private study.

2 I declare that –
   (a) I have not previously been supplied with a copy of the same material by you or any other librarian or archivist;
   (b) I will not use the copy except for research for a non-commercial purpose or private study and will not supply a copy of it to any other person; and
   (c) to the best of my knowledge the work had not been published before the document was deposited in your *library/archive and the copyright owner has not prohibited copying of the work.

3 I understand that if the declaration is false in a material particular the copy supplied to me by you will be an infringing copy and that I shall be liable for infringement of copyright as if I had made the copy myself.

†Signature

Date

Name
Address

*Delete whichever is inappropriate.
†This must be the personal signature of the person making the request. A stamped or typewritten signature, or the signature of an agent, is NOT acceptable.

SCHEDULE 3   Regulation 8

REVOCATIONS

Number	Title
S.I. 1957/868	The Copyright (Libraries) Regulations 1957
S.I. 1989/1009	The Copyright (Copying by Librarians and Archivists) Regulations 1989
S.I. 1989/1069	The Copyright (Copying by Librarians and Archivists) (Amendment) Regulations 1989

9.3 Model licences

9.3.1 Licence to the archive

See 5.4.12–13.

LICENCE

The Agreement is made this [date] day of [month and year]

BETWEEN	1	the Depositor [Name and full postal address of depositor]
AND	2	the Archive [Name and full postal address of the archive]

Preamble

1   The Depositor has deposited the Material in the Archive. This Agreement relates to that part of the Material which is the copyright of the Depositor.

Definitions

2.1 In this Agreement certain words and expressions shall have the following meanings:

Commencement Date	The date of this Agreement
Material	[Specify the documents deposited, as precisely as possible, or refer to the Schedule, and attach a Schedule to the Agreement specifying the Material. If the Depositor makes a further deposit, the Schedule can be amended under clause 11, without changing the terms of the licence.]
Third Party	Any person or body that is not a party to this Agreement

2.2   Any reference to a clause or sub-clause shall be interpreted as a reference to the clause or sub-clause bearing that number in this Agreement.

2.3   Unless the context requires otherwise, words importing the singular number shall include the plural number and vice versa, and words importing the masculine gender shall include the feminine and neuter genders and vice versa.

2.4   Clause headings are for ease of reference only and do not affect interpretation.

Grant

3   The Depositor grants to the Archive the [exclusive] [role] [non-exclusive] licence
      to do the following [delete or add others as necessary]:

    (i)   to grant licences for the use of the Material in [non-commercial/educational]
             publications [in all media *or* specify the media, e.g. book, journal, CD-ROM]
             and related products;

    (ii)   to grant licences for the preparation and publication of indexes to the Material;

    (iii) to grant licences for the exhibition of copies of the Material;

    (iv)   to grant licences for the use of the Material in films, sound recordings and
             broadcasts, and on internet websites;

    (v)   to make use of the Material for similar purposes by the Archive and to make
             copies of the Material for preservation and other archival purposes.

4   All other rights in the Material remain with the Depositor. Applications for licences
      for other uses shall be forwarded to the Depositor who will notify the Archive of
      any licence issued at the time of issue and the terms of that licence. The Depositor
      or his or her heirs shall notify the Archive of any changes of address.

Period

5   Subject to the terms of clause 8 this Agreement shall run for the duration of the
      Depositor's copyright in the Material, unless the Depositor withdraws some or all
      of the Material from the Archive in accordance with relevant provisions of any
      agreement for its deposit in the Archive, in which case it shall terminate, as respects
      the Material withdrawn, from the date of such withdrawal.

Payments

6.1   The Archive may charge royalty fees for the issue of licences granted under clause
      3, at its normal published rates. Income from such fees shall accrue to the Archive
      [or other specified beneficiary].

6.2   The Archive may remit part of any fee due, or waive the fee altogether, in
      appropriate circumstances and in accordance with its normal practice.

Copyright

7.1   The Archive shall require all licensees to acknowledge that part or all of the
      Material is the copyright of the Depositor and shall require that the following
      statement is featured prominently in all copies of works sold using the Material [or
      on screen, in the case of electronic publications]:

    Material in this work that is the copyright of [the Depositor] is published with
      the permission of [the Archive] on behalf of [the Depositor].

7.2 The Archive shall immediately notify the Depositor of any infringements of the Depositor's copyright in the Material that come to its attention. Any action in pursuance of such infringement shall be at the discretion of the Depositor.

Breach

8 The Depositor shall have the right at any time to give notice in writing to the Archive to terminate this Agreement on occurrence of any of the following events:

(i) if the Archive commits a material breach of any of the terms of this Agreement and in the case of a breach capable of being remedied fails to remedy such breach within twenty-one days of being requested by the Depositor in writing to do so;

(ii) [in the case of a company archive] if the Archive's company goes into liquidation either compulsorily or voluntarily or has a receiver appointed over its assets or enters into a composition with its creditors;

(iii) [if appropriate] if the Archive fails to make the payments specified in clause 6.

Termination

9.1 On termination of this Agreement under clause 8 all rights granted to the Licensee under this Agreement shall automatically and immediately revert to the Depositor.

9.2 On expiry or termination of this Agreement under clause 5, the Archive shall be entitled to issue and sell existing copies of any works published by it under clause 3 subject to all other obligations under this Agreement being complied with in full.

9.3 Termination for any reason shall not affect:

(i) the subsisting rights (if any) of any Third Party, or any sub-licence validly issued by the Archive prior to termination;

(ii) the right of the Depositor [or the Archive] to obtain royalties and any other payments due in respect of licences issued by the Archive;

(iii) any claim which the Depositor may have against the Archive for damages or otherwise.

Assignment

10.1 The Archive shall not assign this Agreement or the benefit or advantage hereof without the consent of the Depositor first being obtained in writing.

10.2 The Archive undertakes to inform the Depositor promptly of any changes in ownership of the Archive or any change of name or registered office.

Consideration

11 In consideration for the grant of this licence, the Archive agrees to pay the sum of £1 (one pound) to the Depositor, receipt of which is hereby acknowledged.

Entirety

12   This Agreement [(which expression includes the Schedules hereto whether in their original or amended form)] constitutes the entire agreement between the parties, and no modification or amendment shall be binding on either party unless it is agreed in writing and signed by both parties.

Interpretation

13   This Agreement shall be governed by and interpreted in all respects under the laws of England and Wales [*or* Scotland, *or* Northern Ireland, *or* other specified country] and shall be subject to the jurisdiction of the courts of England and Wales [*or* Scotland, *or* Northern Ireland, *or* other specified country].

Signed   Date
for the Depositor

NAME IN BLOCK CAPITALS

Signed   Date
for the Archive

NAME IN BLOCK CAPITALS

9.3.2 Licence to a user

See 5.4.17–18.

The Agreement is made this [date] day of [month and year]

BETWEEN	1	the Depositor [Name and full postal address of depositor]
AND	2	the Archive [Name and full postal address of the archive]
AND	3	the Licensee [Name and full postal address of the licensee or of the licensee's registered office]

Preamble

1 The Archive is authorized by the Depositor to license the reproduction of Material belonging to the Depositor held on deposit in the Archive which is the copyright of the Depositor or is no longer in copyright. [*or* The Depositor has deposited the Material in the Archive and assigned to the Archive such copyright in the Material as was his or her copyright.]

Definitions

2.1 In this Agreement certain words and expressions shall have the following meanings:

Accounting Periods	The first accounting period shall cover the period from the Commencement Date until .... (inclusive). Thereafter Accounting Periods shall be the periods from .... (inclusive) to .... (inclusive)
Commencement Date	The date of this Agreement
Edition	One publication of the Work in the Language and the Format(s) specified. [In the case of books and CD-ROMs, the edition is defined by the ISBN; if this changes it is a new edition.]
Format	[Specify the format(s) licensed: volume/book form, electronic form (e.g. CD-ROM), video, audio, television, etc.]

Gross Income	Total revenue received by the Licensee generated by the sale (and sub-licensing in the case of electronic products) of the Work throughout the Territory during the appropriate Accounting Period, but excluding taxes, postage and packing, as shown in the signed and audited accounts of the Licensee for that Accounting Period
Language	English [or as specified]
Material	[Specify the documents licensed, as precisely as necessary, or refer to the Schedule, and attach a Schedule to the Agreement specifying the Material. The Schedule can be amended in future if desired under clause 12.1, without changing the terms of the Licence.]
One-time Reproduction Right	The right to reproduce any item of the Material once only in one Edition in the Territory
Territory	[Specify, for instance, the university campus, the World, the European Union, the USA, or a combination.]
Third Party	Any person or body that is not a party to this Agreement
Work	The [publication/product/broadcast] containing the Material licensed by this Agreement [give details]

2.2   Any reference to a clause or sub-clause shall be interpreted as a reference to the clause or sub-clause bearing that number in this Agreement.

2.3   Unless the context requires otherwise, words importing the singular number shall include the plural number and vice versa, and words importing the masculine gender shall include the feminine and neuter genders and vice versa.

2.4   Clause headings are for ease of reference only and do not affect interpretation.

Grant

3   The Archive hereby grants to the Licensee the following rights [delete or add as necessary]:

(i)   the non-exclusive One-time Reproduction Right to publish, market and sell the Material;

(ii) [for electronic publishing] the right to sub-license end-users throughout the Territory to use the Work provided that the Licensee shall sub-license its end-users by means of an end-user licence which shall stipulate that end-users acknowledge that the Material is preserved in the Archive, that the copyright in part or all of the Material is the property of the Depositor [or the Archive] and that they have no right to supply copies of the Material or any part of the Material to others or to authorize the making of such copies without the consent of the Depositor [or the Archive];

(iii) the non-exclusive right to place the Material on a computer network and to permit the making of single hard copies for research or private study purposes only [e.g. by staff and students] throughout the Territory;

(iv) the non-exclusive right to prepare and publish indexes to the Material throughout the Territory;

(v) the non-exclusive right to reproduce the Material in advertising for the Work throughout the Territory;

(vi) the non-exclusive right to include the Material in a broadcast [and ...... repeats] to be received throughout the Territory.

Period

4   Subject to the terms of clause 9 this Agreement shall run for a period of ...... years from the Commencement Date and shall continue thereafter unless terminated by any party giving not less than six months' notice in writing to the other parties.

Payments

5.1 In consideration for the rights granted at clause 3 the Licensee shall pay to the Depositor [or the Archive] [for instance, one or a combination of]:

(i)   a non-returnable advance of £ ...... on the royalties payable under clause 5.1(ii), which sum shall fall due within 28 days of the Commencement Date;

(ii)   a royalty of ...... % of the Gross Income, less the amount of any advance paid in accordance with clause 5.1(i), payable within [time, e.g. three calendar months] of the end of the first Accounting Period;

(iii) a royalty of ...... % of the Gross Income, payable [e.g. annually] within [time, e.g. three calendar months] of the end of the appropriate Accounting Period;

(iv)   a single royalty payment of £ ...... , which sum shall fall due within 28 days of the Commencement Date.

5.2 All payments, together with a copy of the signed audited accounts for the appropriate Accounting Period, shall be sent to the Depositor [or the Archive] in £ sterling.

5.3 Upon reasonable written notice and during the Licensee's normal business hours, the Depositor [or the Archive] or its lawful representative, shall have the right to examine the Licensee's record of accounts at the place at which they are normally kept, insofar as such records relate to sales and receipts in respect of the Work. Such examination shall be at the cost of the Depositor [or the Archive] unless errors are found to the disadvantage of the Depositor [or the Archive] in excess of 2.5% of the amount due to the Depositor [or the Archive] in respect of the last preceding Accounting Period, in which case the cost of such examination shall be borne by the Licensee.

Copyright

6.1   The Licensee shall acknowledge that part or all of the Material is the copyright of the Depositor [or the Archive] and shall ensure that the following statement is featured prominently in all copies of the Work sold [or on screen, in the case of electronic publications]:

> Material in this work that is the copyright of [the Depositor or the Archive] is published with the permission of the Archive [on behalf of the Depositor].

6.2   The Licensee shall immediately notify the Depositor [or the Archive] of any infringements of the Depositor's [or the Archive's] copyright in the Material. Any action in pursuance of such infringement shall be at the discretion of the Depositor [or the Archive].

Complimentary copies

7   The Licensee shall within 28 days of making the Work available for sale, send ...... complimentary copies of the Work to the Depositor [and/or the Archive]. The Depositor [and/or the Archive] shall be entitled to purchase further copies at trade terms for use by the Depositor [or the Archive] and/or for resale by agreement with the Licensee.

Advertising

8   The Licensee shall have the entire control of the manner and extent of advertising the Work save where the advertising material refers to the Depositor [and/or the Archive], when the advertising material shall be submitted to the Depositor [or the Archive] for prior written approval, such approval not to be unreasonably withheld.

Breach

9   The Depositor [or the Archive] shall have the right at any time to give notice in writing to the Licensee to terminate this Agreement on occurrence of any of the following events:

(i)   if the Licensee commits a material breach of any of the terms of this Agreement and in the case of a breach capable of being remedied fails to remedy such breach within twenty-one days of being requested by the Depositor [*or* the Archive] in writing to do so;

(ii) [in the case of a company] if the Licensee goes into liquidation either compulsorily or voluntarily or has a receiver appointed over its assets or enters into a composition with its creditors;

(iii) if the Licensee fails to make the payments and produce the accounts specified in clause 5.

Termination

10.1 On termination of this Agreement under clause 9 all rights granted to the Licensee under this Agreement shall automatically and immediately revert to the Depositor [*or* the Archive] and no further copies of the Work shall be produced, issued or sold by the Licensee.

10.2 On expiry or termination of this Agreement under clause 4, the Licensee shall be entitled to issue and sell existing copies of the Work [*and/or*, e.g., make the broadcast] subject to all other obligations under this Agreement being complied with in full.

10.3 Termination for any reason shall not affect:

(i) the subsisting rights (if any) of any Third Party, or any sub-licence validly issued by the Licensee prior to termination;

(ii) the right of the Depositor [*or* the Archive] to obtain royalties and any other payments due in respect of the Licensee's sale of the Work;

(iii) any claim which the Depositor [*and/or* the Archive] may have against the Licensee for damages or otherwise.

10.4 On expiry or termination of this Agreement, the Depositor [*and/or* the Archive] may exercise the right to purchase all unsold stocks of the Work at a price, no greater than the trade price, to be agreed with the Licensee.

Assignment

11.1 The Licensee shall not assign this Agreement or the benefit or advantage hereof without the consent of the Depositor [*or* the Archive] first being obtained in writing.

11.2 The Licensee undertakes to inform the Depositor [*or* the Archive] promptly of any changes in ownership of the Licensee or any change of name or registered office.

Entirety

12.1 This Agreement [(which expression includes the Schedules hereto whether in their original or amended form)] constitutes the entire agreement between the parties, and no modification or amendment shall be binding on any party unless it is agreed in writing and signed by all parties.

12.2 The Licensee acknowledges that this Agreement gives it no right to authorize or license the reproduction of the Material or any part of it by a Third Party except as set out in clause 3, and the issuing of any such illegitimate authority or licence will be a material breach of the Agreement.

Interpretation

13   This Agreement shall be governed by and interpreted in all respects under the laws of England and Wales [*or* Scotland, *or* Northern Ireland, *or* other specified country] and shall be subject to the jurisdiction of the courts of England and Wales [*or* Scotland, *or* Northern Ireland, *or* other specified country].

Signed   Date
for the Depositor

NAME IN BLOCK CAPITALS

Signed   Date
for the Archive

NAME IN BLOCK CAPITALS

Signed   Date
for the Licensee

NAME IN BLOCK CAPITALS

9.4 Assignment to the record office

See 3.3.8 and 5.4.14–16.

ASSIGNMENT

Parties

1 the Assignor
 [full name and address of copyright owner, or name of the company]

2 the Assignee
 [title (not name) of the archivist or other permanent official]
 of [name and address of the archive]

Definitions

In this Assignment, the following words will have the following meanings

Rights	The copyright, all rights in the nature of copyright and related rights throughout the world in the Material that are the property of the Assignor, for all the residue of the term of copyright and such rights in the Material, together with all accrued causes of action in respect thereof [or specify the limited rights to be assigned, e.g. reference to particular types of use such as educational and charitable].
Material	[Description of the Material, as full as necessary, including archival references as appropriate. The description may be contained in a Schedule consisting of an archival list or similar document if appropriate, in which case include here simply a reference to the Schedule.]
[Authorial Work(s)]	[This part to be used only if the Assignor is the author of some of the works in the Material, and wishes to assert or waive his or her moral rights (see below). It must explicitly identify the works of which the Assignor is the author, e.g. by reference to specific items in an archival list.]

Background

The Assignor is [the author of the Authorial Work(s) and] the owner of the Rights [wherever possible expand to describe the Rights actually owned by the Assignee, e.g. by reference to the family or the company].

The Assignor has deposited the Material in [name of the archive] and has agreed to assign the Rights to the Assignee.

Assignment

The Assignor hereby assigns with full title guarantee the Rights to the Assignee and successors for use throughout the world.

Moral rights [use as appropriate]

The Assignor hereby asserts his (her) right generally to be identified as the author of the Authorial Work(s).

The Assignor hereby [unconditionally and irrevocably] waives his (her) right[s to be identified as the author of the Authorial Work(s) and] to object to derogatory treatment of the Authorial Work(s). [This waiver is made expressly and solely in favour of the Assignee and successors.]

Further assurances

The Assignor shall at any time and from time to time hereafter at the request and expense of the Assignee execute all such documents and do all such further acts as the Assignee may require in order to vest the Rights in the Assignee.

Consideration

In consideration for the grant of this assignment, the Assignee agrees to pay the sum of £1 (one pound) to the Assignor(s), receipt of which is hereby acknowledged.

Execution

The parties have shown their acceptance of the terms of this Assignment by signing at the end of it.

1   Signed by Assignor
        Date:
        [duly authorized or on behalf of
        [name of company]]:

        In the presence of:

[2   Signed by Assignor
        Date:
        [duly authorized or on behalf of
        [name of company]]:

        In the presence of:]

3   Signed by Assignee:
        Date:
        In the presence of:

Date:

9.5   Worked examples

9.5.1   Introduction

The following worked (imaginary) examples try to show how the range of rights, and the duration of them, might apply in particular circumstances. They do not attempt to cover all types of problem, but do indicate the issues that may need to be addressed and what the answers might be. Answers (insofar as clear answers are possible) are suggested in 9.6.

9.5.2   Example 1: file of papers (see 9.6.2)

The file is one created by a local authority concerning a plan to redevelop the town centre. It is dated 1877–1965, but is mostly material from the 1960s and was first made available to the public in the record office in 1996. The contents of the file (except item xii) have never been published. It contains a variety of papers. What rights are there in them and how long will they last?

(i)   Copies of out-letters from Council officers.
(ii)   Minutes of Council committee meetings.
(iii)   Internal Council memoranda.
(iv)   Letters received from the local MP.
(v)   Letters received from members of the public.
(vi)   Letters received from local companies.
(vii)   Letters received from the Ministry of Housing and Local Government.
(viii)   Photographs of the town centre taken by a named local photographer in 1897.
(ix)   Photographs of the town centre taken by a Ministry of Information photographer in 1942.
(x)   Photograph taken by an unknown person in 1962 of a painting in the Council chamber of the town centre, commissioned by the Council in 1910.
(xi)   Architect's drawings of a re-designed square, commissioned by the Council in 1963.
(xii)   Leaflet published in 1962 outlining the proposals.

9.5.3   Example 2: paintings and posters in a company archive (see 9.6.3–6)

A company archive contains paintings and advertisements. Some advertisements are based on paintings in the archive, others are not. All the advertisements carry the company's trade marks. Some advertisements have been reproduced as illustrations on postcards and in publications. What rights does the company have in the advertisements and paintings? What other rights restrict its freedom of action? What rights do users of the material have?

9.5.4 Example 3: copying of works in an archive (see 9.6.7)

An archivist is asked by a reader to make copies of certain unpublished private diaries of a person who died in 1942. Can the copies be made? Consider for each of the following circumstances:

(i)   The reader makes clear that the copies are to be used for reference in the preparation of an unpublished family history.

(ii)   Included in the diaries, as above, are drawings by the diarist.

(iii)   This time the reader has revealed that he is preparing a biography of the diarist for a university thesis, which will contain transcribed extracts from the entries copied. He hopes to have the biography published one day.

(iv)   The reader this time is preparing a commercial biography of the diarist.

(v)   The reader asks for a copy of a manuscript map from a different collection in the archive, showing the estates owned by the diarist.

9.5.5 Example 4: digital copies (see 9.6.8–9)

A reader has asked whether she may take digital photographs of documents in the archive on her own digital camera so that she may read them on a computer at home. She points out that The National Archives permits this. What rights will there be if the photography is allowed, and what should the archive do for the future?

9.5.6 Example 5: ownership of copyright (see 9.6.10)

What rights are there in the following cases?

(i)   Letters from Alexander Bishop, produced as exhibits in a murder trial.

(ii)   Photographs of the Battle of Jutland taken by AB Anthony Jones, contrary to regulations, and by Lieutenant Arthur Nottage, an official photographer.

(iii)   Two sets of photographs, taken in 1958 and 1990 respectively, of Hamchester Castle taken on behalf of the Council by David Ward, photographer of Nossex Street, Hamchester.

(iv)   Private papers of Viscount Nemo, bequeathed to the record office by his sole grandson, who died in 1972.

(v)   Transcript of entries in the parish register of Upshire for 1896.

(vi)   Photocopy of the electoral register of Hamchester, 1899.

9.5.7 Example 6: duration of copyright (see 9.6.11)

Are the following documents in copyright, and why?

(i)   Ordnance Survey map of Kent, 1955.

(ii)   Manuscript musical score by a well known 19th century composer (d. 1900). The work has been published but the score contains material which is different from the published version. Is the manuscript a published work or not? Is it in copyright?

(iii)   Signature of Nell Gwyn on a theatre programme, together with her bill for services rendered.

(v)   Manuscript of Jane Austen's unfinished novel *Sanditon*.

(vi)   Anonymous unpublished treatise found in a new private deposit of papers, explaining why Oliver Cromwell is a usurper and Charles II's reign should be dated from the death of his martyred father.

9.5.8 Example 7: publication (see 9.6.12)

How should the following enquiries be answered?

(i)   Several years ago I obtained from your office a photograph of a poster dated 1845 among the Merfield parish records (Ref P/StMM/15/3). I should now like to publish it as an illustration in a book entitled *Nineteenth-century Agrarian Unrest* to be published by Northchester University Press next year. Could you please give me permission to do so and tell me what fee will be payable?

(ii)   Would you please give me permission to publish a transcript of the letter from Miss Cassandra Austen dated 6 December 1810 in my forthcoming book on Georgian domestic economy?

(iii)   Please may I have permission to publish a transcript of the Southwick Burial Board minutes for 12 June 1854 in an article for the *Nossex Archaeological Society Journal*? I will of course make any appropriate acknowledgement.

(iv)   I am about to publish a biography of Miss Ermintrude Simpson, who was a pioneer in the development of mechanized ambulances in Mesopotamia during World War I. Numerous letters written by Miss Simpson to her family are among the Kirby Papers, deposited in your office by Sir Horatio Kirby in 1954. I transcribed these during a visit to your office last year, and am anxious to use them as sources for my book, together with some direct quotations. Are you able to give me permission to do this? If not, can you put me in touch with the current copyright owner?

(v)   I am writing my family history and hope to circulate about 50 copies among my family and relevant record offices and societies. While I was doing my research I obtained from you copies of the will of John Brown of Tattershaw, proved on 3 November 1847, and the letters of administration of his widow Martha, who died on 23 July 1859. Please may I have permission to include copies of these in my book?

9.5.9 Example 8: copying of records (see 9.6.13)

How would you reply to the following requests from the copyright point of view?

(i)   Please will you supply me with a copy of the entry relating to the trial of William Stubbs in the quarter sessions records for Northchester dated 24 September 1869 (ref QS/35/238)?

(ii)   I understand that your office holds a collection of the sketches made by Erica Calluna, the well known botanist, during her field trips to the Irish peat bogs in the 1930s. I am fascinated by the peat bogs and should like some copies of these sketches for my collection. Please will you tell me how I may obtain photographic copies?

(iii)   I am writing a thesis on the manor of Woodfield in the parish of Wigbrook. I understand that you have on your shelves copies of the *Victoria County History of Nossex*. Please may I have a copy of the three pages relating to Wigbrook in the volume for Merfield Hundred published in 1965?

(iv)   For my geography thesis, I am studying the incidence of snail infestation in market gardens in the Waterbrook Valley. I should be grateful if you would supply me with copies of the relevant pages in the diaries of Arthur Wiltshire (ref D/AW 34/987, pp 12, 56, 79, 465), who joined the Heath Company's market garden in the late 1880s.

(v)   I was delighted to discover that you have in your collection the original manuscript of T S Eliot's poem *The Wasteland*. Please may I have a copy?

(vi)   I am a research student at the Southwick Institute working on a study of the influence of pressure groups on the policies of mining companies in Middlefolk. I should like to order, on behalf of the Institute, five copies of the minutes of the Culpepper Copper Mine Company for 6 March 1938, which I understand have been deposited with your office by the company.

(vii)   I am writing a history of the turnpike roads of Nossex, and wish to include a reproduction of the minutes of the trustees of the Northchester to Tattershaw turnpike for 28 January 1867, when approval was given for the road surface to be improved to prepare for the passage of the Duke of Nihilum's army. Please will you supply me with a good-quality reproduction?

(viii)   I work for the charity Gloop (which protects the threatened habitats of glow-worms). We are planning to issue Christmas cards this year and should like to obtain a copy of the report on glow-worms held in your collection, so that we may use it to improve our publicity strategy for the fund-raising campaign.

9.6 Worked examples: suggested solutions

9.6.1 Introduction

The following suggested answers to the examples given in 9.5 are not comprehensive; much depends on the precise circumstances of each case. Cross-references to relevant parts of the main text have been given where this is likely to be most helpful.

9.6.2 Example 1: rights in the file of papers (see 9.5.2)

The rights in the various parts of the file appear to be as follows:

(i)   Council copyright until 2039 at the earliest (see 2.2.16–17).

(ii)   Council copyright until 2039 at the earliest (see 2.2.19–20, 3.2.12).

(iii)   Council copyright until 2039 at the earliest (see 2.2.16–17).

(iv)   Copyright of the MP personally, then of his or her descendants (assuming he or she makes no assignment of his or her rights, and that he or she is acting in his or her constituency or personal capacity), until 70 years after his or her death or 2039, whichever is later (see 2.2.16–17, 3.2.1, 3.3.8).

(v)   Copyright of the individuals, then their descendants (assuming they make no assignments of their rights), until 70 years after their deaths or 2039, whichever is later (see 2.2.16–17, 3.2.1, 3.3.8).

(vi)   Copyright of the companies, or their successors, until 70 years after the death of the authors (assuming their names are given and are legible) or 2039 whichever is later (see 2.2.16–17, 3.2.12, 7.9). If a letter is from no identifiable author, copyright will expire in 2066 (70 years after being made available to the public, see 2.2.19, 3.2.12). However, the position might be less simple if the letters are from company directors (see 7.9.2).

(vii)   Crown copyright until 2039 at the earliest (see 2.2.21–29, 3.2.28). A PSI licence will probably be sufficient (see 5.4.32).

(viii)   Copyright of the photographer and his or her descendants, unless he or she assigned it elsewhere, until 70 years after his or her death (see 2.3.12, 3.2.1, 3.3.8). If the photographer died in 1925 or earlier (copyright expired before the photographs were made available to the public), the Council has publication right in the photograph until 2021 (25 years after being made available to the public, see 8.3.1, 8.3.6).

(ix)   Out of copyright (see 2.3.23, 3.2.28).

(x)   The painting: copyright of the Council until 70 years after the death of the artist (see 2.3.12, 3.2.20). The photograph: perhaps copyright until 2066 (70 years after being made available to the public, see 2.3.15), but there is no way of tracing the owner and it is possible that there is no copyright in it at all (see 2.1.10).

(xi)   Copyright of the architect, then of his or her descendants, unless assigned elsewhere, until 70 years after his or her death (see 2.3.12, 3.2.1). On the other hand, if the architect was employed by someone else, duration would be the same but ownership would be with the employer (see 3.2.12).

(xii)   Copyright of the Council until 2032 (70 years after publication), assuming no author is identified (see 2.2.19, 3.2.12).

9.6.3   Example 2: the paintings (see 9.5.3)

If the company owns a painting it is the proprietor of the artefact and can refuse permission for it to be reproduced, or even seen (see 3.2.3).

If the artist (and descendants) is the owner of the copyright in a painting (see 3.2.1), the company might have a licence (either express (that is, written) or implied) to use it for advertising purposes, depending on what was said and/or agreed when the painting was purchased (see 3.2.17–18). The company may not give permission to anyone else to reproduce the painting. Copyright subsists until 70 years after the end of the year of the author's death, assuming the artist is known (see 2.3.12).

The company might have secured an assignment of the copyright in a painting from the artist; this must have been in writing and signed by the artist (see 3.3.8). Alternatively, the company might have acquired copyright through a commission placed before 1 August 1989, for example a painting or drawing commissioned between 1862 and 1912 or a portrait painting or drawing commissioned between 1912 and 1989 (see 3.2.20). In these cases the company may reproduce the painting, and authorize reproduction of it, as it pleases. The duration of the copyright is as above.

9.6.4   Example 2: the advertisements (see 9.5.3)

If the company commissioned designers to produce advertisements, it might own the copyright having secured an assignment (see 3.3.8) or because of the type of commission (as above, and see 3.2.20). In that case, it may reproduce the advertisement and authorize its reproduction as it pleases.

If the company commissioned advertisements but did not secure the copyrights, the copyright remained with the artist (see 3.2.1) or his or her employer, such as an advertising agency (see 3.2.12). The company would have a licence (either express or implied) to use the advertisement for the purpose for which it was commissioned, and perhaps for related purposes such as for an illustration in a history of the company, but will have no right to authorize its use by others (see 3.2.17–18). The duration of the copyright is for 70 years after the artist's death, assuming the artist is known (see 2.3.12).

If advertisements were designed based on other works such as paintings, this can have been only under licence from the owner of the copyright in the painting unless the painting was out of copyright. That licence is unlikely to extend to doing (or allowing others to do) anything else with the image. Such licences might have been time-limited and might have become invalid through a later assignment of the copyright (see 5.4.1).

Whether there is a copyright in advertisements using versions of paintings will depend on the circumstances, but any new copyright has no effect on any continuing copyright in the original painting so there could be two (or more) concurrent copyrights. The test for copyright in the advertisement will probably be whether it required 'great talent and technical skill' to use the earlier image or was merely a reproduction of that image (see 2.1.6, 2.1.10). Duration of the copyright in the painting is for 70 years after the artist's death (see 2.3.12). If there is copyright in the advertisement, duration is until 70 years after the death of the employee (or the last of them, if more than one) who created the design; or, if the employees are unknown, until 70 years after the advertisement was published (see 2.3.12, 2.3.15, 3.2.7).

9.6.5   Example 2: trade marks on advertisements (see 9.5.3)

Trade marks must be renewed every ten years or they expire, so if the company has failed to maintain the protection of its old marks it will have no control over their use by others. Some reproductions of trade marks are not infringements if they would not lead to confusion on the part of the public, so reproduction in a picture book of an image bearing a trade mark might not infringe (see 8.6.8).

9.6.6   Example 2: facsimiles (see 9.5.3)

The making of a facsimile (such as a postcard) of an artistic work such as an advertisement might, but only might, create a new copyright, and even then the courts might allow its owner little protection (see 2.1.10). Even if there is a new copyright, it will not affect the copyright in the original work. Thus one company making a postcard can only (perhaps) claim infringement if another company copies its postcard. There can be no infringement of copyright in the postcard by the second company copying the original (see 2.1.7), although if the first company has an exclusive licence the owner of the copyright in the painting might be in breach of contract for giving permission to the second company (see 5.4.1). The copyright in the reproduction, if there is any, will normally subsist regardless of whether it was authorized or not (see 2.1.11). A company reproducing an advertisement as an illustration in a book has no rights of its own over that image, not even in the typographical arrangement of the printed page since the work is artistic (see 2.6.15).

9.6.7   Example 3: copying of works in an archive (see 9.5.4)

(i)   The copies may be made, so long as the reader completes a declaration form (see 5.3.10, 5.3.15, 9.2 schedule 2 form B).

(ii)   The drawings may be copied, but only with the related diary entries. They may not be copied on their own, as distinct artistic works (see 5.3.18).

(iii)   The copies may be made under the exception for examination (see 5.2.15). The use of transcribed extracts is covered by the same exception. The intention to publish is not the current purpose of the copies, but the reader should be advised to trace the copyright owner prior to publication to seek permission for this commercial use of the copies (see 5.3.10) and for the use of the extracts.

(iv)   The copies may not be made under the terms of the library and archive regulations, even if the declaration form is completed, since this is a commercial use (see 5.3.10). However, the copies may be made if the diaries are at least 100 years old; we know that the diarist died over 50 years ago (see 5.3.11).

(v)   The manuscript map must not be copied (see 5.3.18) unless:
   (a)   the person who drew the map is known, and died more than 70 years ago, in which case copyright has expired (see 2.3.12);
   (b)   the person who drew the map is not known, but may reasonably be assumed to have died more than 70 years ago, in which case it may be treated as though copyright has expired (see 5.3.17); or
   (c)   the map is a public record on deposit in the archive (see 5.3.1).

9.6.8 Example 4: digital copies: copying and rights in the copies (see 9.5.5)

The archivist may authorize the making of self-service copies of public records (see 5.3.1). Alternatively, self-service copying might fall under fair dealing or some other exception (see 5.3.20). In many cases, copyright will not prevent such copying, though security and preservation concerns might.

In a straightforward case it is unlikely that there would be any copyright in the digital copies, since there is unlikely to be any originality in them (see 2.1.10). They will attract copyright only if considerable skill, judgment and labour have been used to create them (see 2.1.6). Extensive manipulation might for example need to be used subsequently in the computer because the originals were badly faded and stained. Copyright will continue to subsist in the originals, and permission from the owner of that copyright will be needed for any use of the copies beyond what the relevant exception allows; it is the responsibility of the reader to secure that permission.

9.6.9 Example 4: future policy (see 9.5.5)

The archive would be well advised to:
(i)   set up a service to provide digital copies itself; wherever possible such copies should be protected by some form of digital rights management (see 6.1.8);
(ii)   consider the feasibility and desirability of allowing self-service copying (see 5.3.20);

(iii)　if self-service copying is allowed, ensure that users of digital cameras sign a form agreeing to terms and conditions covering preservation and copyright issues, notably that they accept responsibility for any infringement resulting from their making and use of the copies and that they accept any restrictions placed by the archive on use of its materials (see 5.4.34).

9.6.10 Example 5: ownership of copyright (see 9.5.6)

(i)　Copyright of Alexander Bishop and his descendants. If the records have been in the custody of the court for 50 years they could become public records (see Public Records Act 1958 s8(4)), otherwise they remain the property of the recipient (see 3.2.4).

(ii)　Photographs by AB Jones are his copyright, although he could have been disciplined for taking them (see 3.2.1); if they were taken without official knowledge they could hardly have been taken 'under the direction or control' of the Crown. Photographs by Lieutenant Nottage are Crown copyright (see 3.2.28).

(iii)　Photographs taken in 1958: it depends what 'taken on behalf of' means. If the Council paid for the taking of the photographs it probably owns copyright having commissioned them (see 3.2.20). If it did not pay, the first owner of the copyright was the owner of the material on which they were taken (the negatives, slides or plates) (see 2.3.7). This could be difficult to discover but if the negatives are in the archives that is a good indication of Council ownership. Photographs taken in 1990: copyright of the author (see 2.3.7, 3.2.1).

(iv)　Copyright in unpublished papers by Viscount Nemo will have passed to his grandson and come to the record office with his papers (see 3.3.4). Copyright in letters received by Nemo and in other materials, including publications written by Nemo, remains copyright of the descendants of the authors (see 3.2.1, 3.2.4).

(v)　No rights exist. The entry is merely a collection of facts (see 2.1.4, 7.2.2) and the transcript merely a copy (see 2.1.8).

(vi)　No rights exist. The photocopy is merely a copy (see 2.1.8) while the copyright in the register has probably expired (see 7.8.2). Since the register is over 100 years old data protection considerations are unlikely to be a problem (see 7.8.4, 8.7.2).

9.6.11 Example 6: duration of copyright (see 9.5.7)

(i)　Out of copyright (see 2.3.20).

(ii)　Whether the manuscript is a published work or not depends on how substantial are the differences from the published version. If they are musically significant they are probably substantial (compare discussion of 'visually significant' parts of artistic works at 4.1.9). If unpublished it is copyright to 2039 (see 2.2.17). If the differences are insubstantial (for instance mere correction of obvious errors) copyright has expired (see 2.2.16).

(iii)   Signature is (perhaps) an artistic work, out of copyright (life plus 70 years, see 2.3.12). Theatre programme is a published work never in copyright because its publication preceded the passing of the first Copyright Act (see 1.2.1). Bill is an unpublished literary work of known authorship, copyright of her heirs until 2039 (see 2.2.17).

(v)   *Sanditon* was not published until 1925, over 100 years after Jane Austen died. Copyright in her manuscript expired 50 years after publication (see 2.2.18).

(vi)   Assuming the deposit is now made available to the public, copyright will expire 70 years after the work was so made available (see 2.2.19) though, given that there is no way of knowing who the copyright owner is, the copyright is virtually meaningless (see 3.3.20).

9.6.12 Example 7: publication (see 9.5.8)

(i)   The poster is out of copyright, whether it is regarded as a literary work (as a compilation, see 2.2.3, 2.2.19) or an artistic work (see 2.3.15). There may or may not be copyright in the photograph (see 2.1.10). Whether the archivist is able and wishes to exercise rights over the use of the photograph will depend on the terms of any conditions imposed when the photograph was supplied (see 5.4.34).

(ii)   Copyright of the descendants of the author (see 3.2.1, 3.3.1) until 2039 (see 2.2.17), assuming it was unpublished in 1989. It may be that the present owner, a descendant of the Austen family, could be readily traced so it might be risky to publish without making some attempt (see 5.4.23).

(iii)   Probably copyright of the local authority, until 2039 at the earliest (see 2.2.19–20, 7.1). Whether the archivist may give permission depends on the powers that have been given to him or her by the local authority.

(iv)   The information contained in the letters is not copyright, and may be used as factual evidence freely (see 2.1.4). The letters themselves are copyright, which will expire at the earliest in 2039 (see 2.2.16–17), and this is probably owned by the author's descendants (see 3.2.1, 3.3.1). How substantial are the quotations? If they are insubstantial, permission for use might not be needed (see 5.2.3–6), but the archivist should not attempt a definition of substantiality, save to say that it is measured qualitatively as well as quantitatively. The archivist should avoid offering to help with tracing the current copyright owner unless he or she has definite information on the subject (see 5.4.20).

(v)   The will is copyright until 2039 (see 2.2.17), and the copyright is probably owned by the testator's descendants, possibly even by this enquirer (see 3.2.1, 3.3.1, 7.3.9). In any event, the will may be published without permission so long as the current owner is unknown (see 5.4.23). The Crown copyright in the letters of administration will expire in 2039 (see 2.2.21 and 7.3.4) so permission is obtainable from The National Archives (see 3.2.28).

9.6.13 Example 8: copying of records (see 9.5.9)

(i)   Quarter sessions records are public records, and so may be copied without further formality (see 5.3.1).

(ii)   These are non-public records, and they are artistic works. They may not be copied without the permission of the copyright owner (see 5.3.18).

(iii)   These are publications and may probably be copied under the library and archive provisions (see 5.3.14). If the archive qualifies as a library for these purposes, the library declaration form should be sent and the copies should not be made until it is received back fully completed (see 5.3.15).

(iv)   This is covered by the examination exception (see 5.2.15).

(v)   The copy may not be supplied without permission from the owner of Eliot's copyrights. The manuscript of a work which has been published is a published work and so may not be copied under the archive exception (see 5.3.10), and is not a published edition so the library exception does not apply either (see 5.3.12, 5.3.14).

(vi)   The copies may not be supplied without the company's permission. The library and archive regulations permit only a single copy of any one copyright work to be made for one person, and do not permit the archivist to make a copy in the knowledge that it will be further copied for someone else (see 5.3.10, 5.3.15).

(vii)   The document is over 100 years old and the author may be presumed to have died more than 50 years ago, so the copy may be supplied 'with a view to publication' (see 5.3.11).

(viii)   No copy may be supplied, unless the document is a public record (see 5.3.1) since although for a charity the purpose is commercial (see 5.3.10).

10 Bibliography

10.1 Documents

The National Archives (TNA)

OS 1/6/2: Crown copyright in Ordnance Survey maps, 1883–1911: 5.2.3

T 161/241, file S25383: Copyright in the register of electors, 1924–5: 7.8.2

STAT 14/44: Crown copyright in evidence taken before Committees and Commissions and proceedings of arbitration courts, 1935–54: 3.2.28

10.2 Books

Armstrong, C. J. and Bebbington, L. (2003) *Staying Legal: a guide to issues and practice affecting the library, information and publishing sectors*, 2nd edn, Facet Publishing.

Bainbridge, D. (2002) *Intellectual Property*, 5th edn, Pitman.

British Photographers' Liaison Committee (1999) *The ABCD of UK Photographic Copyright*, BPLC.

Cabinet Office (1998) *Crown Copyright in the Information Age*, Cm 3819, HMSO.

Cabinet Office (1999) *The Future Management of Crown Copyright*, Cm 4300, HMSO.

Canons of the Church of England (Canons Ecclesiastical) (2000), 6th edn, Church House.

Christie, A. (2003) *Blackstone's Statutes on Intellectual Property*, 6th edn, Blackstone.

Cornish, G. P. (2002) *Copyright in a Week*, Hodder and Stoughton.

Cornish, G. P. (2004) *Copyright: interpreting the law for libraries, archives and information services*, 4th edn, Facet Publishing.

Cornish, W. R. and Llewelyn, D. (2003) *Intellectual Property: patents, copyrights, trade marks and allied rights*, 5th edn, Sweet and Maxwell.

Electoral Commission (2006) *Supply, Sale and Inspection of the Register of Electors: changes to 2001 Regulations*, Circular EC06/2006.

Garnett, K., Davies, G. and Rayner James, J. (2005) *Copinger and Skone James on Copyright*, 15th edn, Sweet and Maxwell.

HMSO (1999) *Copyright in Public Records*, HMSO Guidance Note 3, HMSO.

Johnson, S. (1810) *A Dictionary of the English Language*, 10th edn.

Laddie, H., Prescott, P. and Vitoria, M. (2000) *The Modern Law of Copyright and Designs*, 3rd edn, Butterworth.

Law Society, *Directory of Solicitors and Barristers*, Law Society, annual.

Legal Advisory Commission of the General Synod (1994, supplement 1997) *Legal Opinions Concerning the Church of England*, Church House Publishing.

McCracken, R. and Gilbart, M. (1995) *Buying and Clearing Rights*, Blueprint.

Marett, P. (2002) *Information Law in Practice*, 2nd edn, Ashgate.

Michalos, C. (2004) *The Law of Photography and Digital Images*, Sweet and Maxwell.

Monotti, A. and Ricketson, S. (2003) *Universities and Intellectual Property*, Oxford.

Norman, S. (2004) *Practical Copyright for Information Professionals*, Facet Publishing.

Pedley, P. (2003) *Essential Law for Information Professionals*, Facet Publishing.

Post, J. B. (1986) Copyright Mentality and the Archivist, *Journal of the Society of Archivists*, 8 (1), (April), 17.

Post, J. B. and Foster, M. R. (1992) *Copyright: a handbook for archivists*, Society of Archivists.

Public Record Office (2000) *Data Protection Act 1998: a guide for records managers and archivists*, PRO.

Sterling, J. A. L. (2003) *World Copyright Law*, 2nd edn, Sweet and Maxwell.

Sterne, L. (1760) *The Life and Opinions of Tristram Shandy*.

Stokes, S. (2003) *Art and Copyright*, 2nd edn, Hart Publishing.

Stokes, S. (2005) *Digital Copyright: law and practice*, 2nd edn, Hart Publishing.

Whitford Committee (Board of Trade) (1977) *Copyright and Designs Law: report of the committee to consider the law on copyright and designs* (the Whitford Report), Cmnd 6732, HMSO.

Wienand, P., Booy, A. and Fry, R. (2000) *A Guide to Copyright for Museums and Galleries*, Routledge.

Zorich, D. M. (1999) *Managing Digital Assets: options for cultural organizations*, Getty Information Institute.

11 Authorities

11.1 Treaties and EU instruments

1886   Berne Convention for the Protection of Literary and Artistic Works, Paris Act 1971

1948   Universal Declaration of Human Rights

1952   Universal Copyright Convention, Paris Revision 1971

1961   Rome Convention for the Protection of Performers, Producers of Phonograms and Broadcasting Organizations

1971   Geneva Convention for the Protection of Producers of Phonograms against unauthorized distribution of programme-carrying signals

1986   Directive 87/54/EEC of 16 December 1986 on the Legal Protection of Topographies of Semiconductor Products

1991   Directive 91/250/EEC of 14 May 1991 on the Legal Protection of Computer Programs

1992   Directive 92/100/EEC of 19 November 1992 on Rental and Lending Right and on Certain Rights related to Copyright in the field of Intellectual Property

1993   Directive 93/83/EEC of 27 September 1993 on the Coordination of Certain Rules concerning Copyright and Rights related to Copyright applicable to Satellite Broadcasting and Cable Retransmission

1993   Directive 93/98/EEC of 29 October 1993 Harmonizing the Term of Protection of Copyright and certain Related Rights

1994   Agreement on Trade-Related Aspects of Intellectual Property Rights (TRIPS Agreement)

1996   Directive 96/9/EC of 11 March 1996 on the Legal Protection of Databases

1996   World Intellectual Property Organization (WIPO) Copyright Treaty

1996   World Intellectual Property Organization (WIPO) Performances and Phonograms Treaty

2001   Directive 2001/29/EC of 22 May 2001 on the Harmonization of Certain Aspects of Copyright and Related Rights in the Information Society

2001   Directive 2001/84/EC of 27 September 2001 on the Resale Right for the Benefit of the Author of an Original Work of Art

2003   Directive 2003/98/EC of 17 November 2003 on the Re-use of Public Sector Information

2003   Council decision 2003/239/EC of 18 February 2003 on the Conclusion of an Agreement . . . extending to the Isle of Man the Legal Protection of Databases

2004   Directive 2004/48/EC of 29 April 2004 on the Enforcement of Intellectual Property Rights

11.2 Statutes

1710   Copyright Act 8 Anne c21
1734   Engraving Copyright Act 8 Geo2 c13
1753   Marriage Act 25 Geo2 c33
1766   Engraving Copyright Act 7 Geo3 c38
1775   Copyright Act 15 Geo3 c53
1777   Prints Copyright Act 17 Geo3 c57
1812   Parochial Registers Act 52 Geo3 c146
1814   Sculpture Copyright Act 54 Geo3 c56
1823   Commissary Courts (Scotland) Act 4 Geo4 c97
1832   Representation of the People Act 2&3 Wm4 c45
1833   Dramatic Copyright Act 3 Wm4 c15
1835   Lectures Copyright Act 5&6 Wm4 c65
1836   Marriage Act 6&7 Wm4 c85
1836   Births and Deaths Registration Act 6&7 Wm4 c86
1840   Non-Parochial Registers Act 3&4 Vic c92
1842   Copyright Act 5&6 Vic c45
1843   Parliamentary Voters Registration Act 6&7 Vic c18
1844   Marriage (Ireland) Act 7&8 Vic c81
1845   Enclosure Act 8&9 Vic c108
1851   Criminal Justice Administration Act 14&15 Vic c55
1852   International Copyright Act 15&16 Vic c12
1854   Registration of Births, Deaths and Marriages (Scotland) Act 17&18 Vic c80
1857   Court of Probate Act 20&21 Vic c77
1857   Probates and Letters of Administration Act (Ireland) 20&21 Vic c79
1862   Fine Arts Copyright Act 25&26 Vic c68
1863   Registration of Births and Deaths (Ireland) Act 26&27 Vic c11
1863   Registration of Marriages (Ireland) Act 26&27 Vic c90
1877   Justices Clerks Act 40&41 Vic c43
1910   Finance (1909–1910) Act 10 Edw 7&1 Geo5 c8
1911   Copyright Act 1&2 Geo5 c46
1920   Government of Ireland Act 10&11 Geo5 c67
1922   Irish Free State (Agreement) Act 12 Geo5 c4
1922   Irish Free State (Consequential Provisions) Act (session 2) 13 Geo5 c4
1922   Irish Free State Constitution Act (session 2) 13 Geo5 c1
1922   Law of Property Act 12&13 Geo5 c16
1923   Public Records Act (Northern Ireland) 13&14 Geo5 c20 (NI)

1925	Administration of Estates Act 15&16 Geo5 c23
1927	Cinematograph Films Act 17&18 Geo5 c29
1927	Industrial and Commercial Property (Protection) Act No 16/1927 (Ireland)
1937	Public Records (Scotland) Act 1 Edw8 &1 Geo6 c43
1938	Cinematograph Films Act 1&2 Geo6 c 17
1946	National Health Service Act 9&10 Geo6 c81
1948	Cinematograph Films Act 11&12 Geo6 c23
1949	Ireland Act 12&13 Geo6 c41
1949	Marriage Act 12&13 Geo6 c76
1949	Registered Designs Act 12,13&14 Geo6 c88
1949	Justices of the Peace Act 12,13&14 Geo6 c101
1952	Intestate Estates Act 1 Eliz2 c64
1953	Births and Deaths Registration Act 1&2 Eliz2 c20
1956	Copyright Act 4&5 Eliz2 c74
1957	Cinematograph Films Act 5&6 Eliz2 c21
1958	Public Records Act 6&7 Eliz2 c51
1960	Films Act 8&9 Eliz2 c57
1962	Local Government (Records) Act 10&11 Eliz2 c56
1963	Copyright Act No 10/1963 (Ireland)
1965	Copyright Act (Germany) of 9 September 1965
1965	Registration of Births, Deaths and Marriages (Scotland) Act c49
1968	Copyright Act (Australia)
1972	Local Government Act c70
1973	Local Government (Scotland) Act c65
1976	General Revision of the Copyright Law (USA) United States Code Title 17 (with amendments)
1977	Marriage (Scotland) Act c15
1977	Patents Act c37
1978	Parochial Registers and Records Measure General Synod No2
1978	Copyright Act (South Africa) No98
1979	Public Lending Right Act c10
1980	Limitation Act c58
1983	Representation of the People Act c9
1984	Cable and Broadcasting Act c46
1985	Companies Act c6
1985	Films Act c21
1985	Local Government Act c51
1985	Copyright Act (Canada)
1986	Insolvency Act c45
1988	Coroners Act c13
1988	Copyright, Designs and Patents Act c48

1989	Children Act c41
1990	Broadcasting Act c42
1990	Government Trading Act c30
1990	National Health Service and Community Care Act c19
1990	Town and Country Planning Act c8
1991	Copyright Act c8 (Isle of Man)
1992	Local Government Act c19
1994	Local Government (Scotland) Act c39
1994	Local Government (Wales) Act c19
1994	Trade Marks Act c26
1998	Data Protection Act c29
1998	Human Rights Act c42
1998	Regional Development Agencies Act c45
1998	Scotland Act c46
1998	Northern Ireland Act c47
1999	Greater London Authority Act c29
2000	Copyright and Related Rights Act No28/2000 (Ireland)
2000	Electronic Communications Act c7
2000	Freedom of Information Act c36
2000	Representation of the People Act c2
2002	Copyright (Visually Impaired Persons) Act c33
2002	Freedom of Information (Scotland) Act asp13 (Scotland)
2003	Communications Act c21
2003	Legal Deposit Libraries Act c28
2003	Courts Act c39
2004	Civil Partnership Act c33
2004	Copyright and Related Rights (Amendment) Act No18/2004 (Ireland)
2005	Constitutional Reform Act c4
2005	Copyright (Bailiwick of Guernsey) Ordinance
2006	Government of Wales Act c32

11.3 Statutory instruments

SI 1948/567	National Health Service (Transfer of Local Authorities Functions) Order 1948
SI 1948/1292	National Health Service (Dissolved Authorities) Order 1948
SI 1957/863	Copyright Act 1956 (Commencement) Order 1957
SI 1959/1399	Manorial Documents Rules 1959
SI 1963/976	Manorial Documents (Amendment) Rules 1963
SI 1964/177	Copyright Act 1963 (Commencement) Order 1964 (Ireland)
SI 1967/963	Manorial Documents (Amendment) Rules 1967

SI 1973/1861	Local Authorities (England) (Property etc.) Order 1973
SI 1975/659	Local Authorities (Property etc.) (Scotland) Order 1975
SI 1976/1041 (NI 14)	Births and Deaths Registration (NI) Order 1976
SI 1982/719	Public Lending Right Scheme Order 1982
SI 1986/148	Local Government (Property etc.) Order 1986
SI 1986/1081	Representation of the People Regulations 1986
SI 1989/816	Copyright, Designs and Patents Act 1988 (Commencement No 1) Order 1989
SI 1989/1012	Copyright (Recordings of Folksongs for Archives) (Designated Bodies) Order 1989
SI 1989/1067	Copyright (Application of Provisions relating to Educational Establishments to Teachers) (No 2) Order 1989
SI 1989/1068	Copyright (Educational Establishments) (No 2) Order 1989
SI 1989/1070	Copyright (Industrial Process and Excluded Articles) (No 2) Order 1989
SI 1989/1099	Copyright (Material Open to Public Inspection) (Marking of Copies of Maps) Order 1989
SI 1989/1105	Registered Designs Rules 1989
SI 1989/1212	Copyright (Librarians and Archivists) (Copying of Copyright Material) Regulations 1989
SI 1990/1329	National Health Service and Community Care Act 1990 (Commencement No 1) Order 1990
SI 1990/1427	Copyright (Material Open to Public Inspection) (Marking of Copies of Plans and Drawings) Order 1990
SI 1990/1520	National Health Service and Community Care Act 1990 (Commencement No 2) (Scotland) Order 1990
SI 1990/2360	Public Lending Right Scheme 1982 (Commencement of Variations) Order 1990
SI 1990/2540	Broadcasting (Transfer Date and Nominated Company) Order 1990
SI 1992/3233	Copyright (Computer Programs) Regulations 1992
SI GC 316/92	Copyright (Librarians and Archivists) (Copying of Copyright Material) Regulations 1992 (Isle of Man)
SI 1993/74	Copyright (Recording for Archives of Designated Class of Broadcasts and Cable Programmes) (Designated Bodies) Order 1993
SI 1995/402	Local Government Changes for England (Property Transfer and Transitional Payments) Regulations 1995
SI 1995/2499	Local Authorities (Property Transfer) (Scotland) Order 1995
SI 1995/2912	Registered Designs Rules 1995

SI 1995/2990	Performances (Reciprocal Protection) (Convention Countries) Order 1995
SI 1995/3297	Duration of Copyright and Rights in Performances Regulations 1995
SI 1996/2967	Copyright and Related Rights Regulations 1996
SI 1997/3032	Copyright and Rights in Databases Regulations 1997
SI 1999/676	Parliamentary Copyright (Scottish Parliament) Order 1999
SI 427/2000 (Ireland)	Copyright and Related Rights (Librarians and Archivists) (Copying of Protected Material) Regulations 2000
SI 2001/341	Representation of the People (England and Wales) Regulations 2001
SI 2001/400	Representation of the People (Northern Ireland) Regulations 2001
SI 2001/497 (S 2)	Representation of the People (Scotland) Regulations 2001
SI 2001/3949	Registered Designs Regulations 2001
SI 2001/3950	Registered Designs (Amendment) Rules 2001
SI 2002/1871	Representation of the People (England and Wales) (Amendment) Regulations 2002
SI 2002/1872 (S 7)	Representation of the People (Scotland) (Amendment) Regulations 2002
SI 2002/1873	Representation of the People (Northern Ireland) (Amendment) Regulations 2002
SI 2002/2013	Electronic Commerce (EC Directive) Regulations 2002
SI 2003/550	Registered Designs Regulations 2003
SI 2003/2498	Copyright and Related Rights Regulations 2003
SI 2003/2500	Electronic Commerce (EC Directive) (Extension) (No 2) Regulations 2003
SI 2003/2501	Copyright and Rights in Databases (Amendment) Regulations 2003
SI 2004/3089	Freedom of Information (Scotland) Act 2002 (Consequential Modifications) Order 2004
SI 16/2004 (Ireland)	European Communities (Copyright and Related Rights) Regulations 2004
SI 2005/852	Copyright and Performances (Application to Other Countries) Order 2005
SI 2005/1515	Re-use of Public Sector Information Regulations 2005
SI 2005/3176	Civil Partnership (Registration Provisions) Regulations 2005
SI 2006/18	Performances (Moral Rights, etc.) Regulations 2006
SI 2006/346	Artist's Resale Right Regulations 2006
SI 2006/752	Representation of the People (England and Wales) (Amendment) Regulations 2006

| SI 2006/834 | Representation of the People (Scotland) (Amendment) Regulations 2006 |
| SI 2006/1028 | Intellectual Property (Enforcement, etc.) Regulations 2006 |

11.4 Cases

Archivists and records managers unaccustomed to legal referencing in the form required by the Lord Chief Justice may find the full citations of cases given below rather unhelpful. The following notes might assist.

References are to the parties in the (civil) case, usually cited as Claimant (still called Plaintiff in Northern Ireland; Pursuer in Scotland) *v* Defendant (Defender in Scotland), but they are sometimes reversed on appeal. In speech the '*v*' is rendered 'and', not 'versus'. If a date is in (round brackets) it is the date of the case or the report and is supplied merely for information. If it is in [square brackets] it is the date of the report and is a vital part of the reference. There is then an abbreviated reference to the series of case reports in which this particular report is printed (the series cited in this book are listed below) followed by the page or case number. There are also occasional abbreviated references to the court in which the case was heard, also listed below. If two numbers are given, the first is a volume number. Occasionally a case is not reported in an established series, in which case a citation of a report might not conform to this pattern; it might be accessible only by an online service like Lexis, for instance. Cases from courts outside England and Wales might also not conform, and these are identified by the name of the country or court. Each citation is followed by the section numbers in this book where the case has been used.

The footnotes might mention a judge from whom a particular quotation comes. The name of the judge is followed by letters indicating his or her position, J for Mr (Mrs) Justice, LJ for Lord (Lady) Justice, MR for Master of the Rolls and so on. Sometimes in such cases a reference will continue 'at . . .' with a number, which is the page number for the quotation in the report.

AC	Law Reports series, Appeal Cases
All ER	All England Law Reports
CA	Court of Appeal
Ch	Law Reports series, Chancery cases
ChApp	Law Reports series, Chancery Appeals cases
ChD	Law Reports series, Chancery Division cases
ChR	Irish Chancery Reports
Civ	Civil case, unpublished Court of Appeal reports
CP	Law Reports series, Common Pleas cases
DLR	Dominion Law Reports (Canada)
ECDR	European Copyright and Designs Reports

ECJ	European Court of Justice
EMLR	Entertainment and Media Law Reports series
EmpLR	Employment Law Reports
ER	English Reports series
EWHC	High Court unpublished reports
F	Federal Reporter reports (USA)
FSR	Fleet Street Reports series
F Supp	Federal Supplement reports (USA)
HCA	High Court of Australia, unpublished reports
HL	House of Lords
ICR	Industrial Cases Reports
IIC	International Review of Industrial Property and Copyright Law
ILT	Irish Law Times
IPD	Intellectual Property Decisions
IPR	Intellectual Property Reports
IRLR	Industrial Relations Law Reports
JLR	Jersey Law Reports
KB	Law Reports series, King's Bench cases
LJQB	Law Journal reports, Queen's Bench cases
LR	Law Reports series
LT	Law Times Reports
MacCC	MacGillivray's Copyright Cases
ND	North Dakota unpublished reports (USA)
NSW	New South Wales, Australia
NZLR	New Zealand Law Reports
PC	Law Reports series, Privy Council cases, or Privy Council
QB	Law Reports series, Queen's Bench cases
QBD	Law Reports series, Queen's Bench Division cases
RPC	Reports of Patent, Design and Trade Mark Cases series
SC	Court of Session Cases (Scotland)
SCC	Supreme Court of Canada reports
SJ	Solicitors' Journal
SLR	Scots Law Reporter
SR (NSW)	New South Wales State Reports
TLR	Times (Newspaper) Law Reports
UKHL	United Kingdom House of Lords unpublished reports
USCA	United States Court of Appeals unpublished reports
WLR	Weekly Law Reports series
WR	Weekly Reporter

Index

References are to sections